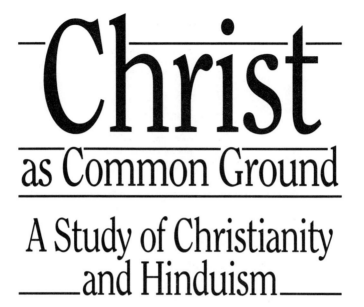

Christ
as Common Ground
A Study of Christianity and Hinduism

Kathleen Healy
Foreword by Bede Griffiths

Duquesne University Press
Pittsburgh, Pennsylvania

Published by Duquesne University Press
600 Forbes Avenue
Pittsburgh, PA 15282

Library of Congress Cataloging-in-Publication Data

Healy, Kathleen.
Christ as common ground : a study of Christianity and
Hinduism / Kathleen Healy.
    p. cm.
Includes bibliographical references.
ISBN 0–8207–0227–7
1. Christianity and other religions—Hinduism.
2. Hinduism-Relations—Christianity.   I. Title.
BR128.H5H42   1990
261.2'45'0954—dc20   90–34260
                                                    CIP

Two hopeful signs of our times — the growing struggle for social justice and the harmonization of Eastern and Western spiritualities — augur well for the future of humanity. . . . Whether we as a species will follow the directions set by these paths, and move toward ever greater harmony, or whether we will retreat into selfishness and fear, is as yet a very real question. . . . Perhaps our present-day crisis of hope results from an inability to understand . . . that the final victory for our species depends less on ourselves than it does on the invincible force of love which draws us onward to completion.

Anthony E. Gilles

Contents

Foreword

There is a growing awareness today that the church, like the rest of the world, is entering on a new age. For nearly two thousand years the church has developed in a Westerly direction. Beginning in the Middle East, the church moved first to Greece and Rome, then to the other countries of Western Europe, developing its structures of doctrine and discipline on Western models. The churches founded in the East, apart from the Syrian churches, which departed from Rome, were all based on these models so that the church in Asia has always had a Western character, its liturgy, theology, and organization being modeled entirely on those of the West. Today, however, things are beginning to change. The Second Vatican Council, by introducing the concept of inculturation, opened the way to a new development of the church in Asia. For the first time the church was brought into contact with the rich tradition of Oriental culture, and it became possible to conceive of a liturgy, a theology, and an organization of the church that would be based on Eastern, not Western, models. The movement is still in its infancy, but on every side there are signs of an awakening of the churches in Asia to their cultural inheritance, and a new model of the church is beginning to emerge.

Sister Kathleen Healy has made a study of the situation of the church in India today in the light of this new understanding of the mission of the church. Based on interviews with the leaders of this movement in the church and on extensive reading in this field, she has produced an extraordinarily comprehensive study of the actual situation in India today. The fundamental challenge to the church in India is, of course, that of Hinduism. India is 85 percent Hindu; Indian culture, in spite of all its diversities, remains basically Hindu. Though the Christian churches after centuries of missionary endeavor remain still a tiny minority, yet it is of particular interest that millions of Hindus, while remaining attached to their own religion, are deeply attracted to Christ and do not hesitate to give him their entire devotion. Yet they will never enter the church, because it bears for them the stamp of an alien religion. Sister Healy sees this as the fundamental challenge to the church in India today. Hindus seek Christ, but they will not accept the Western structures in which the message of Christ is embedded today.

This is the perspective in which she sees the problem of the church in India. Can the Indian church shed its Western character and present Christ to the Hindu in Indian, not in Western, clothes? The answer to this question can be found only if we understand the mission of the church in a new way. Neither Christianity nor Hinduism alone, she boldly says, can save humanity in India today. Christianity as we know it today is a particular form that the gospel of Christ has taken in the course of European history. This form of Christianity cannot save India. What is required, she says, quoting Raimundo Panikkar, is a process of "mutual fecundation." While remaining always true to the essential message of the gospel, the church has to open itself to all that is "true and holy" in Hinduism, as Vatican Council II puts it, so that a new form of Christianity will emerge, expressing the truth of the gospel in a new way. All that the church has ultimately to give to India or to any other people is Jesus Christ himself. This is its message, this is its truth, and every people must receive Jesus Christ in its own way.

Sister Healy explores with great penetration the values in Hinduism of which the church stands in need, particularly those of mysticism and interiority, the vertical dimension of inner experience, which is India's gift not only to the church in India but to the whole world. On the other hand, she recognizes the limitations of Hinduism, especially in the matter of caste and the social dimension of religion. It is only in a meeting and sharing, in which each religion enriches itself and both grow together into a new expression alike of Christianity and of Hinduism, that fulfillment can be found for humanity in India. Nor is this confined to India. The church in the West needs this vertical dimension in its life, and the future of humanity as a whole depends on this meeting of East and West in which each enriches the other. In this lies the hope of a new approach to theology based on experience, the inner experience of the Spirit, the atman of Hindu tradition, and expressing itself not so much in logical systems as in symbols that open the way to a new level of consciousness. In liturgy and theology there is already a movement toward inculturation, but the organization of the church with its center in Rome still remains firmly Western in its character. Only the future will show whether the church as a whole will be able to modify its structures and become decentralized, so as to allow for the creative growth of indigenous churches on the model of the Eastern churches. The Syrian church in India remains an example of an Eastern church with its own liturgy and theological tradition, but like all Eastern churches in union with Rome it has become too Westernized to be a model. It bears witness, however, to the possibility of a church in communion with Rome that would have its own original liturgy and theology, and would be organized along Oriental lines.

This is a courageous and inspiring book, which breaks new ground and opens up the way to a new vision of the future of the church.

Bede Griffiths

Shantivanam Ashram
Tiruchirappalli
Tamil Nadu
South India
May 29, 1988

Preface

This work is an outgrowth of six years of study of the relationship of Christianity and Hinduism in India. In 1976–77 I spent
fourteen months as a Fulbright Professor of American Literature
at the University of Madras, South India, and lectured at many
other universities throughout the subcontinent. Contemporary
developments within Christianity in India offered stimulating
questions, and I continued to study both Hinduism and Indian
Christianity until I returned to India in 1980 as a research
scholar.

During my second Indian journey, I consulted with innumerable theologians, philosophers, swamis, gurus, sannyasis and
"ordinary people." Despite the great diversities within India, I
found certain strong unifying elements among Indian religions
and cultures. (When these unifying factors are repeated, the
process thus occurs within varied contexts.)

The present book is in no sense a "survey" of dialogue
between Hindus and Christians in India. It is an attempt at a
thoughtful integration of what I have learned firsthand about
the spirituality and culture of the Hindus from the Hindus
themselves, about Indian Christians from themselves, and
about what each can offer to the other today in spiritual interpenetration.

It is my firm conviction that the spiritual union of East and
West is crucial in our world. Western Christians can no longer
isolate themselves within the intellectual and geographical limitations of a narrow tunnel view of Christianity. Easterners are
surprisingly open to the extra-Mediterranean Christ whom they
have discovered only partially to date. In the words of one of my
Hindu friends, "Gandhi has taught the Sermon on the Mount

more penetratingly than most Christians have." Indeed, an image of Western Christianity as unique and exclusive is intolerable in the East of the 1980s and 90s.

It is of primary importance for Christians to discover why millions of Hindus worship Christ, but often view the Christian church as "Churchianity." The present book is a modest attempt to answer this question and to point out a possible direction for the authentic follower of Christ in India in interaction with the Hindu — a direction acceptable to Hindu and Christian alike.

A consideration of minority religions in India — of Muslims, Buddhists, Sikhs, Parsees, Jains, Hebrews — is beyond the scope of the present study. Hinduism is the dominant spiritual way in India. It is entwined inextricably with Indian culture.

My gratitude is due to so many Hindus and Christians in India that I can only hope that all of them are deeply conscious of the thanks I have expressed to them personally. I am profoundly grateful, however, to two men. Raimundo Panikkar, of Varanasi, North India, and Barcelona, Spain, perhaps the greatest contemporary East-West theologian and philosopher, not only supported me with enlightening dialogue but read the manuscript and offered valuable suggestions for revision. I have borrowed certain seminal ideas from his creative theology. Dom Bede Griffiths of Shantivanam Ashram, Tamil Nadu, South India, also read the manuscript and offered helpful thoughts for revision. The Introduction he has written for the book is more than generous. It is scarcely necessary to say that no one named above is responsible for the conclusions I have drawn in the text.

I am grateful to my religious congregation, the Pittsburgh Sisters of Mercy, for their affirmation of my work, and to Carlow College, Pittsburgh, for the sabbatical necessary for me to begin research in India. Sister M. Noreen Sheehan, RSM, has been most helpful in the typing of the manuscript.

Kathleen Healy, RSM

Easter 1989

CHAPTER I

The Challenge to Find a Common Ground

O F all the cultures of Asia and Africa, perhaps none can unite in worldwide exchange of experiences and ideas with the Christian church today more richly than Hindu culture can. The time when Christian church representatives approached the Hindu people as evangelists is long past. The contemporary search for a common ground in spiritual inculturation in the East finds a goal in Christian-Hindu exploration, not only because Hinduism represents 85 percent of the Indian population, but because Hindus are perhaps more open than any people in the world to the spiritual experiences of all people. Buddhism, for example, had its birth in India, then moved on to countries all over the world after Hinduism, in its usual fashion, had absorbed the most profound spiritual influences of the Indian Buddha. To an extent, Hinduism has also absorbed some of the best loved teachings of the Christian churches.

The importance of the need to find a common ground for union in spiritual experiences of Christians and Hindus is almost fathomless. Three out of four of the total population of the

1

world are Asian, chiefly Indian and Chinese. Sixty percent of the people of the world live below the poverty level. In actual numbers, the poor, the uneducated, and the starving are more numerous than ever before in human history. Nineteenth century colonialism is finished in theory only. It has given way to economic imperialism. Within the United Nations, 60 countries have expanded to close to 200 within a short number of years, so that the original composition of the international organization is altered fundamentally. Many of the new Asian and African nations challenge as exploitive and unjust the very concepts on which the Western world is built. These concepts are naturally associated with Western Christianity. In short, Asians and Africans frequently do not see the Western church as it sees itself. In India, 85 percent of 883,000,000 people are Hindu. They know as little about Western Christians as Christians in general know about Hindus. The time for a profound Hindu-Christian inculturation is long past.

The most potent challenge to the Christian church in the East is to extend itself to the pluralistic Hindu cultures of India today. Yet Christians in the East and elsewhere often seem to be unaware of the challenge, "to be fiddling while Rome burns." Hindus themselves often seem to have a clearer insight into global spiritual experience than Christians do.

This phenomenon may be illustrated by the attitude of many Hindus toward Christianity. Recently the writer remarked, in a casual conversation with an Indian Hindu engineer resident in the United States for ten years, that thousands of Hindus in the Indian subcontinent are devoted to Jesus Christ. The laughing response was: "You mean millions. I worship an image of Jesus in my own home." Yet this same Hindu would never consider the possibility of membership in a Christian church. Nor is this situation surprising to a Westerner who has spent considerable time in India. The Western resident of India is accustomed to see countless Hindus pray before images of Christ and attend Christian devotions — especially those honoring the Virgin Mary. Hindus who can afford an automobile often display an image of Mary or a Christian saint in their car. But these same Hindus regard an invitation to join a Christian church as strange, alien, and even downright offensive. Hindus believe that they are born to their religion and they cannot change it. They can follow Christ, but they cannot *become* Christian. Similarly, Christians can follow the Hindu God Krishna or Siva or Vishnu, but they cannot *become* Hindu. The relationship between religion and culture is obvious.

How are we to respond, then, when we attend a Christian festival in India and discover that 65 percent of the people present are Hindus? More specifically, what are we to say when we read statements like the following by Mahatma Gandhi, who considered himself a humble follower of Christ, especially with regard to nonviolence and vicarious suffering:

> If you call me a Christian, I shall consider it an insult. But if you call me Christlike, I shall consider it the greatest compliment you can pay me. . . . If I had power and I could legislate, I should stop all proselytizing.[1]

Or another statement of Gandhi:

> I know many men who have never heard the name of Jesus Christ or have even rejected the official interpretation of Christianity, [but who] would probably, if Jesus came in our midst today, be owned by him more than many of us would.[2]

Like a true Hindu, Gandhi resisted conversion. He also expected Christians to be authentic followers of Christ. Was Gandhi more aware of "the other sheep not of this fold" than many Christians are?

If we juxtapose Gandhi's statements to declarations of Western Christians who have lived in India for many years, we are faced with both a startling dilemma for Christians and an urgent challenge to the church. Consider the following judgment of British scholar E. Stanley Jones:

> India is important — very. She is the key to the whole of non-Communist Asia. For whichever way India goes, the whole of non-Communist Asia goes. India has risen to leadership in Asia in a very remarkable way. Hundreds of millions will follow her lead.[3]

Bede Griffiths, Catholic convert and British Benedictine mystic who has been a spiritual leader in South India for more than twenty-five years, goes so far as to say that the future of the world depends on the Christian discovery of the essential tradition of Hindu wisdom based on personal spiritual experience. Hindu philosophy, which is not a separate discipline from theology in India, is based fundamentally on the spiritual experience often represented by the sannyasi or holy man. Not only has God been revealed to India over thousands of years, but the Hindu experience of God, as testified by the Vedas, the Hindu scripture, offers insight into the inner mystery of divinity complementary to Christian revelation. To date, the church has made only a small beginning in its reflection on Christian faith in the light of the cosmic revelation explored by Indian seers. This reflection is extremely urgent today because, while more and more thoughtful people believe that Western Christianity tends gradually to lose the dimension of interior wisdom and become more and more external and active, the world cries out for the reciprocity of Eastern interiority and the message of the Christian gospel.[4]

Raimundo Panikkar, most internationally famed East-West theologian and European-Indian scholar, maintains that in the last quarter of the twentieth century no religious tradition is self-sufficient. Mutual fecundation is essential among the religious traditions of the world. But Christianity and Hinduism as institutions alone cannot bring about this impregnation. Persons are an imperative need, for spiritual fertilization demands love. The new child of faith who may be born of the loving embrace of Christian and Hindu can initiate development in the economy of salvation without compromise to the teaching of Jesus Christ. This development, however, cannot be achieved through a Vatican III or a Chicago I. A kairos, a Jerusalem II, is needed.[5]

The early church, for example, broke away from sacrosanct circumcision, which was a primordial sacrament, in response to the testimony of Peter:

> God, who can read everyone's heart, showed his approval of them [the Gentiles] by giving the Holy Spirit to them just as he

had to us. God made no distinction between them and us, since he purified their hearts by faith [Acts 15:8–9].

In the matter of circumcision, and in other matters, the church of the Apostles was forced to change by the inspiration of the Spirit and by the facts of history.

Today the universal church has problems parallel to those of the Council of Jerusalem: What is Christian identity in a world of pluralistic cultures? What is baptism in the context of a follower of Jesus Christ whose entire culture rejects "conversion"? What does the Spirit want of the Christian in encounter with world religions rooted in spiritual and cultural traditions of thousands of years? The Christian church must have intellectual awareness, prayer and contemplation, detachment, holiness of life, yes — but more is demanded today. The church must have an open vocation not just for Western history but for world history. Christians must take seriously, moreover, the temporal dimension of reality: Christians must seek justice, equality, and peace for all men and women as taught by Jesus Christ.

In India today, a response to the above questions must be made most especially by Indian Christians who, though nurtured in the Western Christian tradition, are more cognizant than Europeans and Americans of the essential requisites for allowing Christ to find his home in India as he desires to find it among all human beings and all nations. "Jesus Christ," said an Indian Jesuit to the writer, "has not yet taken out his naturalization papers in our country. But his application is on file!"

If the Christian church is to go beyond its Judeo-Christian, Mediterranean exclusivity, it must be willing to extend itself to the immense pluralistic Asian and African worlds without prejudice to the diverse cultures of those worlds. It is challenging to think that in India, a country crucial to the future of Christianity, the diversity of peoples and cultures is a call to Rome far more complex than the call of the Roman centurion Cornelius to Peter recorded in the Acts of the Apostles. Christian messengers of the Good News cannot be *merely* messengers: they must understand the mind and faith of the person to whom they offer the Word of God. Peter was made to understand Cornelius, a *non-Jew*, through the action of the Spirit. The Indian Christian today is enlightened by Hindus who welcome and accept Jesus Christ, only to discover that their hospitality has been abused by the messenger of Jesus. In order to embrace Christ, Hindus are sometimes asked to exclude their ancient faith, their tradition, their culture, their family, their caste, their inheritance! They are scandalized. The Christian message appears to them to be sectarian, biased, intolerable. As a result, the encounter between Christian and Hindu is clouded with misunderstanding, ambiguity, and resentment at the start.[6] There are even those who say that it is impossible for a Christian and a Hindu to communicate spiritually unless the Christian learns a new language, not literally but culturally and symbolically.

The sources of conflict between Hindu and Christian are many. Hinduism itself cannot be defined because there are no limits by which it can be circumscribed. Nothing can be asserted about it that cannot also be denied. Nothing can be denied about it that cannot also be affirmed.[7] It has no specific dogmas, no proper organization (though historically many great "schools" or approaches to Hinduism have developed). There are as many Hinduisms as there are Hindus. In short, Hinduism is not precisely an institutionalized system of religious beliefs and practices in the Western sense. Yet it is one of the most profound religions in world history. More than 90 percent of Indians believe absolutely in an Ultimate Reality. If Christians are to speak to Hindus as living witnesses to Christ, they must be aware of the living reality of Hinduism. They must know the person to whom they speak as Jesus knew the blind man, the paralytic, the woman at the well. A worn-out, irrelevant, stereotyped communication will not do. Christians must speak to listeners in words meaningful to them; they must know when to speak in parables; they must speak with the love of Christ.

The types of Hindus in India today reflect the complexity of their culture. The nonorthodox literates, a small percentage of caste Hindus with secondary and higher educations, have broken with Hindu traditions and substituted "democracy" or "science" for the values of their old Hindu beliefs. They respect religion but consider it part of a dead past. The orthodox literates, on the other hand, are high caste Indians who have received a classical Hindu formation in ashrams, Brahmin families, or other institutions. They desire to preserve Hindu sources like the Vedas and the Upanishads, but they have no unanimity as to what should be preserved beyond the basic scriptures.

Finally there are the "people" of India. Eighty-two percent of them cannot read or write. They are a *listening* population with a fine and deep culture. Their values are a naked *acceptance of life as it is*, a sense of the sacredness of all things, worship of their traditional Gods, and a hierarchy of living that implies that who one is, is determined by caste. The above groups can be divided into numerous subgroups.[8]

Obviously, a religious mentality is a fundamental dimension of the character of the great majority of Hindus. Though this mentality is pluralistic, running through it like a dominant vein is a unity grounded in the mystery of the experience of the divine. This sense of unity is so much a part of the daily reality of Indians that they are scarcely aware of its existence. They recognize it only by its absence. Yet it is the still point where alone the Christian and the Hindu can meet. It is the possible point of loving spiritual fecundation. It is the center where Christ can become for India the loving reality that he must become for all men and women. The Indian responds intuitively to the concept of unity in reality. For Indians, God — the Ultimate Reality — is one. "I and the Father are one" is language the Hindu can understand.

Fundamentally, Jesus Christ is not the scandal and the stumbling block to the Hindu that he is to the Jew. He is not the stone the builders rejected. The Hindu never looked for a redeemer. The Hindu was never promised a messiah. The Hindu can accept Jesus Christ as God because Jesus lived and revealed a divine life. In the words of Swami Abhedananda:

> A Hindu distinguishes the religion of the churches from the religion of Jesus the Christ. . . . The religion which is popularly known as Christianity should be called "Churchianity" in contradiction to that pure religion of the heart which was taught by Jesus and practiced by his disciples.[9]

Hindus also recognize Jesus Christ as a man of the East. They can listen to the voice of Jesus, which they feel to be their own.

Gandhi, for example, heard the Word of God spoken by Jesus with an absolutely positive acceptance. Up until the present, the stumbling block for the Hindu undoubtedly has been a church imbedded in a Western culture that seems to Indians to violate all the traditions their people have held sacred for thousands of years. Outstanding Hindu scholars are cognizant of the problem of the church in India and volunteer freely an explanation of the seeming failure of Christianity in India after two thousand years: "Everything about Christians is foreign in India."

To be sure, the alien quality of Western Christianity is only one, though a large, factor in the lack of appeal of the Christian church to the peoples of the subcontinent. Yet it is interesting to note that certain Hindu scholars are willing to express a hope for Christianity in the East if the church will only listen to the above message that Hinduism has literally shouted into its ears:

> Perhaps Christianity, which arose out of an Eastern background and early in its career got wedded to Graeco-Roman culture, may find her rebirth today in the heritage of India.[10]

Fortunately, a diversified population of Christians in India today — theologians, pastors, men and women religious, members of the body of Christ — have opened themselves to the wisdom of their Hindu countrymen. They are studying the ways in which God has been revealed to their Hindu brothers and sisters. They are listening to Jesus Christ speaking in the voices of "the other sheep not of this fold." With humility and sincerity, they are allowing Jesus to incarnate himself in India without resistance from themselves. For these Christians who have ears to hear, "the way to the Father" for the Indian today seems to be the only way the Indian can understand: encounter in love in "the cave of the heart." Christians in India are beginning to understand that the rock-bottom blasphemy for the Hindu is "to protect God from others." Christians have no monopoly on the Christ who existed from the beginning. Without prejudice to either the Hindu or to the church of Christ, I shall attempt to explore in the following pages the call of Christ to India through a possible, perhaps distant, Jerusalem II.

CHAPTER II

Christ beyond Christianity
Jesus Christ, the Hindu, and the Church

1. JESUS CHRIST AND THE HINDU

THE response of the Hindu to Jesus Christ is the clue to a viable response of the Christian church to the challenge of India. For the Hindu who accepts Jesus Christ, it is impossible to conceive that Christ was not present in the long centuries of belief, spirituality, and mysticism of the East. Hindus have little interest in the uniqueness of Christianity, a concept alien to them, but the idea of Christ beyond all time, the God of all humans past, present, and future, is an idea to which they can give a complete response. Many Christians, however, either have not the spiritual experience on integrated vertical and horizontal levels that a Hindu can respond to, or they seem to be incapable of sharing this experience of the transhistorical, everlasting Christ.

The fact that India remains wedded to its ancient religious values is concomitant to the teaching of Vatican Council II that truth and grace are found among nations "as a sort of secret presence of God." As is proved by history, the Indian knows instinctively that the full and real incarnation of Christ cannot come from without. "Christ does not come to India as a stranger. He comes into his own. Christ comes to India not from Europe, but directly from the Father."[1] Hindu converts to Christianity today often regard Hinduism as their spiritual mother. They accept Christ not in spite of Hinduism but because Hinduism has taught them to discern the divinity they find in Jesus. The message they receive is the message of Christ uttered from within, not a message from the Western world.

Hindus who worship Christ without Christian baptism accept Jesus on their own terms. Their devotion is personal, without dogma. Their faith arises from their response to the spiritual values they find in Jesus according to their own freedom of interpretation. For example, simplicity of living is a value of thousands of Hindus. Even when Indians have the means to establish themselves in the comforts of a consumer society, they often do not do so. To the Westerner, Hindus sometimes seem oblivious of their surroundings, to a fault. Yet millions of Indians are happy without nonessential comforts. Some Hindus even wonder why Christians do not see poverty as a value, as Jesus did. "Americans," declared one Indian to the writer, "hate poverty!"[2] The simple lifestyle of Indians crystalizes a Christian value. For them, "the Son of Man has not whereon to lay his head" expresses a luminous spiritual quality.

The thousands of "unbaptized Christians" in India may be said to be of two types. The first have no desire to join the Christian church. They find Jesus to be sufficient for them without the church. In fact, they often find the church to be unattractive. Church members seem to them to be ordinary people with extraordinary claims. The second type would be willing to be church members, but they are unwilling to sacrifice family and friends, community, caste, status, inheritance, as would be demanded of them. A Hindu convert to Christianity is to them like an illegitimate child without heritage.

A professor of Indian philosophy, for example, told the writer about a friend of his who became a baptized Christian, giving up all that he treasured in life except his Christian faith. Within two years he died — and no one attended his funeral. This type of Indian may well ask, "Why should I alienate myself from my own life when I can worship Christ without joining a church?" If he finds spiritual fulfillment in his own oriental Christ, why join a foreign, Western church? The crucial issue for him, then, is whether he can be a faithful follower of Christ without Christian fellowship. The Sermon on the Mount seems to him to be the ideal teaching on a holy life, comparable to — or superior to — the simple and lofty exhortations of Krishna to Arjuna in the Bhagavad Gita.

2. THE CHURCH AND THE HINDU

Other reasons than complete fulfillment in Jesus Christ alone, coupled with the fear of social alienation, prevent Indians who worship the Son of God from seeking baptism in the church. They ponder what seem to them to be contradictions between the teachings of Christian churches and the Word of God in the New Testament. They are scandalized by the variety of churches, all claiming to be Christian, and especially by the conflicts — sometimes violent — among these churches throughout history.

They wonder, moreover, why Christians concentrate on goals that stress values strange to them. The writer was caught up short when a Hindu in attendance at a Christian college inquired: "Why do my teachers focus on order, discipline, cleanliness, and punctuality? Why do they not emphasize the biblical virtues of justice, equality, and love?" The humor of the question conceals a profound truth: Christianity in India is sometimes associated by Hindus with peripheral values that have little to do with the gospel of love. Rather, they reveal cultural customs that are sometimes antithetical to the values of Hindu society. Westerners in India, for example, wonder why the Hindu laughs at their impatience with inefficiency. They do not understand that patience and courtesy are among the highest moral virtues of the Hindu. Efficiency is not a virtue. On a deeper level, the Christian teacher emphasizes that the greatest gift of God is the gift of life itself. Why then, the Hindu asks, has the Christian whose central biblical doctrine is love — even love for one's enemies — so often appeared with a bible in one hand and a bomb in the other? A contemporary Hindu scholar points out, for example, that "the Portuguese came to India with a sword in one hand and a crucifix in the other; finding much gold, they laid the crucifix aside to fill their pockets with gold."[3]

The structure of the church, moreover, presents a problem to Hindus. The organization of the church, juridically and territorially divided, is alien to them. They find its sources in the Roman heritage of the West, not in Jesus of Galilee. They refuse to be captured by institutional structures. Christianity seems to them to be encapsulated, limiting the freedom of spirit of its members. Jesus came to bring life more abundantly, to bring freedom. Baptism, creeds, and dogmas frighten and baffle the Hindu who desires to follow Jesus as a living reality.

The Hindu is also puzzled by endless references of Western Christians to subjects like contraception, sterilization, and abortion. The attempt of Sanjay Gandhi to impose sterilization on the Indian population in the 1970s was offensive and outrageous to the Hindu. Nor do Hindus experience the strong tensions of many Westerners concerning sex life. They accept their body as they accept their total self. To the question of what Christians can learn from Hindus, one Indian Jesuit replies, "They can learn not to be ashamed of their bodies."

In short, Jesus Christ seems to the Hindu to be institutionalized in the Western church, with its own structures, cultures, traditions, eccentricities, and even political backgrounds. Therefore the church has little catalyzing effect on the everyday spiritual life of the Indian. The centralized structure of the papacy, the episcopacy, and the priesthood, together with legalistic restrictions, appear to the Hindu to be foreign, fixed, and closed to development. Even the tremendous service of church members in education, welfare, and social relief often seems to the Hindu to be adapted to maintenance of institutions rather than to societal change with a view to the achievement of expressed Christian values like justice and equality.

The more institutional the church is, in the eyes of some Hindus, the less it is true to Jesus Christ. The Indian identifies Jesus with a way of life, not an established religion; with a theological reality, not an organization. Perhaps this is one reason why many Indians — Christian and non-Christian — have deep devotion to the Virgin Mary. The loving Mother does not make legalistic demands. The concept of God as Mother, moreover, is not rare among Hindus. The Indian always seeks personal spiritual enrichment. Institutional practices create tension between charism and organization. Inevitably, witness and presence — not hierarchy and dogma — are significant to the Indian in seeking Christ.

The Christian church thus appears sometimes to the Hindu to reveal value blindness with regard to the universal dimension of Jesus Christ. The church seems to present itself to the Indian as exclusive, whereas Hinduism is universal. Jesus Christ entered into relationships with all persons whom he encountered, taught them and learned from them, and committed himself to the human community with its limitless social and cultural conditions. He was condemned for his association with Pharisees and publicans. He revealed a universality that seems right and natural to the Hindu, who responds to a Christ beyond the seemingly exclusive body of the church. The Hindu perceives a crucial difference between *hearing* about God through the church and actually *knowing* Christ in an experiential way.

Because Hinduism is syncretic, its assimilative quality offers a natural environment to Indians. They find it difficult to abandon when they choose to worship Christ as their "avatar." Hinduism, in its catholic attempt to provide for the spiritual needs of all human beings in all states of spiritual growth, rejects no one, even the atheist. All human beings are on pilgrimage toward one Supreme Spirit, whatever the differences in the paths they choose at various points in their existence. Christ seems to the Hindu to fit into this assimilative pattern, as the Christian church sometimes does not.

V. A. Devasenapathi, Hindu scholar, quotes Benedictine Bede Griffiths to substantiate the point of view that men and women are saved not by outward profession of faith but by response to the call of grace that comes to them secretly in their hearts. To sin against the Holy Spirit is to reject the voice of God in conscience.[4] This justification of failure to accept Christianity is an excellent example of how Hindu intellectuals may support their following of Christ without membership in a Christian church. They can assimilate belief in Jesus Christ, just as their countrymen of the past accepted belief in Buddha and other religious prophets, and still remain a Hindu. In fact, the vitality of Hinduism over thousands of years is due in great measure to this genius for assimilation. The Christian church, on the contrary, appears to the Hindu as an institution sometimes lacking in the flexibility to which Christ was witness. Indeed, one "educated" Hindu pointed out to the writer as a positive development the fact that the church established by Roman Catholic missionaries in China no longer accepts formal acknowledgment of allegiance to the pope. Thus Chinese Christians can feel free to develop their faith without the restrictions of centralized authority that might impede their following of Christ!

Here again the personal, individualistic quality of Indian faith enters into one's attitude toward Christ and the church. Jesus is a divinity, not an eschatological revelation of God,[5] chosen by the Indian. Just as Hindus can change their devotion from Krishna to Siva or Vishnu, their choice of Christ depends on their human way of seeing the divine. No avatar is unique for them. Their devotion centers on the God or prophet who helps them as an individual to reach the one God who is ultimately unknowable in the present life. If Hindus choose Christ as the way to moksha or liberation, they often see no reason to worship their avatar within a structure centered in Rome. They accept plurality, variety, diversity, with a kindly tolerance for their fellowmen and their chosen Gods. Their one, positive, unchangeable value is centered in the Absolute, the Ultimate Reality. All else is relative. Their own avatar or chosen deity, whether it be Christ or Krishna, is their center of concentration in worship. To be sure, the uneducated Hindu is not always consciously aware of the philosophical "Absolute," but is strongly aware of "Sakti" or "power" as a primordial source.

For the Christian, it can scarcely be overemphasized that the

Indian interpretation of Christianity as lived is crucial to the church in India. Whether or not the Indian interpretation is correct, is less important than the dimensions of Christianity that Indians see and hear with their own eyes and ears within their own cultural background. "Religion" in practice is what people think it is. To the Hindu, it appears that the oneness of God and humanity is sometimes lost in institutionalized Christianity — that the interiority in which humans seek God in "the cave of the heart" through Christ is preferable to membership in a church burdened with hampering restrictions, dogmatic formulations, and centralization of authority.

The church is faced, then, with millions of followers of Christ in India who will neither be institutionalized in the Christian church nor ostracized from their castes or communities. They cannot be encountered as non-Christians, for they accept the gospel of Jesus as their own. They are "other sheep not of this fold." They await Jerusalem II.

3. JESUS CHRIST AND THE KINGDOM

One of the most profound questions of study among Christian scholars in India today is the relationship of the kingdom of God to every member of the human race and to every culture on earth. The Christian teaching of universal fellowship is related to the concept of the Rigveda that the whole human race forms one single family. The gospel teaching that men and women are created in the image of God and that the whole creation proclaims God's glory is related to the Hindu belief that every human being has a spark of the divinity that pervades the entire cosmos.

Since Vatican Council II, Christianity in India and elsewhere has opened itself to a new understanding of its relationship to other religions:

> An ineffable mystery, centre and ground of reality and human life, is active among all peoples of the world. Religious traditions, scriptures, and rites can be, in various degrees, expressions of divine manifestations conducive to salvation. The whole of mankind is within one economy of salvation.[6]

The kingdom of God has no frontiers. It extends to all human beings and to all churches. The whole world belongs to Christ. He is the Word of God, at work in India as he was among the Hebrews. In this particular sense, the scriptures of India — the Vedas, the Upanishads, and the Bhagavad Gita — can be viewed as a Christian as well as a Hindu reality.[7]

The Christian can learn much from the Indian in a reinterpretation of the all-inclusiveness of the kingdom of God. T. M. P. Mahadevan, perhaps one of the greatest living Hindu scholars, asserts that the Christian accepts the teaching "love your neighbor as yourself" because Jesus has said it, while the Hindu accepts the same counsel because he believes a neighbor *is* himself or herself. Behind this subtle distinction is the Hindu philosophical concept of the oneness of the atman or divinity within every human being and the "Brahman," the ultimate Reality.[8] Precisely here is ground for dialogue and philosophical interchange between Christian and Hindu on the question of the kingdom of God. If Christ and the Father are one, the human being who is part of Christ is also part of the Father. This is not to suggest that a Christian can accept the notion of *identity* between the atman and the Brahman. The Christian community in India, however, is sometimes actually less aware of its oneness with Hindus in the kingdom than Hindus are of their oneness with Christians. The social isolation of many Christians, who seem to forget that Christ separated himself from no one, cannot be condoned. Some Hindus have suggested that Christians have kept too much to themselves: they should cultivate consciously a closer relationship with Hindus.

Before Indian Christians speak fruitfully of Christ, they must build up their common spirituality with Hindus in the kingdom of God. They will do so by living and teaching brotherhood and sisterhood in the family of God, in which all men and women are one in union with God. The mystical body of humanity, which fell in Adam, was redeemed in Christ. Christianity cannot be more exclusive than Christ himself. The more Christian one is, the more sensitive one becomes to the grace of God operating in non-Christian religions. Is it fanciful to think that "one flock, one shepherd" is in spirit and intention what the

Tamil mystic, Tirumular, spoke of when he said, "There is but one community [humanity], there is but one God"?[9]

Christians in India are called to unite with all men and women as Christ did, for Christ is found not in a truth imposed by authority but in a truth that is shared. God is heard not only on Sinai but in the voice of the stranger. This is why Orientals attach great importance to the mystery of hospitality. Christology is broader than the history of the Hebrew nation or of the Western world. God has redeemed all men and women, and all other creatures, in Christ: the many faces of Christ have not yet been seen by Christians. The religion of the Samaritan, for example, and the meaning of the parable of the Samaritan have not yet been fully explored. Too often the Samaritan has been seen as a rebuke to the unworthy Christian rather than as a symbol of Christ among "other sheep." Jesus never sanctioned any type of inequality among men and women. He is the *concrete pattern* of God among all — all human beings, every nation, every race. He is also the corrective of all aberrations, uniting all peoples. The union of West and East will arise only from his outgoing, universal love.

When we say that the kingdom extends to the whole human race, it is essential to stress that the kingdom extends to all cultures. Cultures have been perhaps the greatest stumbling block in the extension of the kingdom. Pope Paul VI expressed this thought most cogently: "The split between gospel and culture is the drama of our time."

The church must embody itself and its functions through indigenization in all countries. This truth is so fundamental that the choice is between authentic church and not being church. In India today, however, the church is largely in continuity with the tradition of the Western church, and sometimes in discontinuity with the culture of the country. There is an irony in the fact that Western Christian culture in India today is sometimes anachronistic because Christian culture in the Western countries themselves has changed! Therefore it is essential for the Indian Christian church to welcome its own national inheritance. Only thus will the Indian Christian be in communion with the living Christ. The mission of the church in India must include not only all individuals but the culture of India, which is Hindu. Otherwise, the church will reject the kingdom.

While Christianity claims to be a worldwide religion with a global ministry, its image in Eastern countries is often identified with a nonglobal culture. Western Christian scholars have not yet succeeded in reconceptualizing and incarnating Christianity for the East. Eastern scholars are more successful because they themselves, although they have been trained in Western Christianity, are not so personally embedded in it. They know instinctively that they have no right to identify a particular form of society with the Christian faith. The growth of Christianity in India, nevertheless, will happen less by mere rejection of Western elements in Christianity than by assumption of Eastern elements. This process will constitute the very kairos, or moment of destiny, of the modern Eastern Christian world. Only then will the necessary deepening and universalization of Christianity be achieved and the kingdom of God in the church be equated with the kingdom of God in Christ.[10]

Indian theologians are aware that biblical writers have been both assimilative and corrective. In the past, the mystery of Christ as recorded in St. John has been much studied in the context of Greek culture. Thus the logos — the light out of darkness — has been interpreted in specific Christian terms. St. John's Gospel, however, offers an excellent model to Indian Christian scholars in their efforts to develop an Indian Christian tradition. Instead of the context of the Judeo-Roman culture, they may use that of the Hindu. India has theologians of intellectual acumen — Raimundo Panikkar, Samuel Rayan, Matthew Vellanickal — who have already initiated a changing role in Indian theology. They may help to prevent one of the greatest threats to Indian Christianity: the danger that it may gradually become an Indian subculture. They will do so by attempting to extend the kingdom of God in India beyond its Judeo-Christian exclusivity to the depth and breadth and height envisioned in the gospel of Christ.

4. THE CHURCH AND THE KINGDOM

In India today the church is confronted in a new way with what
many historians call the greatest spiritual tradition of humankind. India throughout its long history has made the "most
searching quest for the divine . . . that the world has known."
In the cosmic revelation of the East, God has been revealed. The
church cannot therefore present the gospel as opposed to the
ancient religion and culture of India. Rather, it is called to purge
itself of accidental historical accretions of centuries in order to
appear in its own truth and universality. For the Hindu, God is
everywhere, in nature and in every living creature. The kingdom of God is unlimited, and Indians are as conscious of this
fact as they are of the shining of the sun. One of India's well
known scholars, M. P. Pandit, director of the Pondicherry
Ashram in Southeast India, declares that he has not practiced
"religion" for years; yet his ideal is "the fulfillment of the
purpose of God: the *kingdom of God* on earth." His goal is to
elevate the collective consciousness of all humans to clear the
ground for God's manifestation. Pandit sees the kingdom of
God as outside the established church, simply because he does
not see the church as what it should be: a dynamism toward
universality.[11]

The mission of the church extends to all men and women, all
religions, all cultures. The church cannot disown truth and
goodness in other religions. The kingdom of God is far more
extensive than many traditions of the established church: revelation and grace are universal; equality and justice belong to all
human beings; salvation is offered to everyone. The challenge to
seek liberation on earth and in eternity may not come to India
from the traditional church today. Only Jesus himself and his
gospel can challenge the Hindu to real, radical conversion to the
kingdom — to transcendence to caste distinctions, concern for
the suffering, freedom, and common humanity. India is open to
the spiritual message it has received from Christianity now only
in part. The church sometimes alienates; Christ attracts. Therefore Christians in India are called to proclaim the Christ who is
already accepted, not those customs of the church that are a

stumbling block, and to allow the Holy Spirit to fill up what is wanting between the church and the kingdom.

Fundamentally, Christianity has no real identity except Jesus Christ and the fraternal love patterned on Christ's love for all human beings to the point of dying for them. All the rest is only cultural accumulation derived from particular societies. Only the incarnation of the Word can determine the nature of the church.[12] Therefore all vexatious Western nonessentials must be removed from the practices of the church in the East. Gandhi knew how to accept and even to preach Christ in India. He did not try to decide who belongs and who does not belong to the kingdom of God. For him, God was the God of all. Fellowship in Christ did not demand rejection of Hindu culture.

Just as Christianity must become a dynamism toward universality in the kingdom, so Hinduism is Christianity in potency. This is not to say that Hinduism should become Christianity. Rather, as Raimundo Panikkar points out, "there is a dynamism within Hinduism itself which leads it toward that peculiar movement of death and resurrection in which we detect the work of the *antaryāmin*, the inner guide, which Christians call Christ."[13] The church in India is called to become more expansive toward Hinduism. It will thus prefer witness to Jesus to mere increase in numbers, and it will embrace new horizons without fear of a universalism that might abrogate basic differences between Hinduism and the Christocentric vision. Unless the church desires to exclude Hinduism from the kingdom — from the action of Christ — it must incorporate Hinduism into the universal economy of salvation through Christ. Christ himself is the universal principle, the beginning and end of reality. The only God found everywhere is the God made known in the word of Jesus: experience of God is known fully only in Christ.

Thoughtful Christians in India are now calling increased attention to the seeming exclusiveness of the church. They are challenging their church to meet the needs of the kingdom of God. Hindus can affirm with total sincerity that Christ is God. But they cannot tolerate a church that narrows Jesus and confines him in traditional Western patterns. The Christian has a responsibility to the non-Christian who welcomes the message of Christ but rejects the institutional church. No one, from the first to the last human being, is excluded from the grace of Christ. In the words of C. S. Lewis, "The truth is, God has not told us what his arrangements about the other people are." He might have added, "Of those to whom much has been given, much will be required."

Jesus Christ is the norm by which Paul looks at other religions: "In Jesus God has spoken." This is the message of the kingdom always. What the church in India sometimes seems not to be aware of is the *practical urgency* of this message today. The fact that Indians know intuitively that the person of Jesus is of deep significance to them makes the message even more urgent. The church is called to go beyond the narrow world of the Western historical development of Christianity and to accept its vocation to develop the gospel message in world history. The church as the kingdom of God is broad and deep and pluralistic.[14]

Yet tensions remain. In order for a person to be Christian, the church insists on certain rites, customs, culture, philosophy, and formulations of doctrines. The church in India is called, nevertheless, to reveal a "living Christ," a Christ who was in the beginning before Abraham, who is the Creator, the Alpha and the Omega, the only Son and the firstborn of all creatures. This is the Christ whom the Christian church recognizes as Jesus of Nazareth and whom it would proclaim to the Hindu, who seeks him and recognizes him but has not yet found his church.

5. THE CHURCH AND BAPTISM

The question of the sacrament of baptism must receive special consideration in Indian Christianity, for it is so often the barrier to the Hindu's acceptance of membership in the church. To the Hindu it sometimes means ostracism from all that is significant in life except Jesus Christ.

Swami Tapasyananda, Hindu scholar, poses some frank questions. If all Indians should become Christian (accept baptism), what would happen? Would the great and ancient culture of India become mere literature? Would the profound spirituality of India deviate interiorly? The implication of these questions is, of course, that Christianity in India today is not Indian. Many Christian scholars would agree.[15]

The nonscholarly Hindu who accepts Christ asks a simpler question: Why is it necessary for me to be baptized and break all roots with my family and culture to become a Christian? Sharda Rao, an Indian Christian, expresses clearly the dilemma of a young woman who sought his advice:

> I know the agony her parents would have to undergo if she decided to receive Baptism. What is the theological meaning of the agony of two loving parents who would not mind their child following Jesus, but would see the whole world crumble before them if that child would break away from her roots?[16]

Consideration of the Hindu attitude toward Christianity leads inevitably to the question of the Christian attitude toward the baptism of the Hindu. How can the church in India be *practical* in the face of acceptance of Christ and rejection of baptism by the Hindu? Many Indian Christian scholars and pastors today emphasize the value of accepting the positive elements implied in the Hindu's desire to follow Christ. Concomitantly, baptism should not be viewed as primary. Admission to the Christian community should not be stressed; the following of Christ should be stressed. Thus a greater good will be achieved. The results of regarding baptism as secondary and delayed can be left in faith to the Holy Spirit. Thus an alternative may be provided for the worshiper of Christ who is not ready to move into a new culture.

It is realistic and practical for the church to teach Jesus Christ to Hindus who respond personally to him as the incarnation of God. The rite of baptism should not be made an unnecessary stumbling block. An experiment in teaching Christ without immediately offering baptism may result in Christ-centered spirituality, individual responses of Indians to private worship of Christ in their own homes, and eventual reception of groups of Hindus to baptism in the church (when they realize that they can become church members together and thus avoid ostracism from community).

More crucial, perhaps, is the fact that the *presence* of the minister of Christ is more important than premature action in formal conversion. While an angel announced to Cornelius the centurion the way to Christ, it was Peter who was witness to Christ and the church. Only a human being can be a witness. In the case of Peter, he was able, as witness, to testify authoritatively to the action of the Spirit.

The concept of delayed baptism is also positive in the sense that, in the process, Christianity in India may mitigate at least partially the Hindu objection to "Churchianity." The poor of India who were converted to Christianity in the past often had mixed motives. They desired real liberation from the low caste that the social structure of Hinduism imposed on them, but they also sought Jesus Christ. The specific mission of the Christian in India is to deepen the dimensions of the church as well as to shed its Western accretions and adapt it to Hindu culture. From this point of view, the Hindu interpretation of Christianity as lived is important, not just the cultural interpretation the Western Christian gives to it.[17]

The Christian scholar in India today is considering the contemporary religious flowering in Hinduism, which is a gift of God. Why did it happen? Why do so many Hindus accept Christ? Why are they accepting Christ without church? Without baptism? What is the special spiritual dynamism at work among Hindu followers of Christ in India? How should the church respond to the problem of baptism? The fact that Hindu worshipers of Christ are relatively close to Christianity does not make it easier for them to recognize the church of Christ — with all its limitations. Yet they continue to follow Jesus Christ, either openly or secretly.

At least four points of view toward baptism are emerging among Christians in India today.

First is the traditional, majority approach, which holds to the necessity of baptism if a person is to be called Christian. Acceptance of Christ and the gospel is not considered to be enough. Rather, this acceptance must include the sacrament of baptism.

The "anonymous Christian" is not even a catechumen, not even a recipient of the doctrine and discipline preparatory to baptism and admission to communicant membership in the church.

A growing number of Indian Christians, however, subscribe to the concept of baptism as secondary or delayed, as already described above. They accept the validity of proclaiming Jesus Christ without baptism, trusting always in the Spirit. This approach they see as an introductory step to membership in the Christian community.

Another minority view is that an Indian can be a good Christian by following Christ without baptism. The *Roman* Catholic way is said to be not the *only* Christian way. An *Indian* Catholic way must be developed before Hindus can be expected to seek baptism in large numbers. The church can no longer bind God within its structures. It is as yet unaware of the face of the Christ who must be proclaimed to India, but not necessarily in terms of the seven sacraments stressed by the institutional church. Belief in Christ is essential. If people have faith in Christ, they will eventually find community and common worship. If the community comes together and develops its own worship, it may find its own way to the sacraments. Also, believers will attract others through their Christ experience. This different approach to conversion, its proponents believe, is now necessary in India.

A fourth approach is a new conception of baptism. Those who follow it believe that the expansion of the present Christian church toward the kingdom of God as envisioned by Christ goes far beyond the problem of baptism alone. They believe that the mutual fecundation of Christianity and Hinduism in India requires a loving reciprocity in faith, theology, society, culture, and politics. This fertilization is only in its beginning stages. When this communion is accomplished, the problem of baptism will no longer exist. The kairos will take place. The hope of Jerusalem II will become a reality. The kingdom will come in India. What form the new initiation rite will develop, which will take the place of the traditional *form* of baptism, is veiled in the future.

6. JESUS CHRIST, THE HINDU, AND THE CHURCH

An unusual triad — Jesus Christ, the established Christian church, and Hinduism — is present in India today. Abbé Jules Monchanin, who together with Henri LeSaux founded the famous Saccidananda Ashram in South India, wrote that India has not yet met Christ, nor have the Christian and the Hindu yet met as they really are. The church, he stated, must therefore enter into Hinduism through purification and transformation. The hidden treasure of Hinduism, the pearl of great price, is the Indian thirst for the Absolute, which reserves for India a providential role in the economy of salvation and in the mission of the church. The seeming ambiguity of the personal-impersonal God in India will be resolved finally, according to Monchanin, through the Trinity as the fulfillment of Hinduism. Jesus Christ, the personal God, the second person of the Trinity, will be the liberator, the one who will guide the hope of humanity in the new India.

Many of the leaders of the Christian churches, on the other hand, do not appear to the Hindus to possess the qualities of the sadhu or holy person. More often the hierarchy seem to the Indian to be administrators, educators, and welfare workers who live outside Hindu culture. The more thoughtful among the Christians are aware of this image. They assert that Christians must stop "giving" material things to Indians and give Jesus Christ himself. Christians must permit themselves to receive from Easterners. Like Augustine, Justin, and Clement of the early church, they must live *inside* the culture of their country. Their task is to proclaim the Lord Christ who was always present in India both before Jesus was born and after his death and resurrection. They would do well to define Christianity as Augustine did:

> That which is called the Christian religion existed among the ancients, and never did not exist from the beginning of the human race until Christ came in the flesh, at which time the true religion, which already existed, began to be called Christianity.

In the words of Joseph Neuner today:

> I do not expect Jesus to say anything really new and different from what others have said. To all men God revealed himself (though, through human error and sin, this revelation has been distorted in many ways). But in Jesus God has given us the *concrete pattern* of what man and humanity are meant to be, and it is for the Church to embody this message and to share it with all men.[18]

Augustine in the year 400 and Neuner in 1980 both echo the First Letter of John:

> Something that has existed since the beginning,
> that we have heard,
> and we have seen with our own eyes;
> that we have watched
> and touched with our hands;
> the Word, who is life —
> this is our subject.

Christ is the epiphany, the real manifestation in history of the mystery hidden since the beginning of time. The Christian teacher in India is thus asked by many of his brothers and sisters to proclaim Jesus Christ and to leave the fulfillment of his message to the Holy Spirit. Conversion as such and baptism can be delayed, for the church of the 1980s is sometimes seen as a Western, alien world movement, a barrier and threat to the Hindu. The whole message of the church in India is Jesus Christ, the incarnation of God. In him, not in the traditional Western church, is the catalyst to Hinduism.

Jesus Christ exercises so profound an attraction for India, in fact, that some Hindu gurus of deep spirituality see the discovery of Christ as the final stage of spiritual evolution.[19] Others, to be sure, refuse to see Jesus as the unique incarnation. The Christ they love is beyond all that the traditional Christian church teaches! The living Christ whom these Hindus seek appears to them to be beyond the historical Jesus Christ (whom, of course, they do not fully know). The Christ for whom they search is the one of whom Paul writes, quoting Isaiah: "I have been found by those who did not seek me, and I have shown myself to those who did not ask for me" (Romans 10:20). This Christ was not speaking of himself as the Messiah promised to the Hebrews. This Christ is a challenge to the Christian to discover the incarnation whom he or she knows only in part, the Christ in whom there is neither Jew nor Greek. Today history is revealing to Christians that they must die to themselves in order to know more fully the Christ who reveals himself to the Hindu: the non-Mediterranean, the universal Christ.

CHAPTER III

Toward a More Universal Perspective
Spiritual Interchange between Christian and Hindu

1. ROMAN CATHOLIC CHURCH AND INDIAN CATHOLIC CHURCH

TODAY in India it is sometimes declared that if the Christian church does not assume the religious and cultural legacy of Asia, it will not survive in the East. It is urgent that it learn from the fathers of the early and the medieval church who assimilated the wisdom and riches of the religions and cultures that surrounded them. If the church in India today is to build up the new creation in Christ, it will listen to Hindu thought on such questions as the human search for the ultimate reality, spirituality as rooted in personal experience, and the unity of God and humankind. Just as Thomas Aquinas adapted the philosophy of Aristotle to Christian teaching in the Middle Ages, Hindu philosophy can be adapted to gospel teaching today. Indian theolo-

28

gians may find an analogy between the Vedantic search for the oneness of humankind with the Absolute, for example, and the study of the evolution of matter and spirit toward the Omega Point in the manner of Teilhard de Chardin.

Whatever else the church in India does, it must seek a new synthesis of the gospel of Jesus Christ meaningful to the Indian mind and heart. It must be willing to learn from the Hindu. India offers the church centuries of the belief, the spirituality, the mysticism of the East. The church can offer the Indian not the uniqueness of Christianity (which the Indian cannot now accept) but the resurrected Christ for all time.[1] Through complementarity, reciprocity, and mutual fertilization, the church can be inculturated in India in the universal Christ. Only thus will an acceptable Indian church emerge.

While most scholars in India today believe that the church is too exclusive in its life, culture, and theology, they also believe that a *genuinely local church* can be created.[2] To achieve it, the church must be willing to change, for it is socially, culturally, and theologically conditioned. Jesus Christ can catalyze Hinduism. A transformed Christianity can arise; a transformed Hinduism can arise.

Christopher Durai Singh, Indian Christian pastor, insists that Christians in India must become "Indian-Christians," not just Christians who happen to be Indians, nor Indians who happen to be Christians.[3] Behind this mental construct or mode of consciousness are centuries of Pan-Indian (Hindu) traditions and two thousand years of Judeo-Christian tradition. The common factor among all Christians in India (whether dominantly Indian or dominantly Western in religious customs and practices) is the decisiveness of their reference to Christ: they are Christocentric. The Western Christian has one scriptural tradition, the Bible. The Indian-Christian has a double scriptural tradition, the Bible and the Vedas. The Indian-Christian is therefore called to incorporate what can be incorporated of the Hindu scriptures within the creation of an Indian-Catholic theology.

As already explained, there are many reasons for the inadequacies of the Christian church in India, as represented in its having reached only 2.5 percent of the population in church membership. The Hindu accepts solutions to human problems that the church has failed to examine; the church has built few bridges to Indian culture; the Hindu rebels against a foreign church; the church has failed to project its spirituality in India. A consensus prevails among thoughtful Christians in India today that the church should take steps to cancel out these mistakes. It is called to affirm the Hindu, to share life and worship with the Hindu, to cultivate cultural interdependence with the Hindu, to develop an Indian Christian theology to which the Hindu can respond. There is disagreement as to whether these actions should originate with the hierarchy of the church, or with grassroots movements, or with both. But change itself is inevitable.

The development of an Indian Christian theology is essential for the development of Indian local churches. The Hindu approach to philosophy requires greater fluidity of expression than the traditional Christian approach to theology. The new Christian theology will require relativization of formulations of credal aspects. Doctrines are faith expressed in cultural terms. Moreover, modes of expression of faith change historically. Traditionally in the West, Christian revelation has been stated in propositions. Definition has been the goal. The object of faith, however, is mystery inexpressible in human terms. The Hindu is confused by precise definitions in the Western manner. The Indian theologian is called therefore to express the Christian faith in terms less intellectual and more experiential.

Thus a central point of meeting of the Christian and the Hindu in India is religion conceived as actual experience of God rather than as intellectual formulation. Personal prayer and meditation, more so than catechism or dogma, are basic in the Indian's learning about God. Indian theologians or pastors who understand the operation of this principle within their own culture can help to create a new Indian Christian society in which all dimensions are Christocentric, yet adapted to the Indian way of life. The "foreign clothes" of the faith will then no longer prevent Hindus from perceiving the universal character of the church. They will understand what it means to be Indian

Catholic, for example, as they do not at present understand the meaning of Roman Catholic. For Indian Christianity will then be based on India's own experience of reality, with Jesus Christ at its core. In fact, Indian theologians who are developing the new theology now offer hope that new Indian Catholic local churches will eventually be recognized as member churches of the universal church of Christ.

2. A NEW ECUMENISM

Vatican Council II defines the ecumenical movement as those activities organized to foster unity among Christians. The council suggests that the church should preserve a proper freedom in the various forms of spiritual life and discipline, in the variety of liturgical rites, and in the theological elaborations of revealed truth.

In India today, a frequent approach to the ecumenical spirit emphasizes that Christian churches should come together chiefly to relate themselves to non-Christian religions, particularly Hinduism, in order to initiate the fermentation of a new religious society. The long-range goal is the mutual fecundation of Christianity and Hinduism through the Holy Spirit.

On a broad level, Asian reality today challenges Christians to seek active cooperation with Hindus, Buddhists, Muslims, and Confucianists in the pursuit of peace and justice. The Asian region has more than half the world's population, of which fewer than 4 percent are Christians. Through the Roman Catholic Church and the World Council of Churches, Eastern Christians have already achieved partnership and cooperation in the fulfillment of certain common tasks. Consultations center on the study of theological bases for Christian cooperation with Asians of other faiths in the struggle for peace and justice in the less economically developed countries. Christian churches in Asia are calling for a spirit of universal inclusiveness, with the goal of overcoming all forms of separation and exclusiveness attributed to them in the past.[4] They seek solidarity with persons of all religions in the struggle for universal human values.

Christian faith centers in salvation, a basic theme of all religions, and in the involvement of God with the liberation of the suffering and the oppressed. Both the Christian and the non-Christian in Asia are confronted by startling realities in the life of the poor and the uneducated. About 50 percent of Asians live below the poverty line. About 500 million, in absolute poverty, struggle to keep alive. Widespread ignorance and unemployment are brought about by economic and political exploitation. Escalation of the arms race develops side by side with authoritarian regimes and the erosion of democratic freedoms. Salvation is not escape from these realities: it means overcoming them to achieve wholeness for all persons.

Cooperation with non-Christians in Asia is therefore not optional for Christians. They have a compelling obligation to aid in the mobilization of all Asians to struggle against dehumanizing forces and to achieve liberation for justice and peace, for salvation in its broadest sense. The Christian ministry demanded is one of reconciliation in Jesus Christ, which will break down the walls of hostility and create one new humanity (Ephesians 2:14–15). Those who call this process a new or extended "ecumenism" are well advised. They are giving a name to a development that has been taking place slowly in the East since the close of Vatican II.

Swami Tapasyananda, president of Ramakrishna Math, Madras, suggests that Christians can become better Christians by recognizing the values of other religions they now appreciate only in "a hazy way."[5] He adds, moreover, that Christians will participate better in the "ecumenical movement" by comparative study of the Bible and the Hindu scriptures. Many Hindu gurus have already done such comparative readings. An example is the well-known *Sermon on the Mount according to Vedanta*, by Swami Prabhavananda.[6] Evidence is thus arising that Hindus sometimes see themselves as a part of the ecumenism originated by the Christian church. The church too is producing expressions of Christian faith through comparative studies.[7] Within this new ecumenism, all religions of the East contribute insights toward a spiritual reciprocity.

The Christian church in India, moreover, is slowly becoming

a nucleus and agent for change through social and economic projects related to ecumenical centers. Paulo Freire's method of conscientization, for example, is carried out to a small extent in centers for lay ecumenical training, community service centers, and Christian industrial centers. Indian Christian leaders, to be sure, know well that Freire's method is directed toward Latin America and that Indians must find their own methods suitable to the development of their own Christian culture. Political, social, economic, and cultural movements in India are now related to diverse types of religious centers. Ecumenism is always carried out on a local level, for the Christian church in India is aware that local roots are essential if concrete results are to be achieved. These results will be most effective, however, when Christians and Hindus can report in one voice their experiences in centers dedicated to both spiritual and social liberation.

Many Christians in India are revealing their insights into the ecumenical process through a new orientation toward small, open communities. A number of large religious institutions are being gradually phased out. In small basic communities or ashrams, often set up in villages rather than cities, Hindus join with Christians in prayer, meals, and social gatherings. Neither conversion nor syncretism is a goal. Rather, understanding, fellowship, and common worship are emphasized.

Since 1970 in India, the ecumenical movement has thus brought a growing understanding between Christian and Hindu. Old attitudes of confrontation are increasingly falling away, and the dialogue approach is becoming stronger. A limited number of Christians and Hindus reveal an increasing mutual respect, humility in claims concerning religious truth, desire for harmony, and willingness to learn from one another. The ecumenical dialogue movement is still in its early stages, but its proponents are full of hope for spiritual exchange between Christians and Hindus. "Ecumenism" in India is no longer meaningful in the context of fostering unity among Christians alone. Roman Catholic, Orthodox, and all types of Christians in India are now more closely united. Their common goal is understanding of and reciprocity with their Hindu neighbors.

3. DIALOGUE AND COMPLEMENTARITY

"Dialogue" is a much abused word in many Western countries today, but in India it is still widely used by Christians in the context clarified by Vatican II. The church, in speaking of Hinduism and Buddhism, exhorts Christians "prudently and lovingly, through dialogue and collaboration . . . and in witness of Christian faith and life, to acknowledge, preserve, and promote the spiritual and moral goods found among these [persons], as well as the values in their society and culture."[8] The church is aware today that in the past every great religion made itself absolute. Hence the encounter with other religions in dialogue poses a sensitive situation.

The process of search for interreligious understanding in India has passed through at least four stages. The first was one of dislike and indifference, during which Christians saw themselves as unique and thus caused ill will among Hindus. The second phase was one of tolerance, which brought a certain growth in mutual acceptance but no real knowledge by each religion of the other. Next came an incipient approach to dialogue, in which the Christian took the lead in an attempt to understand the Hindu. The fourth stage is one of true dialogue and complementarity in which each religion attempts to reach totality and completeness by understanding the other. The latter process is now taking place among a strong minority of Christians and non-Christians. It should be emphasized, however, that the first three stages still exist in varying degrees.

Fortunately, the development of dialogue and complementarity between Christian and Hindu is taking place concomitantly with a wider East-West encounter, which may be called an "Asian-European planetary renaissance." Eastern and Western spirituality are meeting each other finally not as problems but as mysteries. The time is ripe for a deeper Christian-Hindu dialogue, and many members of both spiritual paths are open to its values. Bishop Patrick D'Souza of Varanasi clarifies the goal of the Christian when he points out that dialogue "is not a substitute or mere preliminary to the proclamation of Christ." Rather, in dialogue "we seek together with our brothers and sisters that fullness of Christ which is God's plan for the whole of creation in its entirety and its great and wonderful diversity."

Dialogue thus has a basis in human solidarity and the universal history of humankind. Inasmuch as there is no *complete agreement* among Christian theologians in India as to whether God's redemptive purpose is to manifest Christ within other systems of belief as such, dialogue provides an open ground for search into the fullness of the Christian faith. Serious dialogue in India obliges the Christian to attempt to discover how God has spoken to the Hindu over thousands of years, and to be open to whatever emerges from the dialogue itself. Christians experience a providential invitation to be open to new horizons in their own radical conversion to Christ without yielding to a false universalism that ignores crucial differences in religions. Christian and Hindu together thus experience a shared desire for growth in truth. Each respects the other's core of commitment. Emphasis is on equality of person rather than equality of religion. Spiritual experience is shared. Christians bring to dialogue their experience of Christ; Hindus may bring the Advaitic spiritual experience of India. Because God has spoken to human beings both inside and outside the Judeo-Christian tradition, enrichment in dialogue is mutual. Dialogue has no ulterior or exterior purpose. Fulfillment for all men and women can come only through Christ, the Lord of all. Today, dialogue between Christian and Hindu on the nature and destiny of humankind can give to the confession of Christ as Lord and Savior a challenging significance not known before. Hinduism can be incorporated into the universal economy of salvation in God through Christ. Or, in the words of Raimundo Panikkar, Christianity can seek to "unveil" the "unknown Christ."

Dialogue between Christian and Hindu today is not a choice for the Indian Christian but a necessity. The majority of Hindus are self-assured in both their beliefs and their culture. They do not seek change. A minority of Indian intellectuals tend to take a humanistic stand. Most of the native Indian Christian clergy, on the other hand, are concerned chiefly with the Christian communities they serve. Like the Hindus, they do not seek change. Many young Christian priests and scholars, moreover, believe that their duty as Christians is not so much to seek conversions as to witness to Christ by their presence and their actions among Hindus. Thus there is a second incomplete theological dimension among Christian leaders (in addition to the question of whether God's redemptive purpose is to manifest Christ within other systems of belief). The center of Christian action is not clear: the meaning of "teach all nations" is interpreted on diverse levels. Most Christians in India, moreover, do not speak freely of religion to Hindus. They have an exaggerated respect for Hindu freedom and a fear of misunderstanding because of the burden of the past. In response to this problematic situation, a type of communion not experienced before is now sought in dialogue between Christians and Hindus. A growing number of Indians of varied beliefs are seeking union with one another through prayerful exchange without the slightest hint of debate. They are deepening their faith because dialogue forces them to full expansion of their own beliefs. A special dynamism is at work. Its conclusion is obscured in the future.

Christians recognize that this new dialogue must be approached with absolute seriousness. It cannot be a mere fad or an attempt by Christians to adopt in word or action the externals of Hindu worship. What is properly assimilated from Hindu culture through dialogue must be corrected and introduced with clarity into Christian spiritual practice. This dialogue must be carried out with fundamental sincerity because it rests on the concept that spiritual development can come only through reciprocity of Christianity and Hinduism. Where dialogue has been approached without intellectual preparation and seriousness, it has resulted — as it sometimes has in the West — in mere frustration. As one Indian scholar remarks, "Dialogue is a weak thing, just talk. What does it bring?"[9] A Christian sociologist responds in similar vein: "Dialogue? It does not work. Hindus are not accessible to dialogue. Hindus and Christians speak different languages."[10]

Aside from such negative views, it should be added that the *majority* of leaders of the institutional church in India still believe that the proclamation of the gospel and the mission of conversion comprise their proper approach to the Hindu. Only a minority of creative thinkers asserts the necessity of dialogue as described above.

Bede Griffiths speaks for the strong minority when he asserts that, although dialogue has not always been successful in India, it is imperative that it be continued and developed.[11] Dom Bede believes that "the future lies with small groups of people, Hindu and Christian and also Muslim, who meet together to work for social justice — rather like the basic communities of Latin America — among whom the Gospel works as a kind of leaven, but which are not identified with the Church." Some of the most effective meetings between Christians and Hindus are those in which they join in prayers, hymns, songs, bhajans, and readings from the Gita. Provided the participants are properly prepared, these spiritual activities lead naturally to dialogue of an intellectual type. Serious Christians prepare themselves for dialogue as St. Paul did, by studying what is actually believed by those with whom they wish to communicate.

Indifference to the Hindu faith by the Christian is perhaps the greatest single obstacle to dialogue. Acceptance of the belief of the other without fear of prejudice is essential. The second obstacle is minimization of the actual differences between Christianity and Hinduism. The third is a tendency toward a "universal" religion that will satisfy no one. Yet Christianity can catalyze Hinduism so that a new Hinduism may arise. The end rests with the Holy Spirit. The final goal of dialogue, therefore, can only be surmised.

Complete openness in which Christian and Hindu freely express their spiritual experience is already being achieved in India by those who approach dialogue with the proper orientation. When participants see themselves as pilgrims seeking truth, willing to pray, share, and suffer with others, a spiritual osmosis takes place. They discover that man is more than one; woman is more than one. Reality is more than one. "The Church focusing on herself, or the Hindu focusing on himself, is off-center. The center is not self-centered. Real dialogue happens when the unknown becomes more meaningful than the known."[12] But the unknown cannot be even approached without both tolerance and recognition of the reality of pluralism.

Affirmation must precede sharing, and affirmation cannot happen without love and willingness to understand. Love must be seen as a beginning and an end, never as a mere instrument. At times silent dialogue is more effective than words in the meeting of Christian and Hindu. It leads to intuitive discernment of both unity and differentiation. It can culminate in mutual spiritual fecundation.

Dialogue is more a Western contribution of Christianity to Hinduism than a Hindu concept. It represents the fellowship characteristic of the Christian; it relates to the self-criticism that arises from the Christian concept of sin and guilt, which is somewhat foreign to the Hindu.[13] Also, the Christian missionary idea itself is one of sharing. The Hindu is fundamentally more concerned with the meditative approach to salvation as related to the individual. Therefore dialogue begins with the Christian in India today. The Hindu response to dialogue, when it is affirmative, is testimony to the tolerance and openness of the Hindu approach to life.

M. M. Thomas, in his famous book, *The Acknowledged Christ of the Hindu Renaissance*, enumerates central values to be interchanged through dialogue between Christian and Hindu.[14] Once the theological aspect is clear and the element of a certain degree of mutual exclusiveness in both positions is accepted, greater understanding, coexistence, and cooperation can result. A more profound interpretation at the levels of philosophy and culture can also be achieved. Thomas points out, however, that on the whole a formulated theology of dialogue accepted by both Christian and Hindu in India does not yet exist. Or, in any case, it is not yet time to crystalize a theology of dialogue. But many Indian Christians are convinced that in the pluralistic communities in which they live, dialogue needs no defense. In the very process of dialogue, they hope that a new Eastern Christian theology will evolve.

This mutual enrichment, which is already taking place, provides one of the strongest hopes for the growth of Indian spirituality today. For example, Hindus offer to Christians their emphasis on the values of prayer, contemplation, mysticism, detachment from material things, and awareness of God's presence in the world. Christians are awakening Hindus more and more to social concern for the poor and the oppressed, selfless love expressed in involvement in the world, and a positive outlook toward the modern world itself.

Centers and movements for Christian-Hindu dialogue, despite the disapproval of a number of church leaders, are multiplying rapidly in India. A few examples will illustrate the types of dialogue now accepted.

Aikya Alayam Ashram in Madras, under the direction of Ignatius Hirudayam, is a center for the study of Christian faith in relation to Indian culture and Tamil philosophy. Liturgical rites embrace many Hindu customs of worship. An open pongal celebration, commemorating the harvest festival of the Hindus, is an example of a typical ashram gathering. It consists of sung prayer with karnatic music, a spiritual discourse, a general discussion of the significance of pongal, a closing prayer, and a silent meditation. Both Christians and Hindus participate.

Snehasadhan, a "Home of Friendship" in Pune, Maharashtra, is a house of dialogue directed by Matthew Lederle. It is a center of Christian presence and outreach where members of all religions meet in fellowship. Lectures and discussions are frequent. Here an attempt is made by Christians to establish themselves in a particular Brahmin Hindu milieu for spiritual study and dialogue.

Sebastian Painadath is the leader of Jyothis Centre in Ernakulam, Kerala, where academic courses, meditations, and discussions are held for everyone who wishes to attend. Studies in world religions attract as many as one hundred fifty persons, mostly Hindu but also Muslim and Christian. Ideas of human nature, prayer, suffering, and death are topics of discussion. Eight-day retreats based on the Bhagavad Gita are offered for Christians. Inculturation in practice is found through silence, meditation, and experience of the Gita as a contribution to Christ experience. One-day dialogues open to persons of all religions draw large numbers of attendants.

Aelred Pereira, of Andheri, Bombay, consultor to the Vatican Secretariat for Non-Believers, sponsors interreligious dialogues throughout India. Regular meetings are held in Bombay in which spiritual experiences are shared by Christians, Hindus, Muslims, Buddhists, Hebrews, Parsees, Sikhs, and Jains. Persons of diverse beliefs also share their religious thoughts in two- or three-day meetings called "Indialogues." The ministry of Pereira is related to a movement rather than to a center.

Dialogue between Christian and Hindu is thus a slowly growing phenomenon in India. To many, it offers one of the most sanguine hopes for reciprocity between the Christian faith and the age-old spirituality of India.

4. SPIRITUAL RECIPROCITY AND FECUNDATION

Complementarity, reciprocity, and spiritual fecundation between Christianity and Hinduism in India today extend to individuals, communities, ashrams, and churches. The movement seeks to encompass the minority of educated believers, the minority of educated humanists, and the majority of uneducated believers.

The contemporary situation in India, as described above, poses many questions to Christians: Does "teach all nations" mean to teach all men and women? Does it mean to transform culture? Is direct evangelization necessary? Is it enough for a Hindu to follow Christ personally and witness to him? Does the church itself cry out for change in its approach to the Hindu? The truth about God and humankind remains the truth. How does a Christian maintain spiritual balance in a schizoid situation in which the center does not seem to hold? What is the Holy Spirit asking in the encounter between Christian and Hindu?

Turning to the Hindu, the Christian may also ask questions related as much to the other as to oneself: Why does Christianity appear to be a failure among Hindus after two thousand years in a country with perhaps the greatest spiritual tradition in the world? Are there *profound causes* not yet explored as to why millions of Indians accept Christ without accepting the church? Why does the spiritual interchange between Christian and Hindu carry a special urgency today that it never revealed before?

The incarnation of Jesus Christ is the only touchstone by which the Christian can approach the unique phenomenon of the situation of Christianity in India today. The Hindu does not seek the historic God-Man, the Jewish Messiah sent to redeem the world. But the Hindu is open to the transhistorical Christ who is the man Jesus and more than the man Jesus. The meeting point of Christian and Hindu is the everlasting resurrected Christ. There are not two Christs, however: the Christ who confronts the Hindu is the same Christ who confronts the Christian. Christ is both historical and transhistorical. He is the epiphany, the manifestation, of the Son of God in history, and he is also the mystery hidden from the beginning of time. The Hindu can understand the real Christ who was, is, and will be a living reality. This is the living Christ who can transform Hinduism through his incarnation, death, and resurrection. Reciprocity between Christianity and Hinduism can take place only through the grace of this one everlasting Christ manifested in historical time in Jesus Christ.[15]

The exciting reciprocity that is beginning to take place between Christianity and Hinduism in India is one of mutual enrichment, as already indicated, with an open relationship merging into a larger stream of development. Unless Christians wish to be accused of excluding Hinduism from the action of Christ, they must be willing to include Hinduism in the universal economy of salvation. Hinduism, like Christianity, awaits the radical transformation that will reveal more clearly the relationship of Jesus with the uncreated wisdom of the transhistorical Christ.

Only the mutual realistic love of Christian and Hindu will bring about in India the transformation that will reveal depths of the mystery of Christ *still unknown to the Christian*. The experience of actual loving dialogue in which the Christian and Hindu encounter the Lord, not only each other, in spiritual osmosis demands not so much words on the part of the Christian as witness. Jesus is the concrete pattern. The Spirit is the guide. The growth of an Indian or "Hindu" Christianity will be a new development that will reveal that Western historical Christianity does not own Christ, that the present Christian discovery of

Christ is not at all exhaustive. Just as the identity of the Christian may be defined by stating that he or she is a part of the total Christ who was born, died, and was resurrected in Jesus, so the identity of the new Indian Christian will reveal a oneness with the everlasting Christ still to be unveiled in history.

The great Christian mystic, Abhishiktananda, believed that the extent to which the message of the church in India will be accepted will be in direct proportion to its mystical and contemplative life.[16] If the essential inner adaptation to this fundamental demand of India is lacking, then external forms of adaptation will prove to be fruitless. Rites, musical tones, and dance steps can never be more than signs, which draw their value solely from what they signify. "Only a Church which has fully actualized [its] own experience of faith and has attained to that inner depth where the authentic spiritual life of India is lived, will be capable of entering into a true religious dialogue with [it]." Those who are to be Christian apostles in India, wrote Abhishiktananda, should prepare themselves for this dialogue by serious study of the thought of India and by personal contact with its living spirituality. Their preparation will be most effective if prayer and contemplation hold the chief place in their own lives. These Christian apostles, strong in faith and hope, will study at the feet of the ancient Indian sages, just as the Greek fathers of the church sat at the feet of the rhetoricians and philosophers of classical antiquity:

> When they return, their faith will have been strengthened and enriched by a new depth of experience. A kind of osmosis will have taken place in their souls between the Hindu experience of the depths of the Self and the Christian experience of the depths of the heart of Christ.

Reciprocity in the process of search for loving spiritual fecundation highlights the conviction that neither Christianity nor Hinduism alone can save humanity in India. Salvation will come through the pilgrimage of all Indians, Christian and non-Christian, toward God. This movement will be based on faith in the basic community of men and women, and God's plan for humankind. Each partner in reciprocity must change. The hope of Calvary will be redeemed in mutual love. A new synthesis of the two traditions will be formed in which each will learn from the other. The experience of the double heritage of Christian and Hindu, of death to the old forms and birth to the new, will generate the new reality, the Indian Christian. The common basis to be discovered can have an incalculable influence on the Indian and on the world — without prejudice to the truth of Christ. In such encounter, experience proves that only the outsider, the spectator, can fear danger of syncretism. When persons with the proper orientation enter into spiritual dialogue, they develop almost invariably an increase in faith. Yet Christianity can never be all-inclusive as Hinduism is. Comprehensiveness is the keynote of Hinduism; commitment to Christ is the keynote of Christianity.

Because Christians, more than Hindus, feel the need for reciprocity, it is obvious that the burden of initiative toward mutual fecundation lies with Christians. In order to enrich themselves through Hinduism, Christians must be humble. Perception of the Spirit in Hindus is essential. The ability to discern is a sign of authentic Christians. The Spirit of Jesus is always perceptive. Unfortunately, the historical attitude of Christians in India has often been one of giving — all giving — with nothing to receive. Today, readiness of Christians to enrich their own spirit is paramount. Again, this openness of the Christian to accept the good in Hinduism needs to be personal, communal, ecclesial. Christ is the model. He was not self-sufficient: he sought the help of his Father. The more Christlike Christians become, the more they are ready to see Christ in Hindus and to learn about Christ from them.

In reciprocity, Christians and Hindus become aware that boundaries between their traditions and customs are not always hard and fast. Some boundaries exist chiefly among intellectuals. Not only philosophical concepts, however, but the experiences and articulations of "ordinary people" are essential in spiritual exchange between Christians and Hindus. Religious scholars today are analyzing testimonies, journals, biographies, and even fiction reflecting the spirituality of both sophisticated and folk communities in India. Cities and rural areas reveal differences in religious customs between the better educated and the village populations. Mystical experience of both the learned and the unlearned is explored in imaginative literature. For example, Tamil literature in the South of India would require a lifetime of study to plumb the depths of its revelation of God. Studies of Tamil poetry, like those of A. J. Appasamy, reveal much in Hindu religious thought and worship that is completely in harmony with the spirit of Christ.[17]

Religious festivals, too, offer a colorful expression of Indian spiritual experience. Various methods of prayer are also significant. Sociological surveys and other methods of analysis also help to clarify likenesses and differences among the various Hindu patterns of worship. Judgments differ as to the degree to which the faith of the learned filters down to the uneducated, who form the majority of the Indian population. Yet in spite of all diversity, a unity of manifestations of belief in the one Ultimate Reality maintains a startling consistency throughout India, even to the extent that one will find the learned Hindu scholar worshipping with a simple "puja" before his chosen avatar in a manner that suggests idolatry to an uninitiated Westerner.[18]

Reading and study of Hindu scriptures provide a good basis for spiritual reciprocity between Christian and Hindu. Songs of the Rigveda offer germs of the concept of Christ the Logos and even of the doctrine of redemptive sacrifice. In early hymns, the rishis grope toward the one invisible Being who expresses the Self in forms and qualities that human faculties can apprehend. These hymns suggest a ground for passage from the Vedic God to Christian divinity. They reveal that the Spirit often speaks to the Hindu mystic in a manner similar to that in which the Spirit speaks to the Christian saint.[19]

Although the differing orthodox concepts of Christian and Hindu must be recognized positively in spiritual reciprocity, the goal in any such interaction is the mystery beyond thought and speech. The God beyond all name and description is the God of absolute justice, mercy, and love manifested in Jesus Christ. In seeking the absolute, unknowable God of Eastern tradition, Christianity that has developed in the Western tradition will be only returning to its own past. Indeed, Christianity will remain unbalanced until it has done justice to human solidarity with nature in which the cosmic covenant is revealed.[20] God is not "just one of us." "Our Father" is accessible. "He whose excellence is unsurpassable, who has removed the darkness from my understanding and the cloud of unknowing, is the Lord of celestials." Hindus offer the Christian their own approach to the One Supreme Spirit, whether their Lord be called Krishna, Siva, or Vishnu.

In all exchange between Hindu and Christian, authentic spiritual experience must precede sophisticated analysis of spirituality and of philosophical concepts. Christianity must allow the authentic experience of the Hindu to reveal itself. Expression of faith will develop in the Indian way. Differences between content and method are crucial. In content, Christians have nothing to share but Jesus Christ. Christ offers the concrete example once again: he became human first, then divinized others. As a method, intellectual formulation can never come first. Of central importance is the fact that religious life in the East will *never* appear as it is in the West. Spiritual exchange must always take this fact into consideration.[21]

When Christians engage in dialogue with Hindus in which they hope to tend toward spiritual fecundation, the question of Ultimate Reality will always be side by side with the historical fact of Jesus Christ. Within Hindu culture, it is inauthentic — almost impossible — to proceed from the historical Christ alone. For the Christian, to be sure, the actuality of Christ is unique. But the Christian can always place the truth of Jesus Christ in ultimate reality as well as in history. Christians must surrender not the uniqueness of Jesus Christ but the exclusivity with which Christianity is equated by Hindus. Exclusivity is not the same as uniqueness. It has been the unique dispensation of Indian philosophy to penetrate the question of the Absolute with unparalleled power. In its principal tradition, Vedanta in nondualist form, India offers a viable philosophy that can be operative within Christian thought. The achievement of a thoroughgoing philosophical expression of the Christian faith within the Vedanta tradition (relevant to Platonism in the West) will be a gift not only to India but to the world.

A few Indian philosophers, like Raimundo Panikkar, are now

making strong contributions to the integration of Indian spiritual experience and philosophical thought with gospel truth. Panikkar's *The Trinity and the Religious Experience of Man*,[22] for example, points out the absolute necessity for the deepening and universalization of Christianity today. What we call "Christianity" in the West is *only one form* of living and realizing Christian faith. Panikkar studies the most characteristic forms of spirituality in the majority of great religions: iconolatry (action), personalism (love), and advaita (knowledge). He calls our attention to the fact that the theological problem of the Trinity has been allowed to atrophy. He offers theandrism (unity) as a fundamental attitude through which we can understand and share the basic attitudes of most religions. Only the trinitarian concept of reality permits a synthesis of the above three concepts of the Absolute. The theandric concept avoids both anthropomorphism — of which Western Christianity is accused by both Easterners and Westerners today — and theologism. The human being is a "theandric mystery," and only a theology that relates this mystery to Christianity can bring about the kairos or moment of destiny of the modern world. Only such a theology as related to a way of life can effect the mutual spiritual fecundation of Christianity and Hinduism in India.

The following chapters will explore the possible spiritual sharing that has the potential to bring the discovery of the "unknown Christ of Hinduism" to fruition in India.

CHAPTER IV

Foundations of Spiritual Fecundation

1. PLURALISM AND DOGMATISM

H ENRY ADAMS created a famous aphorism in the nineteenth century when he wrote, "chaos is the law of nature; order is the dream of man." As our global consciousness deepens in the late twentieth century, it is more apt perhaps to say, "Pluralism is the law of nature; unity is the dream of man." Christianity in India, in its historical action of transplanting Western culture together with faith in a universal Christ, has developed a practicing church that is an "island" in the subcontinent of India.

Although the church brought Western culture along with Christianity to many Eastern countries, this anomaly is perhaps most strongly evident in India because of the intrinsic plurality of Indian spirituality. The major current within this plurality is the spirituality of immanence, expressed in the search for the direct experience of the person's innermost being at its very source. This existential quest, which seeks the most intimate reality of the self, is personal, individualistic, and therefore pluralistic. In India, the "natural law" of pluralism is felt to be historically proved. The assimilative quality of Hinduism and the rejection of exclusive religious claims are a part of the very fabric of Indian life. The seeming failure of Christianity in India after hundreds of years reflects the denial of spiritual pluralism among most Western proponents of the Christian message. India brings to Christianity not one but many different ways of looking at human beings and the world, together with a profound sense of the mystery of existence.

The variety of doctrines called Hinduism is bewildering.[1] As stated in the Rig Veda, "Reality is one though sages call it variously." One of the unique features of Hinduism is catholicity and comparative freedom from dogma. The great sages of India have taught that there are as many approaches to God as there are human minds, simply because human minds are variously limited and cannot comprehend total reality. The Christian church in India is therefore exposed in a unique way to its broadest mission, which encompasses all human beings, all cultures, and all religions. An ecclesial pluralism, based on social, cultural, and pastoral pluralism, is needed in the Christian church in India today. Only thus will an essential liturgical pluralism be achieved, as well as the theology of relationship between a universal Christian church and particular local churches.

To be sure, all that is Christianized in India must be subjected to a critique, and false particularism must be excluded. Moreover, there is no question of blame for Christian teachers of the past who had less opportunity to develop a broader vision than church leaders of today who carry a responsibility concomitant with the pluralistic vision possible to them. A providential occasion is present for true Christian renewal as opposed to the practice of Christianity within the residue of imperialist conquest and expansion. One of the larger points at issue, however, is whether local pastors and churches are willing to act. Meetings and conferences of Asian bishops, for example, express in principle many movements toward pastoral and ecclesial pluralism that await the action of local churches.

This demand for action becomes more complicated the more one examines the relationship of Christianity and Hinduism in India today. Despite their differences and divisions, the majority of Christians agree on fundamentals: they believe in one God; in Jesus Christ, the incarnation of God; in his death for the redemption of the world; in the Holy Spirit given to men and women to guide them. Hindus, on the other hand, have comparatively no orthodoxy, no agreement on fundamental questions. Because of the unity of faith experienced by Christians, the church in India would surely sacrifice little by offering its members freedom in matters such as pluralism in social, cultural, and pastoral areas that call forth the diversified Indian national inheritance.

A strong block to social and cultural pluralism is also encountered in India because of the resistance of Christian church members themselves whose families have been indoctrinated through several generations with the experience of Western church laws, customs, and rituals. Because these families became Christian originally through a more or less hostile rejection of "pagan" Hinduism, church leaders owe them in justice an education in the broader meaning of the kingdom of Christ on earth. In short, acceptance of pastoral pluralism makes a strong demand on all Indian Christians as both teachers and witnesses.

Indeed, the two major questions that confront the Indian church today are pluralism of religion and culture, and socioeconomic problems of justice and equality. If the church is to deal with either or both of these questions, it must establish a spiritual base in a pluralism that will welcome and encourage local Indian Christian churches with indigenous roots in Indian culture and society. Christianity in India can sacrifice the "baggage" of Western rituals and customs without the least sacrifice of faith.

The question of pluralism of religions (aside from pluralism within Christianity) is a profound challenge to the Christian church. Philosophical, cultural, and theological pluralisms have always been more or less accepted throughout Christian history, though not often pursued. Justification for religious pluralism implies that other religions have a place in the Christian economy of salvation.[2] It would be gross extrapolation to say that the anathemas pronounced upon pagans in the gospel apply to what has falsely been called idolatry in India. These anathemas cannot be applied to realities other than those intended by the sacred writers. St. Paul's pagans were not Hindus, Buddhists, or Muslims. Hindus were never promised a redeemer. They never desired, hoped for, or awaited a Messiah. Christians have only begun to explore Christianity in the extra-Mediterranean religious and cultural context of India. The Christ who was found by those who did not seek him, who showed himself to those who did not ask for him, requires a new christology in the East. Or, according to Raimundo Panikkar, a new christophany.

The spiritual pluralism found in Hinduism itself offers to the Christian both theoretical and practical values of a high level centered in the ahimsa or nonviolence so sacred to Mahatma Gandhi. Personal depth and a spirit of inner harmony accompany the pluralistic teachings of the Rigveda. "Let noble thoughts come to us from every side." Hinduism reveals the Indian ethos as unity in diversity. Plurality is a gift of God to all in a "counterpoint of concords and discords, opposites and contradictions."[3] No one approach to God is sufficient. The Indian seeks more than Christianity has offered in the Western context. Humankind is larger than the Western, Judeo-Christian concept of humankind. Both Hindu and Christian in India need collaboration, open dialogue, and mutual spiritual fecundation in the search for truth. The Christian is learning that the words of scripture do not exhaust the mystery of God; they cannot describe God completely or circumscribe God.

The hidden working of the transhistorical Christ is at the basis of the positive values of pluralism. The church has authority over expressions of revelation but not over revelation itself. Christian revelation is often expressed in categories that do not negate the mystery, reality, or validity of experience itself.[4] Though Hindus accept all approaches to God as valid, they also believe that not all approaches are of equal value. Without prejudice to orthodoxy, Christians in India can learn a great deal from Hindus about the values of spiritual diversity.

The church in India is called today to reject even a hint of conquest, either spiritual or cultural. Mission is the humble offering of God's truth, justice, and love to free human beings. In a demonstrably pluralistic world, the church cannot live in isolation; it must collaborate with Christ. To be evangelical in the 1990s means to accept the pluralism of local churches in those parts of the world that have no historical relationship to Judeo-Roman Christianity. It also means to accept global diversity as well as differences within each country. Hinduism is the most pluriform religion, both spiritually and culturally, in the world. It is therefore perhaps the greatest challenge to Christianity in existence.

To respond to the challenge of Hinduism, Christian leaders in India are now viewing the historical reality of the incarnation of Christ in the light of the reality of pluralism. Both are essential elements of reality. The mystical body of humanity depends on both. One of the many reasons why Christianity has made little headway in India is that the faith has been presented so often as a "finished product." The truth is that Christ is more inclusive than Christianity as historically developed to date.

It cannot be denied that many Western Christians, as well as Hindus, see Christianity as this "finished product." Western Christians in India are sometimes disturbed by the Hindu emphasis on "seeking" rather than on "having found." The Indian point of view that apparent "contradictions" among religions are merely matters of "emphasis" is also disturbing to some Westerners.[5] What the Western Christian often fails to understand is that the Indian can hold as true two concepts that seem to the Western mind to exclude each other. These concepts are paradoxes. They represent analogies rather than differences. Psychologically, they are arrived at more by intuition than by logic — that is, intuition in the sense of direct knowledge transcending both sensory and rational aspects of experience. In other words, the Indian can accept "contrarieties" that appear to the Western mind as "contradictions."

For example, the Hindu has accepted for centuries the concept of God as father *or* mother. This concept has been introduced into Christian thought only rarely. More fundamentally, the approach to God as philosophically nondual rather than either monistic or dualistic has been accepted by Hindus for centuries. Christian theologians are now calling for a nondualistic approach to explore the mystery of the Trinity, which has long been allowed to lie in comparative intellectual neglect in Western thought.[6] Contemporary Western theologians are also beginning to respond more profoundly to the concept of the early church that one and the same mystery can be explained in seemingly incompatible ways, just as the Council of Florence once recognized two formulas concerning the Holy Spirit. Philosophies are not equivalent. Even differing scholastic philosophical judgments are not radically different views of mystery, as Aquinas and Duns Scotus demonstrated. The Hindu has always understood this lack of equivalence.

In consonance with the Indian pluralistic approach to God, the Bhagavad Gita suggests three major spiritual paths: jnana, the way of knowledge; karma, the way of works; and bhakti, the way of devotion. These paths are not, of course, mutually exclusive. The Indian accepts the fact that each path has interpreters who say that it is supreme. The Indian way is not to argue about the question of supremacy, but to allow for the pluralism that permits all persons to follow their own spirit. The author of the Gita exhorts devotees to pursue all three paths, though in his own judgment the path of bhakti is of the highest value.

In India one observes varied stages of Hindu worship, all acceptable and sometimes even pursued simultaneously by one person: idol worship, incantation, contemplation, mysticism. The snobbery of the Western intellectual who smiles tolerantly at the simple faith of the peasant fingering his rosary is unthinkable in India. Just as unthinkable is the more or less traditional Western attitude that mysticism is the special gift of the rare individual, to be avoided by the "ordinary" man or woman. At an ecumenical meeting in Bombay in 1980, Christians were asked by Hindus to discuss Western mysticism, and no Christian present was able to do so! Among Hindus, reality of experience is the ultimate sanction of prayer and contemplation, and the testimony of the sannyasi is accepted gratefully. Nor do Hindus hesitate to pray in traditions other than their own.

To be spiritually fruitful, the thoughtful Christian in India will use varied methods of prayer that can be adapted to Christian worship. The same can be said of the use of Indian symbols of worship. Methods of prayer and adaptation of symbols sometimes differ in local churches. In India, communities tend to be self-contained. What holds good for worship in one village, for example, may not be accepted in another. Enrichment of Christianity through Indian pluralistic methods of worship therefore requires wisdom of judgment.

An adequate knowledge of Hinduism on the part of Christian leaders is a basic requirement, so that they will not make the mistake of rejecting truth in primordial or cosmic revelation they do not understand. Indian Christians should never be separated from those Hindu religious traditions of their inheritance that are compatible with the Christian faith and offer authentic witness to eternal truth. In short, Christianity in India must purify itself. A pluralistic approach to Hinduism is already taking place through dialogue between Christians and Hindus that is resulting in reciprocity. The church cannot be prophetic as to the outcome of this exchange. It can only rest in faith in the Holy Spirit.

If we turn from a consideration of pluralism itself to the question of dogma and dogmatic formulations in the church, we find that Indian Christian theologians are adopting a new and more viable approach to the formulation of doctrine. They have come to realize that universality of faith can never be achieved by dictatorial edict. They recognize that Christians in the past have often been dogmatic in a bad sense. The special kind of tolerance practiced by the Hindu has helped the Christian to distinguish between a wholesome *relativity* concerning doctrine and an unacceptable *relativism* that implies that all paths to God are ultimately the same.[7] Relativity, on the contrary, suggests that we cannot absolutize in a relative world. What we ordinarily call doctrines are formulations that express mysteries of faith. Recognition of this truth leads to a profound experience of the pilgrimage aspect of the Christian life and a deepening of the theological quest.

The Hindu concept of religion as continual search is thus

conducive to humility in Christians when they speak of dogma. Often the Hindu has reacted negatively to the dogmatism of the Christian as self-righteousness. Thus Gandhi was moved to declare himself a mere seeker of truth with an imperfect experience of God. Acceptance of plurality and diversity seemed to him to reveal the proper modesty of the creature as dogmatic assertion does not.

Indian Christian theologians are now rethinking dogmatic categories. They have concluded that they have dogmatized unnecessarily. Apologetics has been proved historically to be a most ineffective approach to the Hindu. The philosophic mind anywhere can establish the existence of God without revelation. There is no reason why the Christian cannot make use of various approaches to reality to carry on dialogue with the non-Christian. The Hindu has no magisterium. So long as Christians are fully aware of the implications of the dialogue and affirm fundamental differences of belief, they can seek constructive discussion with the Hindu on the latter's basic differences in thought.

Dogmatism in a bad sense is best countered in India through relativization of credal aspects of Christianity. It is sometimes salutary for the Christian to remember that God can be thought of as apart from human beings. One of the dangers in Christian thought that the Hindu is aware of is the anthropomorphic concept of God. The church, on the other hand, has been more aware of the possible danger to the faith of the traditional Western Christian through relativism. Its leaders have practiced prudence in protecting the majority of Christians from confusion. The Indian milieu, however, has made Indian Christian theologians more aware of the majority of humankind than of the majority of Christians. At the same time, they realize that the image of an anthropomorphic God has also alienated many Western Christians, especially intellectuals! They conclude that it is time to state clearly that doctrines are faith expressed in human language. The historical, evolutionary process in the formulation of mysteries of faith can never be expressed absolutely in human terms. Because the church exists in a continuity of historical ages, however, it has the gift of definition of doctrine through grace in its mandate to speak to men and women

until the end of time.[8] The Eastern theologian today is responding to the global mission of the church within the present
time-space continuum.

Christians, through their awareness of this historical process,
can offer the Hindu a sense of the seriousness of temporal
reality. They can help to make the Hindu aware that the search
for the Absolute within each individual is not enough. For many
Hindus, the historicity of Jesus Christ is an accident. Also, the
comparative isolation of India while Western nations developed
on a human level is for Hindus an accident of history. Only in
the late nineteenth century did Vivekananda admit that Hindus,
like the Bourbons, "never learned anything new or forgot anything old" in the context of human development (as parallel to
the search for eternal salvation). The Christian approach to
Christ as both historical and transhistorical can be a gift of grace
to the Hindu. It can lead the Hindu to be more aware of the
general direction of human history over six thousand years.
Christ is living. He is God. When Hindus come down from the
clouds of the Absolute to meet Christians in their mission of
justice and equality for all men and women, and when Christians rise from their earthbound dogmatic rigidities to meet
Hindus in their search for the experience of the divine, a new
Indian Christianity may take its rightful place in the universal
church of Christ.

2. DECENTRALIZATION AND CENTRALIZATION OF GOVERNMENT

The freedom of spirit of Hindus in India has always resisted
strict institutional structures in religion. Hindus are baffled by
the organization and hierarchy of Christian churches, to say
nothing of dogmas, creeds, and baptism. Though acceptance of
Jesus Christ is easy for them, Christianity seems to them to be
encapsulated within a puzzling and rigid system of government. Why do Christians pray together in a church? Why is
baptism necessary? Why should sin be confessed? Above all,
what is a pope, and why does he have such frightening authority over bishops, priests, and people?

Christians allow Hindus to worship Christ in their churches

whenever they desire to do so, to participate in their processions and novenas, to receive ashes on their forehead on Ash Wednesday. Ashes are meaningful to Hindus because they are a symbol they can relate to their own tradition. So they peacefully assimilate what they can of Christianity into their cultural inheritance and brush aside the centralized structure of the church. Some Indians, like the late famous Sadhu Sundar Singh, become baptized Christians and devote their lives completely to worship of Jesus Christ as God and witness to his teaching, but refuse to identify themselves with any particular church.

Personal response is so characteristic of religious thought among Hindus, in fact, that it presents an immediate barrier to the concept of centralized church government. The reasons are complex and complicated. First, personal relationship with God is emphasized. Persons seek to find their own self in the Self of God through direct experience. The Christian, on the other hand, ordinarily seeks God through the structures of the gospel, prayer, and the sacraments. Second, the social life of India, curbed by the caste system, is far from individualistic. Persons do not follow their own social inclinations, but conform themselves to the rules of caste. Some sociologists see the rejection of organized religion by the Indian as a counter-response to the rigidity of the caste system. In this way, the Hindu can transcend social values and become free in spirit by rejection of strict religious structures. A highly organized, centralized church, together with the discipline of the caste system, might become intolerable. To be sure, the *Indian Christian* rejects the inequalities of caste intellectually, but century-old customs die hard.

The Indian spiritual genius is thus basically opposed to the idea of a rigidly organized church. Indian Christian scholars have speculated that if Indian Christians were free to fashion forms of Christianity according to their own natural genius, which is not authoritarian, they would dispense with central authority.[9] They would have no church councils or synods, no huge federations or unions. Power would not reside in holy orders or commissions. "The Indian David cannot fight in the armor and with the sword of Saul." Most ecclesiastical setups would probably be rejected as alien.[10] The Indian would choose to worship in individual local churches and would preach the Word of God according to varying forms and traditions. A centralized teaching authority on scripture would be considered too binding on the believer. It would be thought strange to substitute dicta or creed or dogma for actual religious experience. The foregoing speculations are no more than that, however, for Indian Christians have never had the freedom implied in such reflections. Nevertheless, these theories have been proposed by Indian Christians themselves. They are related to the universal problem of logos and mythos.

It is interesting, moreover, that many Hindus point out to Christians the values they could gain by decentralization of church structures. Hindu philosophers remind the Christian that truth is too complex to be bound in tight logical structures and then promulgated for all to believe. Of more help to the individual, they suggest, is the guru who serves persons in their search of God in a manner for which no structure can substitute. The choice of guru is crucial, for individuals are themselves responsible for finding God. They can then follow the teaching and example of Christ more profitably without the stumbling block of rules and organization. The proper guru, according to the Hindu, can offer the Christian a path to the divine without prejudice to the following of Christ.

It would be false to imply, however, that the institutional religious element is entirely alien to Indian tradition. Lack of organization among Hindus leads to plurality in beliefs, but Hinduism also comprehends ritualistic temple worship of ancient origin. Though its priests are normally only functional today, they belong to hereditary castes. The native Hindu heritage of worship in speech and posture, verse and music, craftsmanship and architecture, has much to offer for adaptation to Christian worship in India. Central hierarchical authority often prevents such developments in Indian dioceses.

There is also a minority of Hindus who offer contrary views with regard to the values of decentralization. According to Swami Ranganathananda, the Hindu can learn from the Western Christian a great deal about the value of centralized structures to human development.[11] A narrow religious concept centered in each individual's subjective path to God can produce a God who is no more than an "image." Indians, the Swami asserts, are often incapable of solving significant problems in union with their neighbors. They do not combine orientation toward God significantly with orientation toward humanity. Master and slave still exist in India because too many men and women do not relate to one another as caring human beings. Because loving service demands some structure of interrelationship beyond that of caste, a central aspect of worship is sometimes lacking. Moreover, Hinduism itself has suffered in its many modern reforms and reformulations because lack of centralization has resulted not only in universal acceptance of all spiritual paths but also in a concomitant indistinctness that renders a definition of Hinduism impossible. To Ranganathananda, these characteristics of Hinduism are negatives. To be sure, the Swami is a member of the westernized Ramakrishna Missions!

P. K. Sundaram of the Institute for Advanced Philosophy, University of Madras, points out that centralization of power, planning, and finances among Christians unites them in their goals, whereas efforts to unite Hindus are normally unsuccessful.[12] Among Christians, social service is institutionalized, even on an international level. India, according to Sundaram, lacks social energy not just because of the caste system. Rather, caste *is* the social system. It does not provide for religious or cultural planning beyond itself.

The organization of the church in India obviously serves to make it a cohesive unit with a focal point in centralized government. Its gospel spirituality is more horizontal than the spirituality of Hinduism, which is strongly vertical in orientation. Education and social interchange are developed readily because of church structures. Also, excellent schools, hospitals, and social service institutes prosper. Team work within the universal church thus enables Christians to contribute much on the social level to countries like India that are financially poor. Social needs and commitments have been learned from Christian institutions by many Hindus. The Ramakrishna Missions, for example, are based on social theories borrowed from Christian organizations as a kind of "appendix" to modern Hinduism. The massive organization of the eucharistic congress in Bombay was amazingly impressive to Hindus. They are also cognizant of the fact that the organizational power of Christians can enable them to pursue nonviolent action as a positive goal. They have observed Christians carrying out peaceful protests and demonstrations on a large scale, such as the disciplined Christian response to the proposed Bill on Forced Conversion in Delhi in the late 1970s. Christians in India are well aware of these positive responses of Hindus to the centralized government of the church.

On the levels of power and politics, to be sure, the value of central organization of the church has been evident to Indian Hindus as well as to Christians throughout Western history. The strength and stability of the established church rests on its centralized government. It is this very identification of centralization with power, however, that has produced a dominantly negative response among thoughtful Eastern Christians. The church is identified with wealth, conquest, colonialism, exploitation, and maintenance of the status quo. Today Indian Christian leaders are aware as never before of the negative effects of centralization of church government.

The majority of Eastern Christian theologians would seem to agree that the organization of the church demands a more flexible structure. Though a strong hierarchy could have advantages if it were utilized for Christian goals like justice, peace, and equality, the official church in India has little catalyzing effect because it is absorbed in maintaining its own traditions — often to the benefit of the economic and political status quo that actually requires change rather than the support of traditional structures. The present structure of the papacy, episcopacy, and priesthood is often felt by Easterners to be fixed in obsolescent forms. The power of the pope is overstressed. New ministries are needed. A much more numerous clergy, who could well be married or female, is in demand to secure sacramental life for the people of God in many Eastern countries. Unfortunately, the achievement of authentic Christian community is often made subservient to the maintenance of a structure centered in its own continuance. Christian community in India today demands structures with a capacity for fermentation toward change.[13] Through such structures, Christians might enrich the church in the East and strengthen its contribution to the church universal.

Thoughtful Christian leaders in India are well aware that emphasis on centralization of power and overorganization of government is repugnant to the majority of Indians. The church, they maintain, cannot organize religion in India as one organizes an army. The Christian challenge to India will never come from a feudal hierarchy.[14] Therefore, the administration of the Eastern church must be more decentralized. Subsidiarity must be implemented. According to Vatican Council II, it is a disturbance of right order to turn over to an authority of "higher" rank functions and services that can be performed by lesser bodies on a "lower" plane. The unique role of implementing subsidiarity belongs to both church leaders and church members.

The more the church presents itself in the East as institutional and structural, the less it appears to the Indian to offer Jesus Christ, the servant of servants. In the mind of the Indian, Christianity should be a theological reality, not a structural development; overemphasis on institutional practices produces unhealthy polarity and tension between charism and institution. Either can injure the other, as witnessed by the historical defection of certain Christians in Kerala from the Roman church.

Until the sixteenth century, the only church in India was the Indian church of the St. Thomas Christians. These Christians are known as the Syro-Malabar Church on the basis of their liturgical language (Syriac) and their place of origin (Malabar). Their metropolitan used the title of Metropolitan of All India for centuries. The hierarchical establishment of the Latin rite in India is closely connected with the arrival of the Portuguese in the sixteenth century. The title and jurisdiction of the metropolitan was suppressed in 1599, and by 1600 the liturgy of the Syro-Malabar Church was mutilated in order to conform externally to the Latin liturgy and rituals. Natural resentment and reaction reached a climax in the mid-seventeenth century with the arrival of a Jacobite Syrian prelate from Antioch who offered episcopal leadership to those Christians who wished to reject Latin administration. Thus originated the history of separated churches in India, to the detriment of the unity of all Indian Christians.[15]

Today Indian bishops who are administrators rather than pastors often injure the church by condemning Christian leaders who attempt to follow the direction of the Spirit toward subsidiarity. For Indians who have practiced a religion thousands of years older than Christianity, the poor Jesus Christ — not the triumphal church — calls forth love.[16] Jesus of Nazareth is the key to the universal Christ of St. John who is not found in structures built by human minds in a small corner of the Western world.

So much has been written of the institutionalization of Jesus Christ, of binding God in history, that the notion is a commonplace in India. Ecclesiastical structures borrowed from the Greco-Roman empire fix Christ himself in an anachronistic system particularly unsuited to Asia (and to Africa). Christ is life itself. Hindus look for the manifestation of this life in Christians, particularly as witnessed in prayer, meditation, and contemplation. They seek the universal Christ who reveals himself in love not to a particular society or culture but to all men and women. No matter how much the church serves the poor, it will not touch Hindus unless it speaks to them of the poor Christ in his manifest love for all men and women everywhere. Historical accumulations of nonessential Western structures must be sacrificed to unveil Christ present in the depths of extra-Mediterranean religious traditions.

The Indian mystic, Sundar Singh, was convinced that India can be evangelized only by holy men and women, not by elaborate church organization and abstruse scholarship: "What are we aiming at in studying theology? What are we doing with scholarship, and what have we achieved by it all? Holy men can move nations. . . . It is better to send a disciple of Christ than one hundred who are not." Christ chose fishermen; there is no need to canonize complex Western traditions.

Presence of the sadhu is of supreme importance to the

Hindu, whereas organized movements can be hindrances. The leaven in the wheat is essential.[17] In the church of power — like that of Pope Innocent III — economic and political, as well as spiritual, forces are in control. St. Francis of Assisi, as sadhu, challenged the very shape of the church. Despite his extraordinary charisms, his accomplishments were defeated eventually and absorbed into the structure of the official church. Many Christians in India feel that a new St. Francis can offer the challenge of Christ to the people of India today.[18]

Institutionalization of the church seems to the Indian to bind God in history; it places men and women in a trap.[19] It legitimizes a Western system associated with economic exploitation. Indians are accustomed over centuries to accept the flow of life. They do not fight it or flee from it. They even value poverty: Western Christians, on the contrary, fight the flow of life. They are highly competitive and oriented toward material success. In the mind of the Indian, this orientation is associated historically with the structures of the Western church.

Decentralization of church structures would help the Indian Christian prove to the Hindu that Christianity is not a finished, unchangeable product, a notion that arises from the observed rigidity of church organization.[20] The church, according to many Indian theologians, is called today to allow each local church in India to unite its theology, liturgy, and spirituality after the pattern of Christianity in its early centuries. Thus diversity of local traditions will be respected. Indian culture will provide models. The humanity of India will become the humanity of Jesus Christ in Indian form.

At present the structures of the Indian Latin church render it predominantly a clericalized institution. To become effective, it must become less hierarchical. The priest is bound up in legal structures, and the life of the church is seen in terms of these structures. The many faces of Christ are indistinct or obliterated. The goal of the priesthood sometimes becomes the maintenance of the traditional diocesan setup rather than the spiritual guidance of God's people.

The type of church just described impoverishes the life of the spirit. Ironically, it is often present today in the West as well as the East. We ask ourselves why so many young Westerners are attracted today to the Eastern religions. Actually, the majority of them are bored with the established churches within their own civilization.[21] Eastern religions attract, for one reason, by the freedom from rigid structures they offer to their adherents. According to Bede Griffiths, young Westerners often go to the Indian ashram to seek their Christian self. The process they experience is a release from rigidities and a return to the rhythm of living in a creative way of life, peace, and wholeness. Once they have found what they are seeking, they come back to the faith and the eucharist.[22] Though permissive Western society is not so condemnatory of violations of law as it once was, the young person still experiences a "guilt trip" because of these violations. The pathos of the situation lies in the fact that the Western Christian church could have provided spiritual food for their hunger in the first place. While the Hindu rejects the oppressive structures of the Western Christian church planted in the East, the young Western Christian goes to the East to find release from the selfsame structures. The fact that Eastern *Christian* ashrams offer the Westerner acceptable spiritual renewal — even on a small scale — gives food for thought. What we actually observe is the quiet influence of Indian spirituality upon Western Christianity!

3. FREEDOM AND RESPONSIBILITY

It is often stated that India is a democracy in its political setup but a medieval feudal society in its lived caste system. By the same token, Western societies are said to be democratic in politics but imperialistic and exploitive in their capitalistic economic systems. We may well ask what are the principles that Hinduism in India and Christianity in the West claim as their courses of action within their religious structures, and which principles they actually live by. Also, in a realistic way, how do these values — professed or lived — provide a bridge for the mutual fecundation of Hinduism and Christianity?

Christians have always professed that living the fundamental principles of faith requires freedom. The full development of the person, the greatest good a man or woman can achieve, depends on free will. If freedom is denied, virtue and sin have no meaning. Total human development and salvation are concomitant goals, even though total development is often blocked by societal systems. Christians have assurance that Christ has overcome the world. They put their hope in God. They believe in personal immortality and the ultimate triumph of good over evil. Their duty is to be loving, just, merciful, and to walk humbly with the Lord.

Hindus, on the other hand, have an explanation for personal fortune and misfortune in karma. Their actions in past incarnations or in their present life result in their deserved happiness or suffering. Sin is for them rather a metaphysical or a cosmic than a moral concept. The need for a savior is not felt. Therefore Hindus do not bring the same sense of urgency to bear on the problem of evil in the world as Christians do. They seek to be meek, forbearing, long-suffering, hospitable, nonviolent, and simple in their life standards. But straightforwardness, public honesty, service, and cooperation with others do not always seem so important to them as to Christians. Sin is not due to a rebellious will but to spiritual ignorance. The famous Hindu philosopher, S. Radhakrishnan, speaks of sin as a "handicap."

Karma is a sound explanation of human inequality, a more acceptable concept than that of an "account-keeping God." Hindus maintain that the negative effects of karma in a past life can be abrogated by present initiative in good works. Yet some scholars maintain that karma in practice can lead to "self-righteousness on the part of the high-born, undue civility among the lower castes, and a strange lack of sympathy toward the unfortunate."[23] Karma can also result in a strong tendency toward fatalism among some Hindus. At times Hindus flow with the current of life because they believe that they cannot alter the current radically.

The Christian can indeed learn from the Hindu the calmness and peace of mind that enables the latter to face all eventualities with comparative serenity. It is paradoxical that the Hindu can often find greater repose in a certain type of fatalism than the

Christian sometimes finds in trust in Jesus Christ. Association with Hindus almost invariably reveals in them an admirable acceptance of unfortunate circumstances that cannot be changed. Their freedom of spirit in suffering is seldom shattered. On the other hand, Hindus can learn from Christians the sense of responsibility to themselves and others that can often change unfortunate circumstances for the better through personal initiative.

In India, then, the concept of human liberation based on redemption and freedom is fundamental in the Christian approach to life. In its prophetic aspect, it results in social involvement. It stresses Christian concern of men and women for one another. It supports social justice as opposed to the human indignities that the caste system sometimes implies.

A contrast is also observable in the approach to freedom of the Eastern and the Western Christian churches. While Christianity in its totality is a *community* of the Spirit, the Eastern churches as compared with the Western have always been more profoundly rooted in the Spirit. Vatican Council II stressed ecclesiology of the Spirit, but the concept has never been strong in Western tradition. Thus the freedom that flows from the Spirit is often felt to be stronger in the Eastern church in India than in the Roman Church with its roots in the West. The effect is greater stress within the Eastern church on the mystery aspect of God, on spiritual pilgrimage as continual search, and on interiority and contemplation, with less emphasis on the horizontal dimensions of faith. The majority of Indian Christian priests and theologians have been trained in seminaries that have been Western in their theological orientation for several centuries. Thus the worldview of both the Hindu philosopher and the minority of the Eastern Christian theologians who emphasize the contemplative is crucial. The *impression* one perceives in India is that Western Christian culture, in its alleged noncontemplative spirit, can be damaging to Indian culture. In this sense, impression is important: in India, there is no culture without religion.[24]

A Hindu graduate student in India, for example, told the writer that she would never attend a university in the United

States because "nobody believes in God there and everybody sleeps with everybody else." She viewed the Hindu family as healthy and secure, while she saw the American family (Christian or non-Christian) as disintegrating on both a cultural and a moral level. This student prefers caste restrictions to the "freedom" she believes to exist among Western Christians. She is not alone in her point of view. While it is comparatively easy to refute charges of this type against Western Christianity, this Hindu impression nevertheless offers Christians a window for reinterpretation of their images among non-Christians and for a possible critique of their own experience of God. One is tempted here to contrast the instinctive sense of the sacred common to most Hindus with the spiritual dichotomy of the "Sunday Christian" in the West, which often produces a strange passivity of uninvolvement with the divine. As T. K. John points out,[25] the primacy of the Spirit is the gift of Hinduism to the world. The Hindu insight into the Absolute Godhead is a great world achievement. Except for St. John and St. Paul, Hindu scripture, according to T. K. John, has a deeper insight into the "dimensions of God" than does the New Testament.

The true freedom and openness of the Christian, the self-giving that discovers God in the total universe, is completely acceptable to Hindus *when they discover it among Christians.* If Indian Christians are willing to learn from the Hindu because they actually believe that Christ is at work in India since the beginning of time, the Hindu will be able to observe in the Christian church and its members a freedom that is personal, communal, and ecclesial. The Hindu will see the Christian as heir to the spiritual and cultural reality of India. The Hindu will even see aspects of Hindu spiritual freedom manifested in the individual Christian. In short, the image of the Christian in India can change.[26]

Unfortunately, Hindus do not observe the spiritual freedom of Christians often enough. They do observe the Christian sense of responsibility and tight control. The Christian life is disciplined: it does not offer an easy way to salvation. Nor can the Christian underplay the cost of discipleship. Definite demands are made by the Christian church, which has expectations and norms. Yet it is an impression of exclusiveness and inflexibility rather than of the authentic demands of Christian faith that alienates the Hindu, who does not reject the teaching of Christ but does reject the exclusivity that isolates Christians from the values that Hindus offer them. Though the freedom of the Hindu often manifests contradictions that seem alien to the Christian, the freedom of the latter is often clouded by lack of openness that hinders free reciprocity between the two.[27] The Hindu sense of spiritual freedom is sometimes seen as offensive by the Christian who cannot shake off traditional restrictions that have their origin in Western culture. (Hindu freedom is offensive also to the Muslim who cannot resist the establishment of an Islamic state.)

If we examine the Christian attitude toward freedom and responsibility more closely, it becomes clear that the apparent exclusivity of the Christian in dealing with the Hindu is contrived and artificial. Insofar as this communal narrowness is the result of a counterreformation mentality still prevalent today, it is inexcusable. However, it is due in part to the insecurity of the Christian who fears to be absorbed by the vast assimilative power of Hinduism, which represents 83 percent of the population of India while Christianity represents only 2.5 percent. Yet Christianity is a worldwide religion as Hinduism is not. It is therefore comparatively easy for the Christian to think in terms of a universal church. But unfortunately the *image* of Christianity in India is not that of a universal church. Therefore Christian theologians struggle to reconceptualize the universality of the church in India. Meanwhile, 60 percent of Christians owe their origins to the Indian lower castes, another factor that renders the image of the Christian church less universal to Hindus. If Christians can overcome their "inferiority complex" as an Indian minority, true freedom in dialogue and reciprocity among Hindus and Christians may emerge.

It is not difficult to demonstrate that freedom from exclusivity without sacrifice of integrity on the part of Christians can result in the acceptance of many Christian values on the part of Hindus. "Responsibility" of Christians to their faith has often been exaggerated to the point of diminishing returns in the search for loving complementarity between Hindu and Christian. Though Hindus are not always as tolerant as their image often suggests, they are much more open to Christians than the Christian response to Hindus indicates.

An honest appraisal of the Hindu sense of freedom and tolerance is apropos here. An idealized evaluation of these Hindu virtues must be rejected. It is a fact that in the caste-conscious character of their communalism, Hindus are often virulently intolerant of castes other than their own. Also, tribals converted by Christians are often declared to be subversive by Hindu caste members. In short, the tolerance of the Hindu must be viewed in a relative sense. Like all other persons, Hindus may be said to have complex personalities! In fact, it is comparatively easy for the Hindu to be tolerant of outsiders in normal situations because of the social security of the caste system. Group distinctions within Hinduism remain, and so does a relative intolerance of the Christian (often with good reason). Moreover, the freedom and tolerance of Hindus have their negative side in the fact that Hinduism often appears as a "conglomeration" of religious beliefs, alive with contradictions. The higher Hinduism of the philosopher (advaita Vedanta) sometimes clashes with the Hinduism of the common man or woman who worships the God of the Puranas. Hindus liberate themselves on their own personal path to God, a doctrine that can result in unlimited eccentricities.

A related negative aspect of Hindu freedom and tolerance arises from the principle that individuals are free to grow at their own pace, even to the point of delaying spiritual growth until a later rebirth. This type of freedom tolerates in practice a person's absorption in private interests. It sometimes allows for dissipation. Free sex, for example, lowers consciousness to the subhuman level. Hinduism thus attracts certain young people from the West because of apparent freedoms that are not practical as a way of growth. These young people often miss the exacting inner discipline that accompanies the outer freedom of Hinduism. Many Eastern gurus who attract Westerners today do not insist on the inner discipline essential for growth of consciousness. The popular gurus, to be sure, are untrue to the Eastern tradition at its best. The acceptance of variations in individual capability of spiritual growth in freedom is not the same as license to lower consciousness below the human level, particularly if inner discipline is neglected. Tolerance has limits.

A further negative aspect of Hindu relations with other religions is the fact that, while assimilation of all faiths by Hinduism is accepted freely, religious conversion is not encountered. Moreover, Hindus have never forgiven the Moghuls for forced conversions of Hindus to Islam. Even today some Hindus tend to call free conversions "forced." More recently, conversion to Christianity has also presented an economic threat to the Hindu. For political and social reasons, the wealthy Hindu wishes to keep cheap labor in the fields in order to maintain servants of lower caste, and also to keep women in their secondary status. Christianity is a threat to these conditions.[28] Marxism and certain modern Western movements, however, may be a greater threat in this regard than is Christianity.

Granted certain negative aspects of Hindu freedom and tolerance, one must still assert that the freedom and openness of the Indian are not myths. The spirit of inner freedom born of poverty and suffering (voluntary or involuntary) and the resultant personal spiritual depth are positive values that contribute to the free acceptance of pluralism and differences among Hindus. The consumer culture of the West has not engulfed this open Hindu culture. Emphasis is still placed on the spiritual awakening of the individual person rather than on dependence on things. Urban Hindus, to be sure, often become alienated from their inner being as does the contemporary European or American in a consumer society. When persons depend on things outside themselves, the resources within them, which can find the springs of their own being, are often untapped. Yet the majority of Indians are still uninvolved in secular realities even to the point of handicapping the development of their society.[29] No philosophy of the secular disturbs the majority of Hindus. Their inner freedom remains as it has been for thousands of years. No institutional structures have been able to invade this openness to spiritual reality over centuries. It presents at the very least an ongoing challenge to both Christianity and Islam in India. Undoubtedly, the Christian has something to learn from the inner freedom of the Hindu.

While keeping in mind that the prophetic aspect of Christian liberation and social involvement is different from human relationship to the divine as expressed in the Bhagavad Gita, one can still examine further the values of the Hindu concept of inner freedom. The idea of the liberation of men and women from history, from the time-space continuum in a cosmic sense (not in the sense of redemption through Jesus Christ), is a Hindu concept. Human relationship with the entire universe as experienced by the Hindu adds a cosmic dimension to human existence, a sense of the unity of reality, a deeper descent into the realms of human consciousness, and a greater awareness in the search for self-realization. The positive value of the Absolute and the relativity of everything else in existence produce a freedom in religious experience that carries with it a basic tolerance for plurality as well as a resistance to dogmatism.[30] The Hindu thus experiences no undue restriction on personal expression. Persons have the right to express themselves as they think right simply because the divine in the human allows this freedom.

A positive result of the Hindu sense of freedom is the supple structure of Hindu worship. Freedom is evident in the Hindu ashram, which is more flexible than most Christian monastic centers and retreat houses. Hindu spiritual traditions and rites are less visible and imposing. The temple is not a place of community worship. Rather, individuals approach God as they choose. The communion of saints is less visible than in the West! One goal only is the pearl of great price in Hinduism: the thirst for the Absolute, "the One without a second," for whom all else may be sacrificed. In search for this goal, the Hindu believes that God is fulfilled in many ways, through different races and persons.

The reputation of the Hindu for openness that results, at least in part, from this concept of freedom is worldwide; it is based securely in history. Hinduism is perhaps the oldest of world religions. For forty centuries it has received on its soil Christians, Jews, Parsees, Muslims, Sikhs, Jains, and Buddhists. The

Bhagavad Gita teaches this spirit of accommodation: "However men approach me, even so do I accept them, for on all sides whatever path they may choose is mine" (14.11). Reality is one. The result of this acceptance of coexistence has been at least comparative freedom from religious quarrels in India. The resultant harmony has given Hinduism a reputation for a relatively peaceful way of life as contrasted with the disharmony experienced historically through both Christian and Muslim religious conflicts. An understanding of the historical background of the Indian heritage is necessary to comprehend Hindu tolerance in proper perspective. Superficial approaches to Indian reality can result in "night and day" interpretations of Hindu genius for accepting all religions and assimilating them to itself. A balanced view of the unity of Hindu reality and the pluralism of Hindu faith are essential to an appreciation of the Hindu way of life.

One of the brightest aspects of Hindu freedom is the alacrity with which it borrows the best of non-Hindu teachings. In the same vein, D. S. Amalorpavadass, director of the National Biblical, Catechetical, and Liturgical Centre, Bangalore, points out that Vatican Council II asked the church to realize its own insufficiencies in this regard and to borrow from other religions when possible without the least hesitation:

> From the customs and traditions of their people, from their wisdom and their learning, from their arts and sciences, these Churches borrow all those things which can contribute to the glory of their creator, the revelation of the Savior's grace, or the proper arrangement of the Christian life. . . . Particular traditions, together with the individual patrimony of each family of nations, can be illumined by the light of the Gospel, and then be taken up into Catholic unity [Ad Gentes, 22].

The fact is, however, that there is little borrowing within the Indian church. All that the church appears to borrow from India is in fact what already belongs to Christ by creation and by resurrection, that which *the church should claim and gather as its own*.[31]

Hindus, on the other hand, have never hesitated to borrow

from Christianity and other religions. The acceptance of Jesus Christ by millions of Hindus, without acceptance of the Christian church, is of course the prime example of Hindu assimilation of the best of other world religions. In the late nineteenth century, Hindus became alive to the values of the teachings of Christ and not only adopted them but pursued research through which they discovered these values in their own Hindu scriptures. Vivekananda, for example, assumed the Christian teaching of care and concern for others to so great an extent that his Hinduism appeared to be Christianity to the majority of Hindus! Christian missionaries discovered in turn that, while they thought they were bringing Christianity to the Hindus, they were often actually purifying Hinduism as preparation for its nineteenth-century reinterpretation.

Gandhi's acceptance of Christ and the Sermon on the Mount is one of the most dramatic assimilations of religion in the history of the world. His teaching of the nonviolence of Christ has had a counter influence in the sense that Christians in India learned about Christ from him! Again, Mohan Roy, under strong Christian influence, opposed the Hindu custom of suttee. Hindu objections to the dowry system, supported by Indira Gandhi, likewise have their roots in Christian teaching. Mother Teresa of Calcutta has helped to build a bridge to Hinduism through her witness to the truth that Christ is for others. Hindus see her as a "holy woman," a concept of fundamental importance to Hindu culture. Examples abound of Hindu assimilation of Christian ideals. Acceptance of Christian values is a relativizing factor in Hinduism itself. This acceptance of Christian ideals and abrogation of certain Hindu customs has indeed operated as salt and leaven in the New Testament scriptural sense.

On a scholarly level, Hindu philosophers have not hesitated to examine the doctrines of Christianity and to relate them to Hinduism. R. Balasubramaniam, director of the Centre for Advanced Study, University of Madras, has studied, for example, Christian interpretations of the doctrine of creation, human nature, the meaning of redemption, and the role of Christ as the human paradigm. He agrees substantially with Christian teaching on human nature. He finds problems in the Christian teaching on creation from nothing; in the meaning of Christian redemption that rejects reincarnation; and in Jesus Christ as unique redeemer, despite his full acceptance of Christ as incarnation of God. Balasubramaniam's interest, and that of other Hindu scholars, in finding common ground with Christianity is of vital significance to the universal church.

To be sure, Indian Christian theologians have studied Hinduism during the last twenty-five years more profoundly than Hindu philosophers have studied Christianity. Scholars like Raimundo Panikkar, T. K. John, Samuel Rayan, and others come to mind at once. It is the church in India, not its contemporary theologians, that is hesitant both in cooperative studies and in borrowing Hindu cultural values.

Within the whole area of freedom, tolerance, and open acceptance of values of the other, Hinduism seems to have profited more than Christianity in spiritual and cultural growth. Hindus believe strongly that God repays them for their acceptance of what is sacred to others. They stand openly for truth always. If something proves to be true in their own judgment, they do not hesitate to accept it. The disciplined training of Christians, on the other hand, often leads them to accept doctrinal formulations blindly without intellectual examination. Also, the characteristic Hindu patience is a natural concomitant to willingness to examine the possible truth of another's religious beliefs. This approach often leads the Hindu to discover more readily than the Christian those beliefs that, despite differences, are common to both.

One of the most profound sources of Hindu freedom and tolerance is the fairly uninterrupted history of the mystical movement in India. Whether popular or profound, mysticism has always been advocated by Hindus. But no sect or philosophical school has ever claimed infallibility on the grounds of its mysticism. Though universally exalted, mysticism in India has never been invested with the authority to overrule reason. A conflict between mysticism and reason has never existed. In the West, claims of religious superiority that run counter to tolerance have been advanced most often on rational or dialectical grounds. For the Indian, conflict between sanity and spiritual ecstacy is impossible. If this attitude seems paradoxical to the Westerner, it nevertheless is a basic source of tolerance among Hindus.[32]

Finally, it must be stated that a concept of *total liberation* is essential for the interpretation of Christianity and Hinduism. Christianity in India is now undergoing a degree of uprooting because of certain changes in attitude identified with "liberation" in a political and economic sense. One result is a tendency among some Indian Christians to disparage contemplatives as if the *only* road to liberation is to overcome injustice and oppression in Indian society. A reactionary response to this tendency is a one-sided contemplative spirit among certain Christians. While Vivekananda's dictum, "Don't try to be a saint before you become a man," is apropos, the thoughtful Indian has no difficulty in reconciling what may appear at first to be contrarieties. To place complete energy in the interior life is to paralyze the social-industrial development of India. On the other hand, to place complete trust in social revolution *as the way to Jesus Christ* is to fail to capitalize on the most profound spiritual riches of India — and also to reject the lessons of history.

A far better concept of total liberation than either of the above is the integration of the most profound approaches to freedom of both Hindu and Christian. Vivekananda's complete political, ethical, and religious message is: "All men are one. This is the meaning of freedom." "In myriad forms," he wrote, "God is present before you. Serve him wherever you see his form. See God in man." It is a privilege to be a human being. Total human development cannot be one-sided. Therefore Vivekananda added:

> Bring light to the world, to the rich and poor, but more light to the rich because they need it more: bring light to the educated and the uneducated, but more light to the educated because they need it more.[33]

The interpenetration of Vivekananda's concept of liberation with that of Christianity offers a challenge. Vivekananda proposed a definition of freedom not always observed in the actual functioning of the caste system. But his ideas (borrowed partially from Christianity) provide a starting point for integration with a Christian approach to liberation in no way contradictory to his Hindu ideals. Christianity should not resort to tricks or gimmicks to make itself palatable to the Hindu in a shallow way. Like Christ and St. Paul, Christians in India must become "all things to all persons." To do so demands a process of self-giving based on the truth that Christ is present in the total universe. There are no frontiers. The more Christian one is, the more one can see Christ in *all* the realities of the world. The more Christian one becomes, the more one is capable of recognizing Christ in every person and every thing. Christ is the Word of God at work in India. Before Vatican Council II, this open Christian attitude was underground in India. Now it is above ground. It represents a radical change in the Christian approach to the Hindu. It is a real, practical recognition that by Christ's incarnation and resurrection the whole world belongs to him. All men and women — Christians and Hindus — are together on pilgrimage to God. This concept of liberation is a *total* concept of freedom that leads directly to universality in Christ. It can provide a center or core for mutual integration of Hinduism and Christianity.[34]

4. AUTHORITY AND LAW

Attitudes toward authority and law within a religious system are crucial to the functioning of that religion as a lived experience. Whether religious government be centralized or decentralized, the concept of law of any religion must be related to the culture in which it is lived. If the law by which members of a religious body relate to their leaders is alien to their way of life, authentic religious experience and participation is threatened. The law that developed in the early Christian church was Greco-Roman and well adapted to the Western membership of the church.

It has been suggested by Indian theologians that Jesus Christ is in continuity with what is best in Eastern cultural tradition, but the authority and law of the Christian churches are not.[35] Jesus gave life. He was committed to the kingdom of God his Father. He was in conflict with existing Jewish structures of domination, opposed them, and paid the price. The Indian Christian appreciates Jesus in his practice of justice and love unto death. Like the Indian Buddha, Jesus rejects every threat to the humanity of his brothers and sisters. In an Indian milieu, one can conclude that he would have rejected unjust aspects of the caste system. Christian church law, however, seems to many Indians to be an important ideological force in maintaining certain principles that Christ would have opposed. The traditional insistence of Christians on the right to private property, for example, seems to be a contradiction to the ideology of the early church established by Christ. At least up to the end of the second century, it was a religion of the poor in which property was held in common. The idea of a bureaucracy of authority is also foreign to the government of the early church.

The structure of Western church law that developed historically, derived from the Roman heritage of Caesar and not from Peter, is alien to Indian culture in its juridical and territorial divisions. Its principles often seem to the Indian to be directed toward efficiency of administration rather than to the life of the spirit; thus it sometimes precipitates spiritual impoverishment rather than enrichment. Since Vatican Council II this type of authority and law among Indian Christians themselves has sometimes resulted in two rather bizarre extremes: first, complete withdrawal from membership in the church to private contemplation even without the sacraments; and second, adherence to Marxism as a spriritual foundation for Christian life (a response quite foreign to the Indian temperament).[36] These extreme reactions sometimes occur because traditional church authority opposes both the proper establishment of Christian ashrams and a positive approach to dialogue with Marxism without prejudice to the church of Christ. Rethinking church law freely without fear of its complete destruction, without magnification of the magisterium, can bring about constructive changes in Christian thought concerning the integration of church law with the response of the Indian temperament.

The Western character of modern Latin Catholicism offers a system of theology and of canon law alien not only to the Indian but to the Eastern mind in general. Thus church law often appears to the Easterner to promote a mission of "spiritual aggression." The mind of the Counter-Reformation, which still often governs the Latin church, gives little attention to the character and temperament of the Easterner. Mere adaptation of Western law will never strike at the roots of basic differences between West and East. In the East, religion has given its form to national culture over thousands of years: remnants of specialized Counter-Reformation church law are unsuited to the needs of Eastern countries. Unfortunately, this type of law extends into many aspects of life, from liturgy and worship to personal and cultural customs. Mutual interpenetration of faith and culture, not adaptation of law alone, is needed to incorporate the people of the East into the universal Christian economy of salvation.

The quality of thought that recognizes the many failures of present church authority and law in India has produced a large number of Christians who are reconsidering the concept of evangelization of Hindus. The uppermost conlusion in their minds is a question: Is church law rooted in a particular Western historical period more crucial to Christianity than the evangelization of millions of God's people? Or why is the Hindu often more aware of the central significance of Jesus Christ to the future of the world than many Western church members are? J. A. Cuttat, Indian Christian scholar of Hinduism, answered these questions clearly when he stated that "the Church will have to give up customs, practices, and formulations she has got used to through centuries and undergo a death experience in order to be born again."[37]

As in other areas, Christians in India are accused of exclusivity in the matter of church laws. Christian ministers "take care of their own." A wider horizon with respect to law is now more and more in demand by thoughtful Indian Christians. If change does not occur, Christian assertion of superiority to all other religions, of being "the only true faith," will continue to imprison Christianity in an ivory tower of exclusivity. This sin of

Christianity in India has been called "violence of spirit."

Opposed to violence of spirit is Jesus Christ who translated his beliefs into action to the point of death. His intensity of love in seeking the will of his Father was never equaled. No one in all history was like him in his total honesty. He is the only great religious leader who can be called the pure spiritual revolutionary because he was oppressed without being also an oppressor.[38] The nonviolence of Christ adopted by Gandhi and thousands of Indians is affirmation of the law of the Spirit as opposed to Greco-Roman or any other type of law that hinders the Christian life. The Indian has always understood — long before Gandhi — the strength of nonresistance. The fundamental violence to the human spirit is human inhumanity. The Indian ideal of nonviolence is essentially the Sermon on the Mount. The Hindu ideal of ahimsa became a dynamic political force with Gandhi: "We practice nonviolence only when we love those who hate us." Suffering for the sake of justice, said the Mahatma, is a Christ principle. Therefore to call nonviolence a "counsel of perfection" is false. The Sermon on the Mount sums up the living experience of Christ, which is the law of the Spirit.

A double implication inheres in the law of the Spirit. Jesus was aware of *existential alienation* as related to the ambivalence of freedom, to individual personal problems, and to the meaning of life and the actuality of death. He responded to this universal alienation, this inward rupture of humankind, with the message of his Father. But he was also aware of *social, cultural,* and *political alienation,* of domination and exploitation. Again, his response was the teaching of his Father. Historically, existential alienation has had structural results in the second type of alienation influenced by the society or culture into which human beings are inserted.[39] The only law by which an integrated response to the above two types of alienation can be achieved is the law of the Spirit that makes all men and women one in their humanity.

It has often been asserted that the point at issue in humanizing the Christian church in India is not so much a problem of authority and law as it is a question of whether local churches are themselves willing to initiate change.[40] In effect, however, the problem is one of adherence by both hierarchy and church members to a historical accumulation of Western principles of law that have a basis in culture rather than in the law of the Spirit preached by Christ. Hope is created by the strong minority of Christian leaders in India who follow the Spirit courageously as they await the abrogation of obsolescent church laws that are a "hangover" from Greco-Roman tradition. Though change comes slowly, these pioneers offer bright prospects for a system of authority and law that can be assumed by both the traditions of Indian culture and the temperament of the individual Indian.

The problem of change in church law is a global one for Christianity, and in each country it must be solved with reference to the culture of the country itself. Fundamentally, Christians must recall that when Christ said "Give unto God the things that are God's, "he was speaking of the law of the Spirit. Just as he never revealed the destiny he planned for billions of Easterners who were never promised a Messiah, so he never laid down church laws for a vast non-Mediterranean world.

5. UNIVERSALITY AND SYNCRETISM

In India today both Christians and Hindus speak of a universal church. Christians hope for a universal faith that is the new creation in Christ. Hindus look toward a universal religion that will assimilate all paths to God, rejecting none. An examination of these two concepts reveals both likenesses and differences that are crucial in humankind's search for a world religion.

India and Palestine are the sources of two of the greatest movements in world religions: Hinduism and Christianity. Both have sprung from the East. Both accept the oneness of the human race. The Rigveda teaches that all human beings are one single family; Christ teaches universal fellowship. Both religions proclaim the principle of ahimsa or nonviolence. However inadequate the practice of this human value may be, followers of both religions at their ideal levels profess love as the conqueror of evil and reject retaliation against those who do evil.

Aside from these two important concurrences, there are a number of religious concepts in which the Hindu and the Christian approaches to truth call for mutual study and dialogue.[41]

Hindus believe that every person has within himself or herself a spark of the divinity that permeates the whole cosmos. The atman, or the divinity within the person, is believed to be identical with the divinity of the Brahman, the Ultimate Reality. The Christian believes in "the indwelling of the Holy Spirit" within the person, whom God has created in the divine image and likeness. The Christian also believes that the whole creation proclaims the glory of God. Although the Christian speaks of seeking communion with God, and the Hindu of seeking oneness with the Absolute, the great mystics of East and West have seldom been troubled by rational analysis of such verbal distinctions. Their descriptions of their spiritual experiences reveal surprising similarities.

Both Hindu and Christian have always been open historically to mystical experience as a culminative goal of spiritual realization. To the Hindu philosopher, spiritual experience is the ultimate test of religious truth. Reverence is therefore given to the sannyasi or holy person because his or her spiritual experience is the ground of spiritual truth. Despite the great Western tradition of the mystical life, mysticism has not been given the same emphasis in the history of Christianity as it has among Eastern religions. While many Western theologians view mysticism as having an integral place in Christian spiritual experience, others do not assign it primary significance, nor do they ordinarily consider it to be a criterion or norm of spirituality. They center the evangelical experience of conversion and sanctification in the sacraments. Rather than personal experience of God, they emphasize divine grace and the fullness of Christian life in community.[42] Today, however, mystical experience is the object of thought and dialogue among many Indian Christians, who realize that their ultimate effectiveness in relating to the religious aspirations of their own people must be centered in spiritual experience, not in theological definitions and formulations.

The reconstruction of society is also a crucial value in the search for a universal religion by both Hindu and Christian. Within Hindu history, the concept of spiritual self-realization has always been stronger than that of the welfare of others, with the possible exception of the members of one's own family or caste. Since the nineteenth-century Hindu renaissance, however, Hindus have become more and more conscious on a practical level of the demand for justice in society. As Indira Gandhi has declared, "the poor of India have not become poorer, but they have become more sharp-eyed in evaluating their place in society." Whether or not Christians, on the other hand, have practiced faithfully the teaching of the Sermon on the Mount, Christianity has always taught love of neighbor as second only to love of God — and as one with love of God. Moreover, a new understanding of the gospel of Christ as the pursuit of liberation of all peoples has been manifested by John XXIII in *Peace on Earth* and by Paul VI in *Development of Nations*. It is finding strong articulation among Christians everywhere today. In short, Hindus and Christians, in their search for a universal faith, have reached a stage in the development of both religions that augurs well for dialogue and reciprocity.

Aside from the above considerations, the question of unity of all religions is basic to any dialogue on world religions between Hindu and Christian. The fundamental Hindu concept is that reality is one. Religions are different paths to the same goal of self-realization, which is a unifying force. On the Christian side, as Francis Acharya points out, Christianity in India since Vatican Council II is indeed opening itself to a new approach to unity among world religions. The whole of humankind is seen to be united within an ineffable mystery of salvation. This Christian attitude corresponds to a certain degree with the inner religious unity of the Indian peoples — a unity most striking because of the multiplicity of Indian races, languages, and local customs. It is dependent on an indefinable spiritual atmosphere present in India for thousands of years.

T. M. P. Mahadevan states that the dominant feature of Hinduism is its acceptance of all religious beliefs.[43] Gandhi declared in 1938, "My Hinduism is not sectarian." This richness and variety of creeds does not imply that there are no basic beliefs to which every Hindu would subscribe — for example, all Hindus believe that "truth is one, though sages call it variously."

Reality is one for Hindus because for them everything is potentially divine. The root of division among men and women is not the human will but avidya or ignorance. Evil is the product of ignorance. Hinduism regards evil as that which stands in the way of human approach to the good. A corollary of this principle is the idea that there are no real contradictions among religions. Only matters of emphasis. Hinduism has respect for both Christ and Buddha. The particular emphasis placed upon a particular incarnation is due to the need of the age and culture in which the prophet appears. The concept that God is one eliminates "a fanatical approach" to any one prophet.

Obviously the type of universal faith suggested by varied Hindu beliefs can never be achieved by the promulgation of any church. Pluriformity is essential to any dialogue with Hinduism that the Christian church, claiming catholicity or ecumenicity as one of its signs, may desire to initiate. It is necessary, then, for Christians in India to examine the real meaning of Christian unity and to propose solutions that may bridge the gap between the Hindu and the Christian concepts of a universal church.

The Christian today is aware as never before of the concept of one world. But this one world is a "global village" in the communication of certain types of events, not in the understanding of peoples. The East does not comprehend the West as the West comprehends itself. Nor does the West understand the East as Easterners understand themselves. Without greater mutual interpenetration, a "higher synthesis" of religions is impossible. In this sense, "one world" in Christ requires re-examination by the church if a viable Christian concept of unity is to be developed.[44] While Hinduism is willing to assimilate the riches and wisdom of the religions and cultures of the East without syncretism, Christ cannot be an object of compromise. On the whole, the East is more aware of the whole of reality by essence, while the West is more aware of different types of unification, such as unification by origin.[45] The Hindu concept of unity in essence offers a challenge to the Christian church to reach out beyond its historical development to a possible universal church.

Christian unity in fact requires dissociation from every sort of particular cultural garment. "The more one lives the Christian faith *subjectively,* the more one becomes conscious of its *objectivity."*[46] "Western Christianity" is only one form of living and realizing the Christian faith. The Christian has no right to identify faith in Christ exclusively with a Greco-Roman form. An oriental form may hold equal validity. Indeed, continued assumption of a Greco-Roman form together with rejection of a possible extra-Mediterranean form may suggest spiritual arrogance.

Raimundo Panikkar writes succinctly of three stages in the process of universalization of the Christian faith. The first corresponds with the mission of Christ in Israel before his death. Jesus' relationship was exclusively with his chosen people. The second stage is that which follows the death of Jesus. In it Christ offers his universal message through Israel. Today we are still living in this historical period. The third stage is about to be born — a period in which Christians will conceive of universal faith in Christ not only through Israel but apart from Israel. The dialectic that took place between the world of the Jew and that of the Gentile during the early councils of the church must be recreated in a sense between the church and the extra-Mediterranean world, particularly that of the East. The Messiah has no meaning for the Hindu. The Christ the Christian must proclaim to the Hindu is "Christ present, active, unknown, and hidden within Hinduism." The Christian who wishes to be understood by the Hindu must be able to declare "with all necessary subtlety" that "Bhagavan or Isvara" was made manifest in Jesus of Nazareth.[47] Only thus will the church be able to build up the new creation of Christ in India. If the whole of matter and spirit is to evolve toward the Omega Point, the true Christ present but hidden in all great religions must be unveiled.

To build a bridge to the unknown Christ of Hinduism, the Christian church is called upon to renounce a type of absolute centrality in rites, rules, and formulations of doctrine promulgated through historically exaggerated insistence on authority. History has demonstrated that this false type of unity has often resulted in passivity even in the Western Christian, who has sometimes accepted the word of authority without thought. The Christian in India is called to reject this narrow concept of unity and to recognize that Hinduism can offer him or her many spiritual riches, some of them unsurpassed in world history. If the church proclaims salvation for all within a closed and rigid tradition that it falsely identifies with unity, it will fail to project a bridge of true unity toward the Hindu living within his or her own spiritual culture.

In order to provide growth toward Christian universality in India, it would seem that the Indian Christian church must therefore incorporate certain principles in its approach to the Hindu. A rejection of exclusivity is primary. The church can no longer view itself in faith and action as God's only chosen people. Within such a concept, the Hindu cannot find access to reciprocity with Christians. The wider horizon of Christ's own openness to all is essential. This openness incorporates a traditional Indian attitude opposed to a rigidity the Hindu senses in certain institutional aspects of Christianity.

Moreover, if the mission of the church is to achieve a universality that will embrace all men and women and all cultures, it must accept an ecclesial pluralism. A pastoral pluralism in practice will result. The church can embrace many Hindu religious traditions within its total reality. All that is true in Hinduism will survive the prophetic critique of the church of Christ, or rather of the kingdom of Christ, which is far more extensive than the historical church.[48]

The universality demanded by an all-embracing Christianity will be realized only through local and particular forms of Christianity. Encounters between God and humans are always particular. The Spirit did not speak to the Gentile in the language of the Jew, nor does the Spirit speak to the Indian in the words of the European. The "language" spoken of here includes lifestyle, local community, art, architecture, spirituality, ministry, worship, service, theology — all of life. In *Ad Gentes*, chapter III, 22, we read:

> If this goal is to be achieved, theological investigation must necessarily be stirred up in each major socio-cultural area, as it is called. In this way, under the light of the tradition of the universal Church, a fresh scrutiny will be brought to bear on the deeds and words which God has made known. . . .
>
> Thus it will be more clearly seen in what ways faith can seek for understanding in the philosophy and wisdom of these peoples. A better view will be gained of how their customs, outlook on life, and social order can be reconciled with the manner of living taught by divine revelation. . . . Thanks to such a procedure, every appearance of syncretism and of false particularism can be excluded, and Christian life can be accommodated to the genius and the dispositions of each culture.[49]

A Christian church that has dogmatized too much needs to see that Hinduism, approached in an open way, will lead to strengthened faith, that *all* ideas can be used in dialogue as instruments to establish truth. Among Hindus, the revelation of the Vedas is traditionally open to the critiques of all philosophers and thinkers. Christians need have no fear of Indian thought on the glories of the revelation of Christ. But a spirit of union between Christian and Hindu in actual living must precede interpenetration of spiritual thought.[50] A gift cannot be forced; it must be received willingly. Gandhi, in his complete acceptance of the gift of the Sermon on the Mount, exemplifies a spirit of universality the Christian can well imitate. Many Christians in India are now appealing to crucial passages in the Bhagavad Gita as one basis for union in thought with Hindus in a manner similar to Gandhi's acceptance of the Christian gospel.

Universality of faith is the goal of Christian leaders in India. It will be the work perhaps of a century to develop a viable Indian Christian theology. Indian philosophical terms must be understood in depth. Indirection or superficiality in theology will be completely ineffective. Fundamentally, the Christian church has no real identity except the Spirit of Christ and the love of men and women for one another patterned on the love of Christ for all to the point of death. All the rest is a matter of cultural identity derived from particular societies. Christ alone must be the basis of Indian Christian theology.

Raimundo Panikkar has pointed out that a trinitarian conception of the Absolute is not an exclusively Christian insight or revelation. The problem of the Trinity is theoretically most important and practically most urgent in the approach of Christianity to a universality that may be meaningful to the Hindu. A cosmotheandric, nondualistic vision of reality in a Christian context is in accord with the Hindu approach to reality. It encompasses the universality of both the experience and the reality of the three Persons of the Trinity as represented in the West by personal pronouns; the radical interrelationship of all things, in spite of artificial separations made by the minds of men and women, and the fundamental unity of reality are not overdshadowed by the diversity of the entire universe.[51] Panikkar's trinitarian approach suggests a bridge to universality as conceived by the Hindu mind. It may also provide for initiation of the mutual fecundation of Christianity and Hinduism.

The Hindu mentality by its very nature can respond more fully to the trinitarian Christ than to Jesus Christ, the man of Galilee, in the historical Christian emphasis. Perhaps the world — as well as India — is ready to respond to a redress of the apparent neglect of the Trinity by many Christian theologians over several hundred years. Western Christians have still much to learn of Christ in the Trinity, and the Easterner can unite with them in this spiritual venture. Today no religion can remain in isolation. The mystery of the church must be seen in universal revelation. Hinduism as well as Christianity leads to transcendent knowledge.

CHAPTER V

Christianity and Hinduism in Spiritual Relationship

WHEN a basis for mutual spiritual exchange is established between Hindus and Christians, a startling response may take place in loving interaction. The gifts of each to the other, once each is ready to accept the gifts of the other, would seem to be as unlimited as the graces given to all men and women through the loving embrace of Christ. The sense of the sacred, both immanent and transcendent; the God of cosmic revelation over thousands of years and the personal Christ of the New Testament; the seriousness of history and the timelessness of the everlasting Christ; the Western tradition of rational clarity in theology and the Eastern centrality of spiritual experience, symbols, and parables — all these gifts suggest a fertile field for holy interchange, with the transhistorical Christ, known and yet not completely known in human experience, as a loving center. Such spiritual interchange may have an incalculable influence on the modern world.

1. SENSE OF THE SACRED

It has often been pointed out that Indians are so inherently men and women of faith that only religion, centered in the sacredness of all creation, is able to move the masses of the Indian people. The Indian awareness of the relativity of all things in the world produces a profound sense of the importance of the eternal. God matters. The world is passing away. But the passing world is sacred. The person, old or young, who leaves his worldly occupation to go to the hills and live as a sannyasi is respected by all. The basic point of contact at which the Christian can enter into dialogue with the Hindu in terms the latter can understand is the sacred, represented in the mystical death to self of the suffering servant.[1]

While Christianity has stressed the sacredness of the human personality, Hinduism has emphasized the sacredness of all reality. To the Hindu, the unseen is more real than the seen. Oriental spirituality, through its sense of the absolute value of the sacred, offers Western Christians an invitation to rediscover forgotten aspects of their own revelation and to reemphasize certain neglected demands of the Christian life. It can also lead them to the very core of Hinduism.

In point of fact, the deepest impression of life in India for many Westerners is the Hindu sense of the sacred pervading the whole order of nature. Perhaps there is nothing the West needs to recover more urgently than this sense of the holy immanent in all things and giving ultimate meaning to life. The sight of millions of people on pilgrimage each year to holy rivers and sacred temples is a natural concomitant of the ever-present sense of the divine that underlies the whole life of the Indian people. Even though the sacredness of all things in India sometimes leads ironically to lack of concern for the individual person, nevertheless this consciousness of the holy can be a balancing factor to the Western preoccupation with the temporal and the secular. "The mighty wave and the tiny bubble both form the same ocean." The Westerner is often unaware of this symbolic relationship, which centralizes the sacredness of all creation. Humankind is in reality bound to God.

Another approach to the same concept is to say that for the Indian *nothing* is profane. The sacred is familiar, natural, normal. Therefore the Indian is more conscious of sacrilege than is the Westerner, but less conscious of sin. Basically, Hindus believe that deep within them is the divine spark, the atman. It is their duty to cultivate its growth until it joins the perfect flame of Brahman. They must become aware actually of this same divine presence in the world around them before they can unite with the divinity that exceeds all form. In order to do so, good Hindus frequently invoke and attempt to realize the divine. They seek stillness and serenity through methods developed by the sannyasi in order to awaken the divine within the self. In every century, over thousands of years, Indians have considered this responsibility for arousing the sacred within themselves to conscious identity with Brahman as their ultimate task, their highest karma.[2]

The immanence of God, the sense of God's presence, is a basic theme of Indian spirituality. Yet the Hindu thought of God and the world is in no sense pantheistic. If they are sure of one thing, it is of the imperfection of the material world: this is a datum of experience. "God is in everything, but God is not everything."[3] Compared with the Christian, the Hindu is less conscious of God's transcendence. When Christians become aware of God's proximate, immediate, and immanent presence, they often see themselves as sinful and unworthy, as distant from God, as "other."[4] Thus their sense of the transcendence of God is magnified. They can therefore learn about the nearness of God from the Hindu, just as the Indian can learn much about the meaning of evil from the Christian.

Indians are quite at home with the immanent God. The concept of a God outside their experience is somewhat foreign to most Hindus. The notion that God dwells in the hearts of men and women is to them a common, everyday idea. It can be compared in some respects with the Christian doctrine of the indwelling of the Holy Spirit. Yet Christians cannot accept that the Spirit dwells in the heart of the rebellious sinner precisely as the Spirit lives in the heart of the saint, nor can they accept the concept that the divine within them is identical with God.[5] The

Hindu notion of the immanence of God is expressed beautifully in the bhakti hymn "Mukundamala," sung daily in devout Vaishnava homes:

Drink life,
Life here and now,
Life whole and endless,
In one long, deep, immortal draught:
God is that draught,
God loving,
God incarnate,
God ever-present
[M. K. Gandhi, *Songs from Prison*].

The Hindu concept of the divinity of humankind is concomitant with the Hindu belief in the immanence of God. It is the nature of human beings to participate in the divinity that permeates the cosmos. This divine principle gives men and women dignity as their birthright, the seed of their spiritual liberation. The individual soul or atman in its essential nature is not different from Brahman. This idea, in its expression, rings strange to Christians. They think of the Holy Spirit as living in their soul. The Hindu can offer the Christian the gift of strengthening the human spirit through methods of contemplation, while the Christian can offer the Hindu a richer realization of the human in humankind, the human ideal in Christ, from whom comes universal love.

The East and West can thus help each other to a more integrated approach to life. Among the Hindus, the old and the new — ritual, music, drama, dance, linguistics, philosophy — are integrated with the sacred. However, medicine, physiology, and the sciences have not developed in the same way as they have in the Christian West. Debates have always been held in the East on a philosophical level, but the East has never developed natural science as the West has. Even today, the myth is maintained by some well-educated Hindus that the waters of the Ganga in Benares are clean because they are holy.

Hindus adore the divinity in humankind. They believe that the sacred appears in a special way in the appearance of avatars at crucial junctures in history (for example, the incarnation of

Vishnu in human or animal form) because humankind is in need of divine help. The idea of the avatar, however, is vitally different from that of the Christian incarnation. The Hindu God intervenes in order to restore dharma when human events go desperately wrong. For the Christian, the living and everlasting Christ is the beginning, the continuation, and the consummation of the holy. But the Hindu can comprehend the reality of the Holy Spirit more readily than the nature of Jesus Christ. Just as the Christian in India has suffered from the Hindu cultural overemphasis of personal salvation, the Christian has also suffered — like all modern Christians — from underemphasis of the Spirit.[6] The Hindu can sometimes teach the Christian, in the words of Vivekananda, that "each soul is potentially divine" through the action of the Spirit.

As a "divine human being," Christ is attractive to the Hindu simply because the Indian is always in danger (as a result of belief in the divinity of human beings) of falling into what the Western theologian calls "angelism" or "divinism."[7] The more a guru abstains from food and laughter, the more a guru rises above human foibles, the more a guru is considered to be a master and superior. Yet both traditional and modern India are drawn to the divine human who is truly human and does not deny his humanity. To the Indian, Christ is not an ascetic of the sannyasi type. Indians have always had an intuitive knowledge of the mysterious union between the human and the divine. This union they find in Christ when they worship him as a historical God who is involved with simplicity in the life of men and women. Reading the gospel, they realize the perfection of his teaching and the perfect confirmation of that teaching in his life. Though they cannot accept the uniqueness of the Christian church, they can readily find unique qualities in Jesus. However they worship Christ, nevertheless, they cannot believe that he is the *only incarnation*, or God come to earth. While millions of Indians prefer to worship Christ rather than Krishna or Rama, the latter two are also seen as God come to earth to help humankind as Jesus did. Yet Christ appears unique to them in his utter renunciation, in his absolute concrete realization of faith in practice.

Reverence for the sacred in human beings and in all creation inspires in the Hindu an attitude of respect that is often puzzling to the Westerner. No angry person is admired in India. Recognition of sham or pretense is characterisitc of simple villagers, even though they do not always reveal this insight. Good Hindus have no respect for pomp or condescension. Their sense of timelessness leads them to be never in a hurry. No matter how much work they have to do, an appointment is normally not necessary in order to meet with them. Their feeling of serenity in relating to others is an outcome of their respect for the other. This quality of reverence is closely associated with the nonviolent, nonaggressive character so often associated with the Hindu. The sometimes overactive Western Christian can thus learn a sense of relaxation and peace from the Indian. Hindus have even been known to remain seemingly passive in the presence of aggressive Christians fighting for the "rights" of the Easterner! The nonviolence of millions of Hindus reflects a quality of spiritual significance that rejects "overnight" change even for a good cause. Cultural responses of thousands of years based on reverence for all creation cannot be changed quickly through doctrinaire logic.

On the other hand, the Hindu observes that respect and reverence for all life is sometimes lacking in the responses of Christians. The capitalistic society of the West, of which Western Christianity is a part, is often passive in the presence of exploitation of persons and of nature for economic gain. The Hindu sometimes hears the Western Christian respond to such exploitation with statements like, "That's what capitalism is all about."

The Hindu sense of responsibility in life, then, lies in belief that men and women are divine or one with God. Life in an Indian village, for example, is regulated like a monastery in its hierarchy, caste, and duties. Who the Hindu is, is determined by one's background. "The stranger without pedigree is an enemy or a God."[8] Everybody has a sacred and particular status and acts according to it. The question is not one of rights but of duties or dharma.

This sense of hierarchy of existence, related to the sacredness of all things, both arises from and results in a oneness of life.

Humankind is sacred, but so is the cow, and so are all creatures. All are united in the cosmic sense. Cultural patterns are sacred just as the religious patterns with which they are woven, as with a golden thread, are sacred. This type of unity often does not reach the consciousness of Western Christians. The Indian does not ordinarily experience a dichotomy between religious and practical life as the Westerner often does. "To see God in everything is the essence of the religious person." The integration of the sacred and the secular is thus taken as a matter of course in Indian life. In the West, the sense of the sacred is not always part and parcel even of the structures of religion. Rather, "fitting into the organization" is often stressed.

The everyday responses of Hindus in their work-a-day world perhaps reveal best their sense of the sacred. The rickshaw driver will stop his autocar for a few minutes, without a word to the occupant, to perform his evening puja. The laborer will take three or four days from work at any time of year to visit the temple of his choice with his family, often on a difficult journey by truck or bus. The father of a family will rise in the middle of the night and wait for hours in a crowded railway station to seek darshan of his chosen goddess on an "auspicious" day, or the mother of the family will open her little closet daily to light a candle and pray before her small household idol. Along the roadside, Hindus will stop to worship their favorite avatar — Ghanesh, or Vishnu, or Kali. Daily rituals are unobtrusively significant. Hindu children, Indian teachers tell us, are often more aware of the immanence of God than their Christian companions are. Asked to go alone into the country to "imagine things," they return with contemplative questions, finding God in birds and trees and streams.[9] Mountains and caves, rivers and trees, plants and animals are holy. Traditional forms of religious worship — singing, dancing, chanting of the mantra — reflect the sacred in daily Indian life. The Indian village, in the midst of poverty and even disease, reflects a sacred character. Birth and marriage and death are still sacred mysteries.

Having stressed the central importance of the sacred in the Hindu way of life, one must point out the sometimes negative qualities of an exaggerated emphasis upon the sacred in India.

The Western Christian sometimes finds in India an apparent lack of concern for the individual life. When *all* is holy, the holiness of the individual can assume less importance! Also, salvation is viewed as vertical, concerning only the person and God, and beyond that only one's family and one's caste. The lives of others have less significance. Thus the life of each person sometimes appears to the foreigner to be valued cheaply. Again, the Westerner finds seeming harshness in the Hindu rejection of converts to Christianity, who are disinherited by their own people. Family, friends, culture, financial stability must all be sacrificed. It is a matter of conscience for the caste to reject the outcaste.

The sense of the sacred, moreover, does not always contribute to temporal development in India. Hindus are subservient to nature as to a god or a goddess, but they do not make nature a controlling motive for worldly progress as the Christian does in the West. Christians explore and control land, mountains, and rivers. They even use power to go to the moon. In everyday life, they are proud of their clean, well-built homes. Christians develop modern medicine, physiology, and science in order to make the world a more human place in which to live. Indians study medicine with Western textbooks and then often cannot practice medicine properly in their own land because they do not have the equipment to do so. They go to the West to learn a profession in order to make more money, and their countrymen complain of India's "brain drain."

Spiritual emancipation can be overemphasized at the expense of deprivation of even the essentials of life, to the injury of human personality. The evils of the caste system and of untouchability, as well as subordination of women through the tradition of dowry, can sometimes be practiced without qualm by the devout Hindu concentrating on the sacred in all things. Thus Hindu spirituality can at times result in a lack of social consciousness. On the spiritual level, moreover, the Indian can accept mystery easily, but mystery for the villager can easily degenerate into superstition. To be sure, the great diversity in Hindu religious customs also reveals that one village may differ greatly from another in religious practices. At the lowest level of concern for the person and of superstition, one can still find the rare practice of human sacrifice among Hindus. There still are annual festivals in which women throw babies under the wheels of chariots to appease their gods. A learned Hindu was heard to remark noncommittally that this practice is expected. Sacrifice to secure blessings has existed for thousands of years![10]

It is frequently pointed out by both Hindus and Christians in India that weakness in applying moral principles in ordinary everyday life is found side by side with reverence for the sacred: rank corruption in social and political practice is common. Therefore many Christians in India refuse to accept the dichotomy of the East as spiritual, the West as either secular or materialistic. A pure cliché, they insist! Moreover, the sannyasi is sometimes found to be materialistic; the sadhu, spiritual. To be sure, generalizations can be made about the people of any society, and generalizations can always be refuted easily. Also, from the time of Vivekananda until now, Hindus have found the highest virtues of Christianity in a "rediscovered" and purified Hinduism.

Granted all human distortions of the Hindu sense of the sacred, the Indian reverence for all creation must still be asserted strongly. It can indeed unite in spiritual relationship with the Christian consciousness of the life of the Spirit in humankind and in the world. A spiritual interchange that can influence the modern world, East and West, toward the peace of Christ is possible.

Only at the basic and central point of spiritual interiority can the Christian enter into dialogue with the Hindu — in fact, with all Indians. The profound Indian sense of the sacred, of prayer, retreat, and recollection, can indeed be an antidote to the lifestyle of those Christians who are too much influenced by secular realities. A young man can spend eight years, for example, in a seminary of an overinstitutionalized Christian church, and emerge with an exaggerated sense of the structure of the church and an inadequate response to the Spirit of Christ. Christians can find in Hinduism a guide to the unfulfilled part of their lives, to too little growth in the Spirit. They can learn paths to serenity, stillness, and peace by means of Eastern ways of contemplation that awaken consciousness of the divine. An emphasis on mystery and ritual learned from the Hindu can also provide a balance to a sometimes oversimplified Christian liturgy today. Since Vatican Council II, Christian worship has sometimes become so simplified that the sense of divine mystery is almost lost.

On the other hand, Christianity can offer to India the gift of a sense of the seriousness of the temporal. The Hindu has always been overoccupied with spiritual self-liberation. Christ can offer the ideal of the beautiful balance of the spiritual and the temporal. Christianity can lead India to the Christ who encompasses time and eternity. The Christian balance can allow for greater progress and development on a human level. This Christian impact has been strongly felt in India since the nineteenth century, but has not always been acknowledged. The West is teaching discipline to the East on a material level that is leading to exploration and control of nature for the welfare of human beings. While contemporary Western men and women may have lost to a great extent their sense of the sacred, Hindus often blame the stars to explain away the events they find undesirable. Perhaps these are the reasons why one hears a poignant appeal for a modern St. Francis of Assisi in India today. The medieval saint combined a cosmic reverence for all creation with the Spirit of Christ, which gives both divine and human meaning to all that is sacred in the universe.

2. COSMIC REVELATION, ANTHROPOMORPHISM, AND NONDUALISM

Cosmic revelation is the revelation that God makes to all men and women through nature and the soul. It is the basis of all primitive religion. With regard to nature, St. Paul wrote that "the invisible nature of God was made known through the visible things which he has made" (Rom. 1:20). Concerning the soul, Paul said, "the Gentiles who have not the law have the law written in their hearts" (Rom. 2:15). Hinduism stands today as a witness to the whole world of the length and breadth, the height and depth, of this universal revelation.

In the cosmic tradition of the East, nature is mother, teacher, healer. Divinity is the depth dimension of the cosmos. Primitive peoples saw an equation between the macrocosm and the microcosm. The sun was related to the eye; the wind to the breath; cosmic reproduction to sexual reproduction. Cosmic rejuvenation was related to death and rebirth. Thus developed the concept of identity between the ultimate ground of the cosmos (Brahman) and the ground of humanity (atman). Philosophers later transformed this experiential identity into ontological identity. The Hindu scholar, T. M. P. Mahadevan, traces the origin of the world to this spiritual principle, Brahman-atman, the all-inclusive ground of the universe.[11] The cosmos is a unity in which humanity shares: the eternal within man and woman is one with the eternal ground of the ever-changing cosmos. It is not possible to conceive of a Hinduism that is not cosmic. To the Hindu, existence is irreducible. In fact, Indians are less aware of the beauty of nature than is the Westerner simply because they themselves are nature. They do not worry about the purpose of existence. The important idea is to live, to experience life.

Inasmuch as the variety of beliefs called Hinduism is bewildering and unlimited, the Hindu philosopher relies on both reason and revelation. Metaphysics is a sustained inquiry into the nature of ultimate reality, whereas experience is the ultimate test of truth. Reality is known through "intuitive" experience, which transcends the sensory and the rational. Hindu scripture offers knowledge of the real. Reasoning functions at the relational level. It cannot comprehend Ultimate Reality. The truth of scripture, however, is the direct outcome of the intuitive or mystic experience of the ancient seers, or of wise and holy persons. Such wisdom is self-certifying and self-revealed. Thus, in the philosophy of India, "the philosophic absolute and the religious absolute are one and the same."[12] Primordial cosmic revelation is a different way of looking at the world than that of the Western philosopher. The Hindu philosopher sees no problem at all in speaking of earth, fire, and water as cosmic sacraments.

The Hindu God bestows self-revelation on many levels of revelation. God is worshiped as idol or physical object, as avatar, as the one supreme transcendent Spirit, as God immanent in nature, or as Jesus Christ (in all sincerity). "All our talk with God is baby talk," says a Hindu holy man. "So why are Christians so afraid of plural approaches to God? All names are sacred to him. Does he really need *our* protection?"[13] Moreover, the sannyasi declares, in all lands and ages and religions, holy men and women have described their experience of God with impressive unanimity. Knowledge revealed by scripture must become experience: only then does revelation fulfill its purpose. And the one who has experienced God needs neither external authority nor scripture.

For the Christian, revelation is a direct communication from God, who spoke to men and women through the prophets and through Jesus Christ. For the Indian, revelation is what holy men and women have heard *within* themselves. It speaks through the atman within the holy person, which is identified with Brahman. It is a direct experience of human innermost being at its very source, a pure perception of the self beyond differentiation. Thus the major current of Hindu spirituality is one of immanence, while that of the Christian tends to stress transcendence. In the judgment of many *Indian* Christian scholars today, the East is concerned too much with the immanent, the West too much with the transcendent. Each can balance the other in approach to divinity. To the Hindu, the prayer of the Christian often seems to be "the sound of mouths"; to the Christian, the Hindu sometimes lacks the social dimension of love and care for the other. The Hindu is not heard to petition God to respond to the needs of either his own brothers and sisters or those of the hungry and oppressed throughout the world. Nor is the Christian seen as an exemplar of the prayer of simple union with the Spirit.[14]

The Hindu can indeed teach the Christian a broader vision of cosmic harmony in the approach to God. In the past, Christians have often tended to see God as imprisoned in places, times, and formulas. Because of a dualistic attitude, they have sometimes projected their own images upon the reality of God. Hindus know that they do not have to create an image in order to enter into God's presence to pray: they have only to become aware of God's presence whenever and wherever they choose.

God, humankind, temple, and world are a single whole in such a vision, even though each remains distinct. The vision of the Western Christian is certainly not that of the Hindu who once lived and often still lives today in constant dependence on raw nature, sun, and rain for a livelihood, and even constant fear of the influence of the stars. Science and technology have brought a radical change in the West, manifested in a heightened sense of productive creativity; a greater mobility and "pronounced dynamism" as expressed in the papal encyclical *Pacem in Terris*; and a certain sense of "powerlessness to consecrate the forces released by technology solely to human ends," often accompanied by alienation and threat to the integrity of selfhood.[15] Therefore, the gift of cosmic perspective that the Hindu offers the contemporary Christian is not the "magic world" created by the belief that wise persons accept difficulties passively because the temporal is not important. The Hindu contribution is rather a deeper awareness of the immanence of God, always and everywhere. It can be an antidote to human alienation in the West.

The Christian contribution to the Hindu, on the other hand, must always begin with the fact of Christ to be integrated with ultimate reality in a cosmic sense. Indian philosophy, principally nondualistic Vedanta, becomes viable here. The fact of Christ is not inherent in the thought of ultimate reality, nor is it derived from logic. The division between the universality of ultimate reality and the particularity of Christ can be overcome through a nondualistic philosophy completely compatible with Christian faith. Philosophers like Raimundo Panikkar are today developing such a philosophy, which respects both cosmic revelation and the gospel of Christ.[16]

Today God invites the Christian to rediscover the aspect of cosmic sacrament in the Orient. The East tells the West that the universe is a symbol of God; the West tells the East that this symbol is also message. "The cosmic function of the Word, brought to light again by Teilhard, is enhanced by the Orient." Christian spirituality is deepened and enriched by the "cosmic component." If in the East the world is manifested as the cosmic side of the godhead, in the West interiority does not eliminate

transcendence. Every human being is a synthesis of interiority
and transcendence. And Christ is the "place" par excellence for
the meeting of the richnesses of East and West. The West will be
psychologically unbalanced until it integrates its spirituality
with the cosmic covenant of its own past through Christ.[17] Primordial revelation in its purest form reveals elements of truth common to Christianity. This revelation is not false religion. It bears
authentic witness to truth. Therefore the Christian must approach
cosmic revelation as revelation sharing in the truth of Christ.

The unique Hindu experience of God, as revealed in the
Vedas, the Upanishads, and the Bhagavad Gita, gives insight
into cosmic revelation as complementary to Christian revelation.
Each can be a catalyst to the other. Christ enlightens both Hindu
and Christian through love expressed in his death and resurrection. Because primordial religion existed all over the world
before the advent of Jesus, the great Eastern prophets —
Buddha, Confucius, Lao Tzu — can well be considered as
pointing toward Christ. Born between East and West, Christ
must become incarnate in the East as he became incarnate
among the Jews. India, China, and Africa may well develop
their own Christian rituals, differing from those of Western
Christianity, but essentially one with it. Christianity does not
reject but confirm much of the wisdom of primordial revelation.
Nor need it reject many of its age-old rituals.

One of the outstanding values of cosmic revelation for contemporary Christianity is that it can sometimes lead Christians
to think of God as apart from humankind. Christians are often
in danger of suggesting indirectly to non-Christians that the
God of the scriptures is an anthropomorphic God.[18] The Hindu
insight into the Absolute godhead through advaita Vedanta
philosophy is a great world achievement. It presents a great
awareness of the *mystery* of God. To say that God is a Person is
not necessarily to deny that God is also nonpersonal. The values
of the godhead exist in God in a manner beyond our com-
prehension. Each revelation has its own perspective, and each
has its own insight into the eternal mystery.[19]

Hindu prayer, for example, is often found to be an experience of utter openness to the divine, whereas the Christian sometimes loses sight in prayer of God as mystery. A similarity to the Western mystics — Dionysius, Eckhart, Teresa of Avila, John of the Cross — is found in the Indian sannyasi, who makes a relentless search for the Ultimate. Deep silence in prayer represents a break from an anthropomorphic approach to God. In wordless prayer, the imcomprehensible opens up, and God comes to men and women. Christians are often strongly aware in prayer of the image of the personal Christ in the New Testament, but not always of Christ "beyond" Christ, the everlasting Christ who is nearer to us than we are to ourselves. Divine action in history is real, not just an appearance of the real. The danger in the modern world of a personal God's becoming an idol or an image of glorified humanity is also real. The problems presented by Paul Tillich and by J. A. T. Robinson are examples of this danger. God in se transcends all our concepts of God. The Absolute God of the Hindu and the Trinity of the Christian open a way to cancel the concept of God as idol.

In both East and West, to be sure, distortions appear in worship. The cosmic experience of God in the East degenerates at times into magic, occult ritualism, and even alienation from the divine. A one-sided devotion to the human person of Christ of the New Testament can at times cloud the Christian awareness that God is transpersonal. Magic and anthropomorphism are both dangers, but one suspects that the greater danger in our time may be the Christian loss of divine mystery. A pastor in Gujarat, who is an Indian national and a Spaniard by birth, has clarified well the plight of many Christians today who are closed to the boundless mystery of the eternal Christ whom they do not yet know:

> Hinduism can enrich Christianity by purifying the Judaeo-Christian concept of God heavily laden with anthropomorphism in theory and practice, which is prompting some Christians today to abandon the idea of a God they cannot defend. The Vedantic concept of God, and the consequent ascesis to be one with him, is one of the deepest religious facts in the world and lies at the root of the great appeal India has for the West today.[20]

While Hindu philosophy may be dualist, nondualist, or qualified dualist — even all at the same time — the most profound
Hindu philosophy is the nondualist advaita Vedanta. It is open
to subtleties that often appear to the Westerner to be contradictions. Yet the Hindu always maintains that all gods are but
manifestations of the one Supreme Being: "They speak of Indra,
Mitra, Varuna, Agni; the one being whom the wise call by many
names" (Rigveda 1. 164). The profound Hindu insight into the
ultimate mystery of being is the nondual Absolute. This one
being is known as Brahman, or as Saccidananda, which is Being
experienced in pure consciousness as absolute bliss. Precisely
here is the essential truth of Hinduism. The Brahman, the
ultimate ground of being, is one with the atman, the ultimate
ground of the self, and this in turn is one with the Lord, the
personal God. Reality is nondual. This doctrine can be related to
the Christian teaching of human destiny:

> In the Spirit we are all one in the Word, each one unique in
> himself, reflecting the light of the Word, and in that Word we are
> one with the Father, the source of all. "That they may all be one:
> even as thou, Father, are in me, and I in thee, that they also may
> be in us." This is our destiny, to be one with God in a unity which
> transcends all distinction, and yet in which each individual being
> is found in his integral wholeness.[21]

The great mystic, Abhishiktananda, has taught that unless
human beings experience the nonduality of being, they have no
true experience of God or of themselves. This truth is one of the
major contributions of India to the West. Joseph Mattam points
out succinctly that while a distinction between a spirituality of
identity and a spirituality of communion may be justified on a
conceptual level, the whole thesis of solitary and reciprocal
interiority is somewhat academic. The solitariness of the sannyasi can be compared with that of the Christian mystics. Christ-
centered spirituality always tends to union, not to distance and
separation.[22]

The experience of mystic union underlying the doctrines of
the Trinity and the incarnation parallel the Hindu nondual
vision and offer a framework for incorporating it within Indian

Christianity. The fathers of the church regarded human union with the divine as the end and aim of life. They described mystic union as mutual indwelling through the Holy Spirit. Nonduality is an intuition of oneness, of unity, in which there is an awareness that can be described as "there are two, but *they* are not two."[23] Trinitarian theology is the starting point of Indian Christian theology.

No one has developed to date a trinitarian theology parallel to advaita Vedanta and yet interpenetrating with it so profoundly as Raimundo Panikkar has.[24] This theological development cannot be described completely here. Panikkar insists that the relationship between Christianity and Hinduism must be one of mutual fecundation. The trinitarian paradigm allows for infinite diversity. Panikkar proposes both the traditional advaitic solution to the problem of "the one and the many" and the equally traditional Christian answer: "religious truth is existential and nonobjectifiable." There is only one Christ, but this Lord who is, this one and everlasting Christ, is more than the Christ we comprehend. The Indian Christian can only attempt, on pilgrimage to God, to unveil "that unknown *reality*, which Christians call Christ, discovered in the heart of Hinduism, not as a stranger to it, but as its *principle of life*, as the light which illumines every man who comes into the world."

With regard to existential knowledge of God, Panikkar offers a thought for profound meditation: "There are ex-Catholics, ex-Marxists, ex-Buddhists, and so forth, but I know of no ex-mystic. Once the transformation due to an authentic mystical experience has happened, it is irreversible." Precisely here is an indirect definition of knowledge of God that reduces rational clarity to a child's primer. Similarly powerful is Panikkar's statement on the revelation of Christ in others: "you discover Christ in all those who have reached the Mystery, even if their ways have not been the Christian one." The above two statements place Panikkar's creative theology in the realm of mystical theology: those who have ears to hear, let them hear.[25] "By his own powers man cannot see God, yet God will be seen by men because he wills it. He will be seen by those he chooses, at the time he chooses, and in the way he chooses, for God can do all

things. He was seen of old through the Spirit in prophecy. . . .
As those who see light are in the light sharing its brilliance, so
those who see God are in God sharing his glory."[26]

3. SERIOUSNESS OF HISTORY

Hinduism has been called the most searching quest for the
divine that the world has known. The Hindu experience is of
God as absolute, infinite, eternal. Yet the Hindu has never been
able to find, in the eyes of the West, a true relation between the
Absolute and the relative world of time and space. The
Easterner does not have the same concern for actual history as
the Westerner. "What is history?," asks the Hindu philosopher.
"It is subjective, relative. Even the distant past changes in the
perspective of time. Just as human beings have different appearances in different pictures, so God has different appearances in
different ages: Krishna and Christ are the same."

As a result of his comparative indifference to history, the
Hindu concept of fate becomes frozen over the centuries.[27]
Because they often believe that they cannot alter history, Hindus may miss much of the world that confronts them. Because
of their concern for a higher reality, they may be fatalistic when
they could be creative. In the harsh reality of suffering, they
normally do not know the Christ who is near to the human
sinner. In India, said Vivekananda, the human attitude is sometimes the least privileged. As a result, human development has
been neglected: "the pure soul of India contrasts with the
bruised body in society."[28] India remained isolated for centuries
because of its concern for the Absolute combined with its social
stagnation. Although it developed major philosophical systems
in the past, it is only now generating a new life corresponding to
the pulsing, palpitating world around it. It has been left centuries behind in development by countries that have made a larger
synthesis of experience through concern for the multifarious
aspects of human life. Most of the great minds of India have not
reached beyond Himalayan barriers.

The Hindu today has no common historical religious symbol

to appeal to, and the educated Hindu sometimes appears as a secularist in society. The Hindu's concepts refer to no institution or authority. The Hindu sees the Christian as too insistent on the historical approach to spirituality. Religion based on incidents of the past they see as detrimental to the spiritual life. There is no pure history, and the history we know must be taken only for what it is worth. Religion must be accepted only on eternal principles.[29]

Hindus have no difficulty in accepting the historicity of Jesus Christ. Their difficulty is centered in the nature of history itself, especially spiritual history. Can we gauge God's manifestations with our own narrow measures of human history? Is the historical time-scale adequate to measure eternity? A Hindu wonders whether God's revelation can be limited for all time to the manifestation of Jesus. Is it not one and the same incarnation that rises up in one place as Krishna and in another place as Christ? The real problem with traditional Christianity, then, is that it cannot separate the personality of Jesus from the universal principle of Christhood he manifested.[30] In this approach, the historicity and the personality of Jesus are accidents, and should be held as nonessential to the gospel of Christ.

On the other hand, it has been maintained by Hindus that the *teaching* of Jesus is in continuity with the best in Indian tradition. Many Hindus adopted the teaching of Buddha on love, righteousness, and the anti-caste tradition, so that Buddhism is no longer a separate stream of life in India today. Parallels exist in the teachings of Jesus adopted by such Indian leaders as Mohan Roy, Vivekananda, and others. The real history of the development of Hinduism in India, it is said, has not yet been written.

One of the most cogent answers to the problem of the relationship between the Absolute and the relative world of time and space is that of Christian Swami Abhishiktananda.[31] Jesus, he points out, revealed the Father as both the source and the term of the cosmos. He came from the Father to redeem time and bring it to completion. He manifested the divine fullness in the world of time and space, and in his return to the Father he continues to be present to every moment of time through his metatemporal existence as the Risen One. Thus he provided at last the solution to the paradox of advaita Vedanta. The jnanis had sensed the solution but were unable to express it. In reality, wrote Abhishiktananda:

> Redemption is neither something past nor something yet to come. It is wholly and entirely realized in the present moment, in which I actually am. . . . And it is also in this moment that I "pass from non-being to being," from time to eternity, crossing to the further shore of death, and attaining to Immortality, beyond the darkness.

Yet, adds the mystic, it is always possible for being to fail to develop in me. I can become a "slayer of the self."

History is real, and God works within history. The Christian is called to be immersed in history in an actual existential situation. Philosophical or theological concepts are not enough. Mystical union alone is not enough. The temporal here and now must be reconciled with interiority. Christians are responsible for the historical situation in which they find themselves. Christians take history seriously: their experiential situation is crucial.

The Christian West thus offers to the Hindu the rediscovery of the value of history. Salvation history can unite with Eastern cosmic revelation and the revelation of the heart, vertical spirituality with horizontal. As the church should surrender accidental elements of historical circumstances, so the Hindu should recognize the need to "come down to earth" in history. And since the event of Christ is already placed in history for Christians, they must concomitantly place it in ultimate reality. Jesus Christ and ultimate reality are both of fundamental importance. The two must be integrated simultaneously. Fact must be metamorphosed into truth.

A problem arises for the Christian because historicity can be its own undoing. Precisely because of the philosophical categories that have bound Christianity, a spiritual restlessness results. Today there is a tendency among Western Christians to turn away with scorn from clearly nonactive philosophies. At times, more intense action is offered as the cure for ills that are the outcome of action. As is sometimes the case in psychiatry, the disease is presented as the cure.

Aside from the reconciliation of history and ultimate reality, emphasis must always be placed on the truth that history here and now is profoundly serious in itself. Salvation history implies that not individuals alone but the whole of creation is to be renewed. If the new creation comes into being only beyond history, what is the meaning of history? God is the ground of Christian hope in history. The Christian must offer the Hindu this sense of temporal reality as crucial. The kingdom here and now for the Christian is the realization of God's plan in history. The human city is a part of salvation, and a just society for all is necessary as well as the salvation of the individual. Hindus, on the other hand, reveal a certain irresponsibility as regards concern for the world because for them what matters is the individual person's realization of identity with the Absolute. For the Christian, the temporal has a real and purposive unity for all men and women, and historical reality is an essential element of all reality. Christ, the ultimate reality, is divine-human; all that is related to him, divine and human, makes the temporal profoundly serious.

Christians themselves have still much to learn of the seriousness of history. Christianity is allegiance to Christ fundamentally. Anything that is not Christ is secondary. Therefore, the entire historical development and present condition of Christianity itself in its positive and negative elements are relative, except insofar as they are part of faith in Christ.[32] Only Christ is the norm, the concrete pattern of God in history. He alone offers the basic dimensions of salvation. But Christ must be lived in a specific culture in a concrete historical situation. Christians are only beginning to see in its profundity this truth that centralizes the seriousness of the temporal. "If Jesus is the Christ, he must live today in all cultures, and unleash a new history in our much more varied world."

Christianity, moreover, is engaged in an evolving, historical pilgrimage. All men and women are engaged in this journey, which will redeem all of humankind. The encounter of all human beings gives form to Christianity. Christ made total entry into Christianity through Jesus, a historical human. His historicity is crucial; his Semitic origin in history is secondary.[33] Because of the seriousness of the temporal, men and women are

responsible in common for the secular historical situation in
which they live. They are responsible for their own destiny and
the destiny of their world. Growth in fuller responsibility for life
is discerned at various levels in the evolution of history. Freedom gives persons the responsibility to discover both their
unique selfhood and the reality of being human in a community
of persons. Thus all human beings create a purposive history
moving toward its goal, and a fuller promise for human life.

Despite collective and individual egoism, confession of Christ
and defense of human rights are integral to each other. Human
choice and decision in the face of existential problems have
made it almost impossible to ignore Jesus Christ. Revolutionary
ferment in the world today is in great part due to Christian
values — often in Marxist garb! Redemption is today more than
ever redemption of the whole world. Christian creative presence
today strives to extend itself to the whole cosmos and to lead all
peoples toward ultimate fulfillment in Christ.

This hope for the fulfillment of history is the enduring basis
of human responsibility to mold the future of the world. And
this sense of responsibility for total humanity is at the root of
one of Christianity's most significant offerings to the Hindu in
mutual fecundation: a sense of the seriousness of the temporal
described above as related to every individual and to corporate
humanity. In India, the bullock cart and the jet plane, and the
responses to history that they represent, continue to coexist.
Everything new is assimilated; nothing is rejected. But in the
West every new historical event, whether it be landing a human
being on the moon or orbiting a shuttle in space, is full of
significance and movement toward a goal. This type of decision
and commitment are gifts of the Christian West to the Hindu.
Whether Christians use these values to their own spiritual
growth is another question!

These gifts are essential for India because the Hindu has not
yet developed a strong synthesis of goals related to development of the social dimension of Indian life. The significance of
historical development, of commitment to society and secular
reality, is not yet integrated with the religious life of the Hindu.
Thus India has a two-tier society. The outside tier has accepted,

for example, Western industry and Western technology. But the inside tier maintains the traditional social structure. Authentic Christianity can offer freedom in Christ as against this double approach to life: integration of the spiritual within and the temporal without.

Christianity itself can return to its own historical past in integration with the great cosmic religions like Hinduism. The reflective consciousness of Westerners often finds them isolated today from nature, from their fellows, from their ground of being. Modern humans are perhaps more isolated than any humans in history. They will be saved only as the body of Christ, not only as individuals. The myth of the God who dies and rises is revealed as actual history in Christ, so that the meeting of myth and history in Christ offers revelation of the ultimate meaning of life. The incarnation of Christ in history in its dynamic aspect means that the destiny of humanity itself is transformed. It becomes what it was not. The church too must commit itself to the total human community. It must descend into a deeper level of its own being so that it can become, together with other religions, a co-worshiper of the Father.

In order to become a partner with Hindus, the church must therefore recognize first of all that for them mere historical veracity can never be the last word of true spirituality. The Hindu cares for the teaching of Jesus Christ, not for the facts of his life. In the words of Swami Asheshananda, "The historicity of Christ is not of much concern to Hindus."[34] The Christian, however, insists that God in history changes history. Indeed, divine action in history, because it is reality and not appearance, is an actual guide to the integration of the spiritualities of East and West. Though the God experience of the Hindu differs from the unique historical experience of Jesus, the transhistorical Christ unites the experience of Jesus with that God experience that the eternal Father has granted to Hindus within their own time and culture.

To present Christ as only historical event would therefore destroy the meaning of Christianity for the Hindu, but Christ as the epiphany, the real manifestation in history of the mystery hidden since the beginning of time, is entirely comprehensible to Hindus. With this approach, the Hindu can understand why Christianity cannot do without history. The Hindu cannot accept the present sociological crystalization of Christianity, but can respond to an everlasting Christ who became an incarnation of God in history. In the words of Raimundo Panikkar, "Historical order is not all that there was in the beginning nor all that will be in the end. India understands this very well."[35]

Therefore the Hindu may accept the idea that time is conquered by the historical process itself when it reaches a culmination in which time and history are transformed and enter a new dimension of eternal life (Eph. 1:10). Thus the whole universe and human history will be transfigured (and not merely disappear as in the teaching of the Hindu philosopher Sankara).[36] The old plant must be cut, the new seed must fall to the ground to produce the transforming revelation concretely manifested in history through Christ. By means of a mutually enriching epiphany, the historical reality of Jesus Christ and the interior universality of God's action in Hindu life will join in transforming unity. Christ will be the center of the mutual fecundation of Christianity and Hinduism.

4. RATIONALITY AND SYMBOLISM

Thinking persons respond negatively to oversimplification of the notion that the West and the East represent diametric opposites: rational clarity and intuition, action and contemplation, materialism and spirituality. Nevertheless, both scholarship and human experience reveal over and over again that the contrasts implied in these opposites are often not mere appearances. An understanding of them is essential if interaction between Christianity and Hinduism is to occur in any significant degree.

The contrast between the Eastern and the Western approaches to reality has been analyzed endlessly, especially within the last hundred years. The Indian scholar K. M. Munshi established the Bharatiya Vidya Bhavan in the major cities of India in 1938 in order to bridge the gap between the spiritual culture of the East and the technological one of the West.[37] Bede

Griffiths, an Englishman who has spent more than a quarter century in India, maintains that the West must assimilate the *mode* of Eastern thought, for the difference between the thought of East and West lies primarily in mode: the West is rational and discursive, the East is intuitive and contemplative. This difference, he adds, is primarily psychological, so that a true marriage of East and West demands a union of *animus* and *anima*. Gaspar Koelman, a German in India, sees great value in uniting the Western search for intellectual enrichment with the Eastern penetration of pure consciousness.[38]

Christian thought over centuries has acquired categories that are distinctly recognized as Western. To some extent, Christian thought is limited to this circle of realities: person, world, action, faith, creation. It is difficult in the West to raise questions concerning ultimate reality outside these categories. At times this type of thought is reduced to axioms without alternatives. For example, the West could well consider more profoundly the thought that, while the event of Jesus Christ in history is not open to denial, Christ can be placed alternatively in ultimate reality. Hindu Swami Tapasyananda points out perspicaciously that Christianity, in its dogmatic expression, has overemphasized the personal and "watered down" the absolute.[39] Today Christianity is beginning to recognize in a cloudy way that Christ can be centered in eternity even apart from humankind.

Individual Christians in India are turning to a more balanced approach to the infinite. An example is Francis Acharya, a Belgian Trappist dissatisfied with the Western monastic tradition, who found in India a deeper dimension of Christianity.[40] He is now director of Kurisumala Ashram in Kerala, South India. The symbols, images, and parables of the East touched him as the rational clarity of Western theology and the obligatory character of Western prayer did not. For two centuries, he declares, the West thought that demythologizing was the only acceptable way of spirituality. The result was a paradoxical loss of contact with reality! Conceptualization in Christian thought is today driving Westerners increasingly to the spirituality of the East.

The problem-solving Western mind will comprehend the

Eastern mentality when it responds more directly to the Eastern concept of experience of reality. "Experience," says Raimundo Panikkar, "is the act through which the person becomes aware of himself in relation to the world, to himself, or to God."[41] Experience is immediate contact with reality. Supreme experience is identification with reality itself. In such a venture, the logical and the dogmatic are not part of the Indian charism.

The Indian experience of reality, then, is not characterized through any categories, but it is not characterless.[42] Its significant negations actually affirm by denying. Its metaphysical speculation is not theoretical only, but practiced. The actual goal of men and women is liberation or salvation. On another level, to be sure, India's intellectuals have not yet been able to translate what they know from experience into significant actual measures for human development in social and industrial areas.[43] Here a little rational clarity would be beneficial! While the Hindu cannot respond to the Christian's rational statement concerning the meaning of life, the Hindu can learn from the down-to-earth response of the authentic Christian to the enslavement of human beings in poverty, unemployment, and illiteracy. The Hindu knows that social planning, where it exists in India, is related to the practical rationality of the Western Christian.

In the realm of ultimate reality, of the Absolute beyond form and formlessness, however, the Hindu can teach the Westerner to go beyond direct logic. For the Indian, subtleties enhance the Hindu sense of the unity of all religions in their goals:

> We ought to remember that both of us may be true, though apparently contradictory. There may be millions of radii converging towards the same centre in the sun. The further they are from the centre, the greater is the distance between any two. But as they all meet at the centre, all difference vanishes. There is such a centre, which is the absolute goal of mankind. It is God.[44]

When the Indians hold as true two doctrines that *seem* to exclude each other, they are speaking in paradox.[45] They deal in analogies and identities rather than distinctions and differences. Plurality is for them a gift of God to all men and women, East and West.

Aside from the question of rational clarity and intuition, it is essential for the Western mind to understand the actual priority of religious belief in India. Indians are not skeptics. They believe in God, immanent and transcendent. Despite the weakening of religion in India because of the powerful impact of the contemporary areligious mentality, the religious attitude is still a fundamental dimension of Indian life. The Hindu cannot do without religion. Unlike the doubting Western Christian, Hindus find it easy to believe in God. Because of the element of mysticism in their character, they have a strong sense of dedication to the God they worship, and they believe that the power of God affects the events of their daily life.

In recent years it has been suggested that Western education and the growth of the scientific spirit in India will bring a change in the faith of Hindus, that they will continue to practice the externals of worship, yet cease to believe.[46] But such a radical change would be ahistorical and untrue to the Eastern tradition. There is little ground for controversy between science and religion where pluralism as a value offers place for all points of view. Centuries of spirituality are at the roots of this attitude. Holiness begins with faith, which leads to knowledge and wisdom. Reason offers no final verdict, but the holy person is known as holy, and the believer recognizes him or her as holy.

In reconciling the seeming conflict between the rational clarity attributed to Western Christian theology and the pluralistic existential faith of the Hindu, Raimundo Panikkar reminds us that pluralism in doctrine is evident even in traditional Christianity. For example, the Council of Florence accepted two formulas concerning the doctrine of the Holy Spirit. Aquinas and Duns Scotus suggested theological formulas that were not equivalent. Today the church must be guided by the Spirit in its awareness of the general direction of human history over six thousand years. Christ is living and can therefore be made credible to Hindu and Christian alike. A new Christianity in India will be a development brought about through mutual fecundation of Christianity and Hinduism. The Christian discovery of Christ is not, to date, exhaustive. Jesus is Christ, but Christ is not *only* Jesus. God in the Hindu tradition can reveal more than the Christian now knows about Christ. If the Christian can discover Christ hidden within Hinduism, then his message will be intelligible to the Indian, and the Hindu will understand the Christian act of faith.[47]

It cannot be emphasized too much that the Hindu can be appealed to only through the intuitive Indian mentality. Analogy satisfies the Indian as logic does not. Back in the seventeenth century, Jesuit missionary Robert De Nobili attempted to write Christian theology in the Tamil language to appeal to the well-educated Brahmins of South India. He opened up a gulf of misunderstanding. He therefore abandoned his original intention and used Hindu parables and illustrations to teach the Christian message![48] Today, too, the interaction of Christianity and Hinduism must come within Indian culture itself. And culture refers here to art, music, epics, folklore, proverbs, architecture, and sculpture as well as to De Nobili's parables. Inculturation of Christianity is a common goal of thoughtful Christians in India today.

In the process of inculturation, it is wise of the Christian to begin with God, not humankind, for the Hindu has a passion for the wonder and depth of God. Hindus seek reality through symbols, images, and parables of the sacred that touch them in their emotional experience as doctrine does not. A symbol is not effective unless it produces an echo in the people. For example, the sound of *om* is symbolic of God for both the Hindu and many Indian Christians. It is now used in Christian prayer because it suggests the manifestation of God in history. Assimilation is thus taking place in the use of symbols where mutual response calls forth worship of God from both Hindu and Christian. The more the church responds to the age-old Hindu symbols of the sacred, the more the interpenetration of Christianity and Hinduism is possible. The holy history of India provides inspiration through these symbols.

A special dynamism is evident in India today among many Hindus who respond warmly to Christian acceptance of their approaches to worship. Christians themselves are listening to the Spirit in this response. They are also aware that the Hindu respects the elements of Western Christianity that relate more closely to Indian culture. For example, the celibate Christian is highly respected in India because the celibacy of the sannyasi has been esteemed for thousands of years. Veneration of statues, feast day celebrations, and religious processions also relate Roman Catholic Christianity to the Hindu. The cultural areas in which integration can be initiated more deeply are art, song, dance, and architecture.

Because of the basic unity among life, religion, and art in India, art is at the service of the Hindu religion. Sculpture, painting, music, and architecture are all proof of this basic unity. This spiritual atmosphere is hard to define, but always present. On the other hand, the role of art in spirituality is almost totally absent in Indian Christianity. This situation prevails despite the fact that much of the literature, art, and music of India's heritage can be related readily to the teaching and example of Christ. Yet a certain isolation of Indian Christians has precluded their identification with the art of their own countrymen. Christian converts in the past were socially ostracized from Hindus and developed a "mission-compound" mentality. Foreign missionaries often completed a process of westernization in dress, food, names, and social customs. These changes were symptomatic of internal transformations. Indian Christians often became strangers to their native art and folklore.

Excellent attempts at Christian inculturation are found today in certain Indian villages as well as in city ashrams. An Indian nun points out, for example, that her sisters celebrate the Feast of the Maternity of Mary in a village of Hindu converts to Christianity by adapting the Navratri festival of the ancient fertility rite of worship of the Mother Goddess. A Gujarati dance called Garba, in which women dance in the streets with lights on their heads, honors the image of Mary that leads the procession.[49]

But Indian Christian art has scarcely begun to develop. Instead of Indian symbols, one sees in Christian churches mediocre statues and pictures of the Anglo-Saxon Jesus that ironically are being removed gradually from churches in the West. Authentic symbolism lifts Indians above everyday life and helps them to see God in unexpected places. The Indian symbol of the lotus, for example, is significant. The lotus represents the notion of God touching earth as incarnation. In a Christian context, the lotus is man or woman remaining incorruptible in a world of sin and temptation; "in the world but not of it," as the water in which the lotus blooms does not wet the blossom; rooted in God, the lotus plunges downward to reach sustenance. The peacock as a symbol of resurrection is also meaningful to the Indian, whether Hindu or Christian.

In architecture, Christian church construction can well incorporate features of the Hindu temple. A Christian cathedral at Dornakal in Hyderabad reveals exquisitely carved Dravidian stone pillars and courtyards suggestive of South Indian Hindu temples. A cross is central. A Japalaya, or house of prayer, in Tirupattur is built like a Dravidian temple with outer walls enclosing rectangular space. The outer wooded door is a duplicate of the heavy panelled doors of the Dravidian temple, and the gateway is crowned by a Gopuram, or carved tower, of brick. The building has no walls, so that worshipers move freely in and out for private prayer. The atmosphere created leads Hindus passing by to enter and worship, something that seldom happens in churches of closed-in Gothic style or in the Puritan fashion of a Western public hall! Hindus also respond favorably to Christian themes portrayed on church walls in the manner in which Buddhists revealed spiritual images on the renovated temple at Saranath near Benares. In the furnishing of churches, Indian Christians resist the Western tendency to make fetishes of uniformity and standardization. They accept pews, but they prefer to kneel or sit on mats on the floor. One of the finest examples of incorporation of Indian art and architecture with Christian worship is found at the National Biblical, Catechetical, and Liturgical Centre at Bangalore. At this centre, emphasis is given to interpenetration of Hindu and Christian customs of worship in all areas of liturgy and art.

Ceremony, movement, and incense attract the Indian. Hindu worship exercises the whole self — mind and body, emotions and rhythmic sense, the sensuous and the suprasensuous, the social and the personal.[50] Christian Indian worship would seem less formal, lifeless, and wooden, for example, if churches would increase the use of Indian lyrics in preference to poor translations of Western hymns. Selections from the Upanishads, the Bhagavad Gita, and the epics of Rama can also be used. What could be more beautifully Indian than a chant of lines like the following from the Upanishads:

> Lead me from the unreal to the real,
> from darkness to light
> and from death to immortality.

Hindus also respond to reverential use of silence in worship. They are adept in meditation, contemplation, and intense concentration. Westerners are amazed to observe Indians motionless for hours in silent prayer in their temples. Contemporary Indian Christians are today studying and incorporating Hindu indigenous forms of worship into their own worship.

Another example of Christian efforts in inculturation today is particularly apropos. George Proksch, director of Gyan Ashram in Andheri, Bombay, spent thirty years as a missionary in India before he decided to found an ashram with the goal of offering the mystery of Christ through Indian art and culture. He translated the Psalms into Hindi and set them to Indian classical music. The Psalms were presented as an Indian dance for the Feast of the Assumption. Then Proksch composed a drama on the life of Christ in Hindi. The play was the first dramatic life of Christ ever presented in Varanasi. The Brahmins of the holy city thanked Proksch for presenting *"the real Christ."* To date, the drama — which includes an Indian dance before the eucharist — has been performed eight hundred times in both India and Europe. Always it is received enthusiastically, by audiences that do not understand Hindi as well as by those that do. Now Proksch has conceived the idea of establishing an Indian secular institute to proclaim Christ through Indian culture.[51]

One of the finest contemporary Indian religious artists is Jyoti Sahi, the son of a Hindu father and an English mother. Like the creative thought of philosopher and theologian Raimundo Panikkar, son of a Hindu father and a Spanish mother, Sahi's art combines the best of two cultures. A Westerner approaching

Indian art for the first time can learn a great deal from Sahi's views on indianization of Christianity through art.

The above examples are minimal. The sad truth, however, is that the Hindu temples all over India are centers of art and culture, while most Christian churches in India do not represent even the art of the West, much less Indian art. Uneducated Christians in India sometimes express a fear of idolatry in the Hindu use of images. However, scholars of Hinduism, like the Spanish Adolf Esteller who has studied the Vedas for fifty years, point out that the "idolatry" of the Hindu is often closer to Christian truth than a sometimes "magical" use of Christian images. And Ramanuja's teaching of the world as the body of God is more Christian than the rejection of the world as evil by some Christians.[52] Even studies of illiterate villagers in India show that the great majority, as they worship their favorite idols, understand clearly that the image is not the absolute God whom they adore.

Christian scholars also reveal that, while Christian art is almost nonexistent in the majority of Indian churches, this situation did not always prevail. At one time the original St. Thomas Christians in Kerala worshiped in architecturally beautiful churches that resembled the Hindu temples of their own culture. The sixteenth-century influence of the Portuguese Christians put an end to that influence.[53] It would be inaccurate to declare, however, as some writers do today, that Christianity has no bridge to developed Indian art and culture. While this statement may have been true in the recent past, all over India today new and promising initiatives toward Christian incultura-tion through all forms of art are evident. Their slow and quiet development throughout the country is less impressive to the native than it is to the Westerner in India.

CHAPTER VI

Eastern and Western Paths in Conflict and Complementarity

THE meeting of East and West in spiritual interpenetration is in its early stages among Christians and Hindus in India. Words are inadequate to define what is happening and what will continue to happen, but actions associated with words can help to describe the human interchange of all those who seek truth in the Spirit. Pairs of ideas that may seem to suggest certain contradictions, while not actually doing so, highlight the changes that the meeting of spiritualities in different cultures may produce in world religions. Pairs of ideas vital with meaning that come to mind when one explores the relationship of Christianity and Hinduism are: mysticism and human service; interiority and action; vertical spirituality and horizontal spirituality; experience and suffering; karma and person. To be sure, the exploration of terms such as mysticism, interiority, spirituality, and experience in the above context can be academic, but it need not be. It can produce significant concrete statements about Eastern and Western responses to truth and reality. The

119

existential relationship of these responses is at the core of what Bede Griffiths calls "the marriage of East and West."

1. MYSTICISM AND SERVICE

Mysticism implies that even in this life it is possible to enjoy a certain degree of experience of God. Without images or concepts, God may be present in the soul, and the person may know God by immediate presence. The ordinary Christian teaching is that the human being cannot enjoy the perfect and full vision of God until transfiguration by the Spirit in the resurrection. Hinduism teaches that truth is the direct outcome of the mystic or intuitive experience of ancient seers. Persons who have realized this integral experience need no external authority in the form of scripture. Their wisdom is "self-certifying and self-revealed."[1] A mystic is one who "surrenders to a power that is greater than human and advances toward God in a darkness that goes beyond the light of reason." The experience of God is solitary but not isolated. There is a consensus among students of mysticism that the experience of God is highly similar among mystics in all advanced religions.

According to Bede Griffiths, mystical theology seems to have originated in India, as found in the Upanishads (about 600 B.C.), and to have reached a peak in the Bhagavad Gita (about 300 B.C.). If a genuine Indian Christian theology is to be developed, this tradition must be incorporated within the Christian vision.[2] The infused wisdom that unites the human being directly to God is the basis of all Eastern spirituality. This mysticism offers a richness and depth not excelled in the influence of Greek and Roman culture. Today Christianity is called to assimilate the intuitive and contemplative mode of Eastern theology to the rational and discursive mode of the West. The Eastern mode is found in its deepest profundity in one of the greatest of the mystical classics, the Gita, which provides a fruitful starting point for dialogue between the Eastern existential approach to the immanent God and the Western rational approach to God as transcendent. Spiritual retreats for Christians based on the Gita have been found fruitful in India in recent years. In the Gita, a divinity-humanity encounter is described. The Lord Krishna and the human Arjuna open themselves to each other in mystical union. Silence and meditation on the texts of the Gita by Christians have been found to lead to Christ experience.[3]

In fact, behind Indian spirituality lies a profound mystical experience, just as behind Christianity lies the profound experience of God in Israel. The Indian mind is not ordinarily analytic; it responds to symbols, not concepts. The desire to see and know God is normal and natural to the Hindu. "In return for thy great and good gift [of thyself], I have wholly yielded up my spirit to Thee," wrote the mystic Nammalvar. Throughout history, Hindus at their highest level have sought the direct experience of innermost being at its source. Liberation to them is a pure perception of self beyond all differentiation and relativity. The reality of this experience is itself the sanction of mysticism. Moreover, mysticism and death to self are seen by almost all Christian scholars as the basic and central point of contact between Christianity and Hinduism. Nowhere else can Christians enter into profound dialogue with Hindus in terms the latter can understand. In fact, Christian mysticism is sometimes seen as the fulfillment of Hinduism.

The contrast between Eastern and Western spirituality is most evident in this consideration of the mystical life. While the East has preserved the contemplative dimension over centuries, the West has turned outward since the Renaissance and has thus created an imbalance through its emphasis on technology, sociology, economics, and even psychology. Yet a concomitant materialism has also produced a reaction in the West — a need to rediscover interiority, sometimes expressed as a forced awakening to the mystical vision. On the other hand, the East is today moving forward in technology. To many, a synthesis of Eastern intuition and Western rationality is an imperative in today's world. Both Christian and Hindu scholars point out the need for study of the great Western mystics: Teresa of Avila and John of the Cross, Eckhart, Ruysbroeck, and Tauler are seen as central. The Western Christian needs to consider the *within* of both the Hindu and the Christian traditions of mysticism as well as to focus on the *without*. The Christian must also learn to go beyond the concept of God as Father and Jesus as human person. A less anthropomorphic approach to God will help to restore the balance between immanence and transcendence in the prayer of the Christian.

While sannyasis or mystics in India are regarded as so far above the requirements of ceremonial religion that they need not worship in the temple, it would be false to say that the ordinary Indian seeks mystical fulfillment as a daily way of life. Yet the search for union with the Absolute is basic to spirituality. The sannyasi who seeks God in the solitudes of forest or mountain is so reverenced by all as to be identified, in a sense, with God. The average Christian, Eastern or Western, on the other hand, is not profoundly aware of implications of the mystical life. The Christian reaches God through faith, grace, and the sacraments. A member of a Christian family converted from Hinduism writes that "the average Christian teacher scarcely rises above the ABC of Christianity because he has reached only that in his own life." The writer adds that he learned the mystical life from a Hindu sannyasi because no Christian mystic was available. Eventually he moved on to study Eckhart and Tauler.[4] The educated Christian in India is only now becoming aware of the need to renew the mystical life, which is basic to the Indian temperament.

This meeting point of Christianity and Hinduism is crucial to any approach to the interpenetration of the spirituality of the Christian and that of the Hindu. In the Vatican II document, *Ad Gentes*, we read:

> Working to plant the Church, and thoroughly enriched with the treasures of mysticism adorning the Church's religious tradition, religious communities should strive to give expression to these treasures and to hand them on in a manner harmonious with the nature and the genius of each nation. Let them reflect attentively on how Christian religious life may be able to assimilate the ascetic and contemplative traditions whose seeds were sometimes already planted by God in ancient cultures prior to the preaching of the Gospel.

Christian mystic Bede Griffiths believes that the real point of meeting between Christian and Hindu must be mystical experience, in the ground of the soul, beyond images and concepts. The comparative study of religions makes it clear that there is no form of religion without some elements of truth. A continuous tradition coming down from primitive revelation given to humankind in the beginning has been developed with profound insight in Hinduism and Buddhism. In its purest mystical forms, it comes astonishingly close to Christianity. Griffiths also holds that Christ cannot have a true birth in the Indian soul until he is accepted as the point at which God enters history.[5]

The mystic Abhishiktananda also insisted on the primacy of spiritual values and contemplation as the meeting point of Christianity and Hinduism. The church today can no longer be concerned with the external aspects of its being rather than with its spiritual aspects. Abhishiktananda states boldly that the encounter of the church with Hinduism in our times is the most formidable challenge the church has ever met in the course of its history. Hinduism offers it the challenge of interiority and spiritual depth. The particular mission of the church in the East today demands the priority of those values because of the traditions of the Hindu mystical life.[6] The call of the Spirit to contemplation in the church of India is addressed through the Hindu tradition.

Samuel Rayan points out that Hinduism has integrated an immanent transcendence and a transcendent immanence in its traditional spirituality, whereas Christianity has often stressed God as "wholly other." The Christian lack of due emphasis on the divine as immanent has resulted in a moralistic conception of divine-human relationships. If we are not what Christ is, we are nothing. If we are what he is, we have no limitations. Authentic religious experience is beyond the level of reason: myth, symbol, and ritual are its best expression. God language is the human expression of the divine experience of humans. Therefore the gospel is a more authentic expression of spiritual experience than "seventeen volumes of Karl Rahner."[7]

Christian scholar M. M. Thomas reminds us that Vedic Hinduism generally regards mysticism as "the common factor in all religions" and "the goal to which religion is directed." While many Western theologians give mysticism "an integral place in Christian experience," it is not generally considered a criterion or norm of spirituality. Nor does it lead necessarily to the community consciousness of the Christian. Nevertheless, many Indian Christian theologians today believe that Indian Christianity must lay emphasis on mystical experience in its attempt to relate itself to Indian thought and to become a living force in the country.

Abbé Jules Monchanin, one of the founders of Saccidananda Ashram in South India, understood Christian mysticism to mean a direct experience of the sharing of God's life — of the trinitarian relationship, an intuition above image and concept. He distinguishes between mysticism founded on the immanence of God (illustrated by St. Francis of Assisi) and mysticism founded on the transcendence of God (illustrated by the Greek fathers: Basil, Gregory of Nazianzen, Gregory of Nyssa, and John Chrysostom). He sees Eckhart and Ruysbroeck as related to the latter.[8]

Raimundo Panikkar maintains that Christianity and Hinduism meet in Christ. The concrete and historical dimension of Christ is inseparable from his cosmic action. The Christ who is present in Hinduism has not yet unveiled his whole face. Christianity must incorporate Hinduism into the universal economy of salvation by God through Christ. The meeting in Christ of the two religions will be to their mutual enrichment. The future is open. "Nobody knows how Christianity will look when the present Christian waters and the Hindu river merge into a bigger stream."[9]

Apparently the crucial difference between the Hindu mystic and the Christian mystic, whether the approach is analogical or not, is the sharing of the trinitarian relationship in the experience of the Christian mystic. Panikkar sees the trinitarian relationship as the final meeting point between Christian and Hindu. The relationship of human being to God in mystic union is an experience that is neither monistic nor dual, but nondual. Only the mystery of the Trinity — the mystery of the Father in loving shared relationship with the Son and the Spirit — gives clarity to the mystical experience. For the Trinity reveals that the human being is, in a sense, part of the living Christ. "Every being is, and is only, a Christophany."[10]

It is apropos to state here that Hindus in dialogue with Christians in India today are requesting Christians to tell them of the experience of the great Western mystics, of Teresa of Avila and John of the Cross, of the Greek fathers and the Rhine mystics. Without the trinitarian approach to mysticism of scholars like Panikkar, the experience of the Christian mystics cannot be related fruitfully to that of the Hindu mystics. If the true meeting point of Christianity and Hinduism lies in the mystical experience as related to Christ, the trinitarian approach is absolutely essential.

Not only are Hindus today seeking knowledge of Western mysticism; Western youth is seeking knowledge of Eastern mysticism. After World War II, two directions were signalized, two revolutions were preached: the political and the mystical. The latter discovered the significance of the East for the West. It clarified the value of the mystical dimension in human existence as over against the functional dimension of Western culture. The division between East and West was seen as actually a division within humanity, creating the tension that can be resolved only in the recognition of humanity as a Christophany sharing in the loving relationship of the Trinity. Only thus will the spiritual experience of the East and that of the West meet in fruitful fecundation.

Nevertheless, Indian scholars admit that Hinduism has tended to exalt mystical experience in its higher aspects over the need for moral and spiritual transformation of human beings in their everyday life. And there are Christian scholars who believe that Hindu contemplative methods are inhibiting to outgoing thought. The goal of pure consciousness is sometimes seen as an inadequate basis for reaching out to others in love. Thus mysticism, when it lacks a horizontal spirituality, is seen as self-centered in its more or less exclusive relationship to God. There may be something to be said for this point of view, but the lives of the great mystics consistently reveal deep concern for others.

The spirit of service is the new commandment of Christ, a positive value that Christianity can teach many Hindus today. It is basic to Christianity that men and women should minister to one another in love, in the sense of the community of all God's children. The self-sacrificing love of person for person is the second commandment of Christ, second only to the love of God. This commandment is based on the equality of all humans before God. Such equality does not exist among many Hindus because of the preconception of a divinely established order, or caste system, which does not change. Thousands of "untouchables" still exist in India even though India's political democracy outlaws the concept of untouchability. While not all Christians indeed observe the commandment of love of neighbor, Christianity has never subscribed to inequality as a religious principle. The service of "any of these little ones" is equivalent to the service of God. From a certain perspective, it is opposed to the Hindu principle that teaches that humans deserve what happens to them because of their past existence: "Do not blame the arrow that strikes you. See who has shot it. It is *yourself* of the past."[11]

The clear demand for service to one's suffering brothers and sisters is not found in the same terms in the Hindu scripture as in the Christian. Buddha, on the other hand, challenged human beings to a concern for suffering that transcends social class. The mission of Christ to humanize the world is the call to Christianity in India today. Otherwise, Christianity will have no relevance to life. While there is no clear recognition of the social character of religion among many Hindus, Christians must live Christ's teaching of fellowship through service — or bear no fruit in India. For many Christians in India today, the concept of helping others is closely related to the intimate presence of Christ in the eucharist, a mystery unknown to Hindus. Their concept of incarnation as represented in their gods is different in essence from that of the incarnation of Christ. Jesus combined service with prayer, presence, and contemplation. Christians who follow Jesus in India today therefore encourage the harijans, the untouchables, to seek their human rights. As a result, both the harijans and their Christian protectors suffer atrocities at the hands of wealthy Hindu landholders who refuse just wages to the poor and react against the social awakening of the untouchables. An organized, strong hierarchy working together with Christian leaders can help the lowest castes in their struggle for justice.

How, then, do we account for the repeated statements of modern Hindus that love and service of one's fellows is an essential part of the Hindu tradition? As long ago as the tenth century A.D., we are told, the Bhagavata Purana (VII, IX, 49) complained of the failure of Hindu bhaktas to love humans and minister to their needs as an essential part of their duty to God: "Sages generally, O God, desire their own salvation, and practice silent meditation in solitude. Leaving the pitiable folk of the world, I do not desire deliverance for my single self." Similarly, Tagore writes that devotion to God must find outlet in service to men and women: "Come out of thy meditations. . . . What harm if thy clothes become tattered and stained? Meet him and stand by him in the sweat of thy brow." Vinoba, founder of the great Sarvodaya, a movement to awaken enterprise and cooperation in Indian villages, and Gandhi, who followed the Sermon on the Mount in seeking justice in social and political life as no one before him in India had ever done, were more Christian in their loving service of others than most Christians. And the Hindu man of God, Pandit Daba Saheb, declared that mystical knowledge without social service is meaningless![12]

The answer of many Christian scholars is that the services offered by Christian missionaries in all areas of Indian life compelled Hindus to a critical evaluation of their religious and cultural heritage. Thus a major stimulus was provided for the Hindu renascence of the nineteenth century. The Christian ethical challenge played a major role in the rediscovery of social values in Hindu scriptures and culture. The values of service based on equality and human dignity of all men and women as children of God were emphasized. Faith and hope supplemented a tendency toward fatalism. In the words of the modern Hindu scholar, Radhakrishnan, "If, in our eagerness to seek after God, we ignore the interests of humanity, we will not elevate the race. We have shown how high individuals can rise by spiritual culture and how low a race can fall by its own one-sidedness."[13] Vivekananda was the strongest exponent of the new Hinduism. Like many Hindus, he refused to acknowledge the Christian influence that stimulated the Hindu renascence. Gandhi, to be sure, spoke freely of the influence of Christ on the morality of his social and political principles. The burden of 70 million untouchables lay heavily upon him.

The influence of Christian social service in India is of course unquestionable. The achievement of Christian action in every type of service over a century and a half has been monumental. Christian colleges are among the best in the country. Fields of service often neglected by others are pursued by Christians: nurses' training; aid to the blind, mutes, lepers, and the handicapped; orphanages; help for the illegitimate and the unwanted; education of women behind the purdah; adult education in health and hygiene, crafts, civics, community life, music, and folk dance. Counseling service in India is a comparatively new field for Christians.

Hindu education is what it is today because of Christians. The major benefits of all Christian services do not go to Christians in India. More than 65 percent of educated Hindu women owe their education to Christian women. Centers of education — primary, secondary, and collegiate — have their sources in Christian action in India in the nineteenth century. The majority of activities in behalf of harijans are carried on by Christians. P. K. Sundaram, of the Institute for Advanced Philosophy, University of Madras, points out that social service has been institutionalized by Christians in India, particularly because they are united in their goals, while Hindus are not. Christians have social energy and social consciousness, while caste among Hindus *is* the social system.[14]

Caste and communalism are the two greatest obstacles to social concern in India. Therefore it is imperative that Christians stress practical fellowship in the church of the living Christ who was poor, not in a triumphal church. It is absolutely essential that Christian education, relief, and welfare be pursued for the sake of justice, not to maintain an unjust order. The Hindu often views the Christian as qualified only for administration and service in institutions, not as spiritual leader. Further, Hindus who are converted to service of their brothers and sisters sometimes practice social service only with the goal of achieving personal liberation and happiness for themselves through spiritual motivation! Both Christian and Hindu in India, like all human beings, are called to examine their motives in practicing love for others. It would be a sad indictment of Christianity if its dominant contribution to the Hindu in India were social service only, without participation in the profound search for union with God, which is at the core of Hinduism.

2. INTERIORITY AND ACTION

Today one speaks of "mysticism" chiefly as related to the sannyasi in India or to the deeply contemplative person in the West. But "interiority" in the spiritual life is applied normally to even very "secular" Hindus in India who meditate an hour or two each day, while Western Christians are often accused of rejecting the interior life in their emphasis on action.

Perhaps the essence of interiority as understood by the Hindu is expressed best in symbols. Ramakrishna Paramahamsa wrote:

> Behold the bee buzzing and circling round and round near the blown lotus, how it buzzes and circles again and again:
> But now it goes inside the flower, it settles down and drinks of the honey in silence:
> Even so, disciple, man talks and argues before he has found his joy in the Lord, before he has tasted of faith:
> But when he finds the nectar at last in the opened lotus of his heart, at once he settles down to drink it, and babbles and talks no more.[15]

Interiority is the descent into human consciousness in search of self-awareness of the immanence of the Absolute in creation.[16] It is simply openness to God in peace at every moment. It is being present to God within oneself and within God's immersion in all creation. As such, it is not prayer only, but an act of human becoming. It gives to man and woman the capability to see meanings beyond the surface in persons, relationships, and things. It confers both depth and mystery. Social structures can endanger or destroy it. It has little meaning when considered in the light of dogmatic and juridical emphases.

When we speak of interiority as being more characteristic of the Hindu and action as being more characteristic of the Western Christian, it is important to point out that neither characteristic is totally absent in either Hindu or Christian, and that either can be evoked or developed in any human being. Indeed some scholars warn against the "myth" of Eastern interiority and Western activity, insisting on approaching these two characteristics rather as "dominant features."[17] On the other hand, there are those who contend that the West, in its intoxication with technology, has lost much of its contact with *reality*, and that an awakening of the West to the spiritual interiority of the East is the last hope of humankind.

On the whole, however, the common view in India is that the Hindu way is to look inward to discover God and *afterward* to look outward, which is not the Greco-Roman Western way of spirituality. The need to be alone to think and pray is an Eastern characteristic. Disinvolvement from the actions of everyday life is seen as a value. The need for the *effort* to reach God interiorly is normally within the ordinary awareness of the Hindu.

While the concept of the search for union with God interiorly here and now is accepted by most schools of philosophy, one finds rather extreme contrarieties among modern Indians in their judgments of the spiritual interiority of contemporary Christians. For example, an Indian Christian scholar once greeted the writer with the bald statement, "Western Christianity is dead!" This type of Indian points to the scorn for interiority and the spiritual restlessness that turns to action among Western Christians. He suggests that the "conquering world of the West is dead to awe and wonderment, the tangibility of God in creation, the need to withdraw in contemplation."[18] He calls attention to the "pitiful lack of prayer in the sense of communion with the living Christ" found among many Western Christians. He even goes so far as to say that Christ called fishermen because he knew that educated Westerners would repress their native intuition and substitute for it an artificial intuition. "Do not indianize Christianity," this type of Indian chides. Rather, "christianize Christianity!"[19]

Among some Indians, it is an accepted idea that Christians do not seem to be a deeply praying people, that they are taught about God but not taught to know God. Among most Hindus, even those who are not deeply spiritual persons, one finds the attractiveness and the resonance of interiority, while Hindus observe in the life of the Christian an abundance of activity, a quality they do not greatly appreciate. Some Indians even rejected Gandhi because of his dedication to active service of his fellowmen! Even Hindus who respect Christians for their service to others often feel that Christians exaggerate this value at the expense of interiority, contemplation, and presence. Bede Griffiths points out that the church has somehow lost its capability to grow, and that the West will remain psychologically unbalanced until it has done justice to the orientation of the East toward interiority.[20]

One concludes, at the very least, that the Christian church must be contemplative if it is to impress either the Hindu or the Indian Christian. It must develop an interior awareness of the immanence of God as a source of inner strength. In this respect, Christian sannyasis may be a needed corrective for the whole church. They may help to bring about the necessary dialogue between East and West. Through their presence, through their spiritual dialogue within the ashram, they may guide Christians to interiority. In the eyes of many Indians, then, the challenge to the church is to interiority, to death to self in the living Christ. If the church meets the challenge, it will unite itself not just with Indian culture, but with all cultures.

If we turn now to the response of many Western and certain Indian Christians to the above judgments, we find a more positive appraisal of Western Christianity. M. M. Thomas, for example, maintains that "true spirituality is the possession of moral excellence," that the Christian must expose tendencies in many non-Christian religions to minimize or eliminate the urgency of moral demands on individuals and communities. In fact, "the central importance of the personal and the historical dimensions of faith lies in the affirmation of the sphere of morality."[21] More concretely, in the words of T. K. John, Christianity proposes a question to the Hindu conscience, "Why is humanity fragmented and rejected in India?" Or, "Who rejected the leper and threw out the untouchable?"[22]

A noncondemnatory answer is offered by Joseph Neuner. The entire historical development and the present condition of Christianity in its positive and negative aspects, he declares, is *relative*. The crucial question is: "What is the significance of Jesus Christ for Hinduism *today?*" The Christian must bring to Indians what they need and understand. If they seek interiority, the Christian must bring them the interiority of Christ, for "in Jesus, God has spoken." The *form* in which the truth of Christ is presented must be learned from the traditions of nations, for Jesus Christ is true only in concrete historical situations.[23]

Christians in India have also responded to the charge of lack of interiority by distinguishing between two paths to Christ. G. Gispert-Sauch points out that Western Christians, attached to Christ by faith, trust themselves to God and thus attain infinite distance without exploring the depths of their own being. Indians, on the other hand, come to consciousness of the interior reality of their own being. They find Christ in silence and emptiness at the bottom ground of their own being. "The first crosses the abyss to Christ: the second lets himself fall into the depths of the abyss."[24] Bede Griffiths also speaks of two ways of interiority. The Hindu seeks detachment from everything, isolation of soul in pure interiority. Christians begin with repentance and discovery of the abyss that separates them from God. Their encounter with God as Person in love and forgiveness leads to their full realization of themselves as persons made for communion with God.

This is the distinctive character of Christian experience. The fruits of the Spirit are the criteria of Christian sanctity, which demands the recognition of *others* as *persons*. This distinction provides an important contrast between Hindu and Christian interiority. Christians discover that for them the abyss of the heart of Christ is closer to the ultimate than the experience of the self in "the cave of the heart." Christians must die: they must be detached from the world and at the same time be immersed in history in their existential situation.

If spiritual interpenetration is to take place between Hinduism and Christianity, Eastern and Western spiritualities must be seen as complementary. The "mutual" or "open" interiority of the Christian will relate to the "solitary" but not isolated interiority of the Hindu. A common concern today is the possible erosion of the interior life in *both* East and West. A perhaps temporary eclipse of contemplative experience, however, seems now to be accompanied by an underground resurgence of concern for the interior life. It may result in a fruitful synthesis of the contemplative experience with that of the active life of service.

If there is to be a resurgence of the interior life among Christians in India, it will indeed be related to the search or the pilgrimage aspect of Christianity. The Hindu concept of religion as continuous search can be conducive to humility in the Christian. Perhaps more than any other people, Hindus have devoted themselves over centuries to the *search* for God. They have developed techniques for spiritual concentration and for contemplation known to all the world. Their prayer traditions are almost always based on the return to the sources of being, an approach that makes them adept in meditation and deep contemplation. The Hindu aspect of continual spiritual search, however, is often disturbing to Westerners, who tend to believe that Jesus Christ has given them the truth once and for all. Western Christians may be surprised to learn that the Eastern search for God as mystery can enrich their prayer far beyond their present conceptions. When persons seek for God experience in complete openness, the incomprehensible opens to them. Christians who thus open themselves to the mystery immanent in all existence can learn much from the experience of St. Augustine, who embraced both Neoplatonic interiority and the Pauline gospel only to discover that Christianity can be purified to reveal an innermost nature in which contemplation and action are reciprocal.

The margas, yogas, and diverse methods through which the Hindu searches for the Absolute within are many and profound.

Hundreds of books and manuscripts explain them to the Westerner who desires to explore them. Today the interest of Westerners in Eastern modes of contemplation is more extensive than ever before, sometimes on a profound level, sometimes as a mere fad. There are those who see the Eastern offering to the West in prayer as merely a series of techniques developed over three thousand years. Others see the Hindu margas as an essential part of the interfaith dialogue that will lead to mutual fecundation of Christianity and Hinduism. These latter are the Christians who believe that it is essential for Christians to pray together with the Hindu. The Indian way of prayer, to be sure, is different from that of the West, and will never be completely identical with it. The prayer of the Indian Christian must develop in its own way within Indian culture. Many Indian Christians believe that the great margas or forms of spirituality (karma, bhakti, jnana) are essential for the development of Indian Christian spirituality. Raimundo Panikkar sees them as universal objects of the spiritual search, as guides for men and women in a pluralistic world. Ignatius Hirudayam has done a scholarly study of prayer in the traditions of the various margas.[25]

The term "yoga" has been denigrated in the West because of the adoption of yoga as a method of physical and psychological growth unrelated on the whole to spiritual development. The classical treatise on yoga, of course, is the ancient Sanskrit text, Yoga Sutras, written or compiled by Patanjali. One of the finest modern descriptions of yoga as "the transformation of body and soul by the Spirit" is Bede Griffiths's "Yoga, the Way of Union." A. S. Appasamy offers an excellent analysis of yoga as the teacher of the secret of concentration necessary for contemplation. Yoga is a valuable discipline that can be used by the Christian as well as the Hindu, in fact by anyone.

Inquiry and experiment is now taking place among Indian Christians concerning Hindu methods of prayer. As far back as 1942, A. J. Appasamy based his entire study of the gospel and India's heritage on the bhakti approach to the spiritual life. Praying Seminar, edited by D. S. Amalorpavadass, is one of the best recent publications on adaption of Hindu ways of prayer for Christian spirituality today.[26] And Abhishiktananda's small volume, *Prayer*, is already a classic.[27] Its special value is that it not only reveals secrets of living contemplatively, but also demonstrates that there is no conflict between contemplative spirituality and concern for others. Discussion of the prayer of the name, the prayer of silence, bhajans, mantras, and many other Eastern practices may be found in both Eastern and Western publications today. Many studies of the Gita reveal it as the highest Indian contribution to Christian spiritual life, particularly as a basis for interfaith prayer of Hindu and Christian. Examples of Hindu-Christian prayer services, especially for religious festivals (Dipavali, for example), are easily available. Francis Acharya has published *The Book of Common Prayer*, "Adapted with Seeds of the Word from the Spiritual Heritage of India."[28]

One should be aware too of the simple, spontaneous adaptations that are taking place among Christians and Hindus in Indian villages today. Ancient fertility rites, for example, are sometimes transformed into reverential dances and processions in celebration of Christian feast days. Finally, Christians must consider that they have scarcely yet offered to the Hindu *the prayer of interiority of the West*, which the Hindu has often requested of them.

A word must be said of the prayer of silence in any comparison or contrast between Hindu and Christian interiority. The Hindu response to silence in prayer has always been more profound than that of the average Christian. Among Hindus, silent, wordless prayer is common. A visit to any Hindu temple reveals many persons sitting cross-legged in quiet prayer, often for hours on end. The prayer of silence is considered a value in itself among Hindus. For the Indian Christian, it is a welcome break from the strong tendency toward oral prayer among Western Christians. Though human beings cannot experience *total* silence, the incomprehensible opens itself to humankind in silence. The Hindu prayer of silence — without words, without action — has been sometimes compared to the prayer described by St. Teresa of Avila in the Fourth Mansion. Western Christians are aware, for all their concern with service of others, that Christ left even Peter, James, and John to be alone with his Father in silence.

The relationship of the guru and the ashram to Hindu spirituality is also related to any consideration of interiority and action. If there is to be mutual fecundation between Christianity and Hinduism, the Christian ashram may become more and more significant. An ashram has been defined as a group of disciples gathered around a master who have put the search for God-realization above all other goals. Bede Griffiths believes that personal prayer, in which one seeks to discover one's own center, and to experience the presence of God in the ground of his being beyond all thoughts and images, should be the real center of the ashram. The basic features of ashram life are: experience of God, an atmosphere of quiet peace, an open community of men and women, a simple and poor community, and freedom and flexibility of lifestyle. Secondary goals and perspectives of ashrams may differ. An extension of the original idea of the ashram as just described may be, for example, the goal of transforming the social consciousness of villagers through continual processes of learning and teaching.

While prayer is always essential, activities may be initiated to help very poor villagers to change the perceptions they have of themselves and to participate in changing the conditions of their desperate lives. Such Christian ashrams have been compared with the "basic communities" of Paulo Freire in Latin America. To be sure, ashrams sometimes face the danger of becoming "fads." It is essential to remember that they should be a spiritual leaven in human lives, never a movement. They should provide time and space for prayer attuned to the spirituality of the culture.

The relationship of the disciple to the guru in the Hindu ashram is of fundamental importance. Holy persons become gurus only because they are chosen by their followers. They can be neither appointed nor self-selected. Their task is to lead their disciples to the experience of God. Their presence is more essential than their teaching, and their disciples approach them with trust, confidence, and openness of mind. For Hindus, gurus are divine. Their wisdom is transferred to their followers by a kind of spiritual osmosis. In the East, when gurus die, their disciples may disperse. Their spirit is not necessarily passed on to another.

The Hindu guru is an intermediary between the inconceivable God and weak man or woman. Gurus are really an incarnation of God, so that respect for them is compared with respect for God. They are equalized with God by their followers. In the Christian ashram, the spiritual leader is of course reverenced but not identified with the divine in the Hindu sense. Gospel-centered spirituality is stressed, with strong emphasis on loving service to others. Shantivanam, the famous ashram in Tiruchirappalli, under the guidance of Bede Griffiths, brings together the Christian tradition of monasticism and the Hindu sannyasa. Dom Bede's ashram is definitely an Indian ashram, developed within the Indian spiritual tradition. He has entered into the *roots* of Indian culture. He states that a Christian ashram may be a place for union with God through liturgy, common prayer, and social action. But it must be above all a place of contemplation, of the "realization" of God. Nothing can take the place of "the knowledge of the love of Christ, which surpasses all knowledge."

Ishwar Prasad describes the goal of the well-known ashram Krist Panthi, which he founded outside Varanasi, as witness to Christ through gospel life, prayer in the Indian tradition, and humble service.[29] This ashram is somewhat like a neighborhood meeting place for prayer and spiritual discussion in which anyone may participate, whatever his or her religion.

Many Christians are drawn today to ashram life. They respond to a simple spiritual lifestyle apart from church institutions. They discover a special appeal in ecumenical ashrams where small groups of Christians and non-Christians pray and reflect together for periods of time. They find the Hindu tradition of spirituality, which respects the wise and peaceful spirit of pluralism, to be compatible with their own spirituality. Some feel that they must shed "institutional Christianity" for a time in order to discover Christ.

At present the number of ashrams is growing, and Indian-style Christian ashrams dot the landscape throughout India. This expansion suggests the need for spiritual preparation for ashram direction, always keeping in mind that one does not found an ashram: it happens. Westernized ashrams in India are not authentic. Cultural alienation caused by them results in conflict. Indeed, Western Christians are strangers in India still! Their inculturation must come slowly by trial and development.

If there is criticism of the Christian ashram in India today, it is that some ashrams, in their emphasis on contemplation, overlook the problem of starving and oppressed millions. Community is a central Christian experience resulting in devoted action for others. The Christian is involved in the realities of life always. Indifference to social distress among Hindus has appeared to the Christian as a lack of civic responsibility. Even educated Hindus have been seen to think largely in terms of themselves, their families, castes, and communities.

The Hindu thus appears to care more for inwardness and metaphysical speculation than for the moral transformation of everyday life. The Christian, on the other hand, believes that all work is valuable, all work has dignity because of the equality of all humans. If Hindu swamis participate in manual work, they are seen as losing dignity. The authentic Christian ashram, however, must combine concern for others with its central goal of experience of God through personal prayer and contemplation. God has initiated a new beginning in history through Christ, a new creation that values all persons and their human freedom of action. Yet Jesus Christ revealed perfect symmetry in his life through combining contemplation with active service of others. Hindus are conscious of the active service of Christians, but they often fail to appreciate the Christian concept of a union of contemplation and action — of action growing out of contemplation.

Of course, the type of Christian action practiced is crucial whether the Christian lives an ashram life or not. A few years ago, a survey of Hindu reaction to Christian service in India revealed that Indian Christians were considered to be guilty of cultural alienation, religious domination, service of the upper classes, extraterritorial loyalty, and managerial rather than human values![30] Yet the Hindus who were questioned also recognized the contrast between the charitable activities of Christians and their own passivity in face of the need for social action.

However, if the lives of Hindus and Christians are to inter-penetrate one another in spirituality, Christians must be ready to live what they believe. Christians have brought social service, education, health, and humanitarianism to the Hindus, but Hindus are not always aware of the Christ life in the persons who serve them. The Hindu looks for Christ in the Christian servant. Because many Christians now appreciate this Hindu insight, a new attitude toward non-Christian religions and a deeper appreciation of Hindu spirituality are influencing the lives and activities of Christian leaders in India today. The relationship between evangelization and human development, between evangelization and dialogue, between evangelization and contemplation, is taking on new meaning. Social action of Christians in India is becoming more and more complementary to spiritual interiority. Thus the way is being paved for a meeting of Christian and Hindu on deeper levels of religious inter-penetration.

3. VERTICAL AND HORIZONTAL SPIRITUALITY

In India, it is almost a cliché to speak of the vertical spirituality of the Hindu and the horizontal spirituality of the Christian. More often the two spiritualities are seen as conflicting, sometimes as complementary, but seldom as united. If we examine first the significance of the vertical, then the meaning of the horizontal spirituality, it becomes clear that the two terms are used most often in a sense of contrast. For many Indians, the implications of the two words are by their very nature opposed.

To be sure, a purely vertical or a purely horizontal human activity is inconceivable. The two elements meet in human nature. Christian theology discerns and confronts the relation-ship of the two more profoundly than Hindu philosophy does because it takes historicity more seriously. The goal of freedom in Christ is for the Christian both eternal salvation and a more human society.

The goal of Hindu spirituality is self-realization related directly to God. Moksha, or salvation, is liberation from the human condition, from the bonds of time and space. Moksha implies a spiritually free life. The fundamental ethical idea of Hinduism is therefore nonattachment.[31] According to some writers, Hindus must liberate themselves through their own efforts because Hinduism has no concept like that of Christian redemption. There is no doubt, however, that the concept of grace is pre-Christian. It occurs in the Katha Upanishad around 500 B.C. According to most Hindu scholars, grace and effort are both required for moksha.

It is pointed out, even by Hindus themselves, that the Hindu is too much concerned with personal salvation. Just as interior silence with the goal of pure consciousness is a Hindu religious ideal, social work for others is sometimes considered to be even an "irreligious" goal. While the Christian views equality and humanitarianism as actually derived from Christ, the Hindu tends to regard religious experience as individual, with social service added as a kind of "appendix."

Prayer for the Hindu is dominantly an individual matter. God is not a "father" to whom one prays for favors for one's brothers and sisters. The communal is not emphasized in Hindu prayer experience, whereas it is basic to Christianity to express concern for others in prayer. While worship for the Christian is both corporate and personal, congregational worship does not exist for the Hindu. In fact, one caste may prevent another from approaching the "holy of holies" in the Hindu temple. Attempts to assert their rights of worship by depressed classes have often been ineffective. The Christian would say that grace, the life of God, is communicated through love in worship and in action. The Hindu would say that, theoretically, one loves one's neighbor as oneself, not because God commands one to do so, but because one's neighbor *is* oneself in a metaphysical sense. All creation is one. For the Hindu, the difficulty in the practice of love rises within a social system based on caste. It is interesting to note, nevertheless, that Hindu children in Christian schools respond strongly to concepts of love, forgiveness, and the prayer of healing. Though Hindu prayer is on a vertical level, the social aspect of Christian prayer is very attractive to Hindu children.

If we consider "horizontal" spirituality as characteristic of the Christian experience of God, we find quite different emphases in Hindu worship. Christians believe that "human individuals do not exist in isolation but as members of a body, or organic whole, which develops in time and space toward its final consummation in eternal life."[32] The ministry of the church depends upon its being truly a community of persons rooted in the Word of God, a new creation seeking communitarian salvation. There can be no Christianity without a fellowship of love and concern. Christianity thus enjoys social cohesiveness, which the Hindu actually admires. It has a focal point in community as opposed to a certain divisiveness in Hinduism. This centeredness is evident in worship, education, and social interchange among Christians of many different cultural backgrounds. Its lack is evident in the inequality of the Indian masses. The duty of the Hindu to the caste to which he or she belongs is qualitatively different from the love of the Christian for brothers and sisters. Because of caste, the immobility of Hindu society is justified by religious sanction. Therefore Hinduism, so long as it sanctions the caste system, is said to have the capability of producing great individuals, but not a just society.[33] St. Francis of Assisi, who practiced Christian love to perfection, once refused to give alms but instead sat down with beggars to teach the equality of all persons before God.

Christians believe that where two or three are gathered together in the name of Christ, God is with them. They invite God to direct their lives in community. They stress the reading of scripture, the reception of the sacraments, the proclamation of the gospel. Christian emphasis on community leads to concern for the rights of others. Hindu prayer, on the other hand, lacks the element of seeking salvation within community. The Hindu most often goes alone to the temple to pray. The Hindu pattern of worship is individualistic. Even when thousands of Indians go on pilgrimage to holy shrines or sacred rivers, they do not worship as a congregation. This Hindu emphasis on exclusive personal relationship with God rather than worship as community sometimes leads, in its want of mutual concern for the rights of others, to a devaluation of personal human life.

The practice of family worship among Christians is also communal, whereas the Hindu family does not pray as a group. It is considered appropriate for the Hindu wife to perform puja alone and call down the blessings of her chosen god. Nor does the Hindu participate in prayerful reconciliation services with others, as do Christians. The example of the Samaritan ministering to the outcast, related by Christ in the gospel, is a Christian practice unknown to the Hindu. The Brahmin does not bind up the wounds of the harijan.

Indian Christians who desire to pray with Hindus are now devising new programs of prayer as a solution to the differences between the vertical and horizontal approaches to worship. S. Suviseshamuthu, for example, suggests a combination of congregational and individual prayer, which is now acceptable to many Hindus, especially Brahmins.[34] Because Hindus appreciate fellowship socially in their caste, this value can sometimes be transferred to prayer, thus making worship within community more acceptable. It should be added that Hindus who, like Gandhi, respond profoundly to the Sermon on the Mount, are more likely to welcome the practice of community prayer in ashrams open to all — Hindus, Muslims, and Christians.

The Christian practice of community prayer frequently leads to discussions, seminars, and symposiums on religious topics. The Hindu admires the positive effects of such organized activity, but does not always view it as spiritual in essence. A Hindu professor was heard to remark, for example, that the social cohesiveness of Christians leads to success in business, thus offering Hindus an example of how to succeed in monetary ventures! Spirituality, so understood, is a personal venture — vertical, not horizontal.

A concern expressed today by both Christians and Hindus in India is that the East is now telescoping into a brief historical period much that has happened in the Western past. The danger is that India may pass from its traditional Hindu sense of collectivity (manifested in the caste system) to a technical mass society without discovering the Christian values of the human community. On the other hand, there is throughout the world today a growing sense of human solidarity expressed in the struggle for human rights and the endeavor to build structures for a stable world community. This trend highlights personal and community freedom rather than nationalism. For the Indian Christian, this human community is one of forgiven sinners in which love replaces sometimes self-defeating "duty" according to one's state or dharma. It is also a community of the redeemed secular collective human life. Christ embraces the world and all who are in it. The true Christian speaks of redemption of the whole human race, not of a rebellion against communism or secularism. In this context, the Christian can provide a framework for a new integration of relations between Christians and Hindus.[35] It can be a framework leading to the unity in worship of God sought by all great religions.

4. EXPERIENCE AND SUFFERING

Christ and Krishna are often contrasted in analyses of Eastern and Western approaches to God. Bede Griffiths believes that the crucial question in this context is: "Can Hinduism accept a God who suffers and dies, who enters history, whose love is experienced in suffering and dereliction?" Krishna is the Supreme Being who pervades creation and dwells in humans. Yet Krishna belongs not to history but to the archetypal world beyond time. Hinduism centers in the human ascent to God; Christianity in God's descent through the cross. In all great religions, renunciation has been recognized as the path to the Absolute. Detachment is a universal law. In the modern world, balance and harmony between the human ascent and the divine descent are almost lost. Some scholars see the cause of this alienation as a conflict between the demands of spiritual interiority and those of social action. Others view it as a demand for justice and love, beginning here and now in both contemplation and service of others, and ending in eternity. Still others see it as a historical event: it is the Marxist conflict between capital and labor.

For the Hindu, balance and harmony are restored in our personal experience of God. In the Gita, the man Arjuna opens himself completely to the experience of the God Krishna. This experience is scarcely available to the person who has not the capability of responding with his or her whole being to the Other who is presented to humankind through the created universe. The Upanishads teach that humanity is brought gradually to that state of peace, receptivity, and expectancy that alone will permit the Absolute to be manifested. This personal knowledge of God is essential to Indian spiritual experience. Indians seek it at the very source of their innermost being. It has complete primacy over any concept, dogma, or orthodoxy. It is the goal and end of all religious experience. I am not speaking of a matter of emphasis: the unanimity of all Indian seers places personal experiential knowledge of God at the center of human existence. Spiritual experience is counter to logos; simple religious consciousness is more central than philosophical analysis.

Though the Hindu margas encompass knowledge, devotion, and action as paths to the Absolute, the emphasis on personal experience leads to acceptance of infinitely varied ways to God simply because personal experiences differ greatly. To be sure, comfort and convenience are excluded: one must pay the price of suffering in the search for the unknown. Horizons open to persons who renounce their own ego. And there are some sannyasis who insist that this renunciation extends to the horizontal level of service of one's brother and sister.

If some Indian Christians believe that the strong Hindu emphasis on subjective religious experience is a source of lack of social consciousness, others are willing to include "immediate experience of the ultimate reality" in a broad definition of prayer experience. To this subjective element they would add "the relationship among persons in total self-gift and belonging" and "the fellowship of persons within the reality of our life, world, and history."[36] In other words, true Christians cannot experience themselves as separate from the rest of humankind, living in a world of one's own. The Christian finds union with God and with all other men and women, a union experienced centrally in the sharing of the eucharist.

When we attempt to reconcile the Eastern and Western no-tions of spiritual experience, it is well to keep in mind a statement like the following by A. J. Appasamy:

> The spiritual life of an Asiatic is not just simply the same as that of a European. The Asiatic sees, hears, feels, expects, experiences, believes, hopes, loves, and suffers differently from the European. What we consider imagination is reality for him. What appears to be reality to us is for him often imagination.[37]

The Christian frequently appears to the Hindu to be dogmatic and intolerant in the refusal to bring religion to the test of experience. For the Hindu, as I have insisted above, the meeting point with the Christian is in the experience of God. No dialogue is possible between the two except on the basis of such experience. Hindus can accept Christ on their own terms, but they will never accept Christ on Christian terms except through an authentic *Indian* experience. Because of abstract ideas taught to them by Western Christians, Indian Christians sometimes cannot well explain Christianity in an English idiom understandable to the Hindu. Hindus can understand a personal loving Christ, even if they cannot understand a catechism definition of the incarnation. It is fundamental that the Christian in the East accept the fact that truth must be approached by different routes by different peoples.

When Indian Christians say that "where the West ends prayer, the East begins," they are probably unfair in their judgment.[38] But at the same time they are suggesting an avenue of approach to the Hindu. The latter rejects words alone in interchange with the Christian. One of the most powerful values that the Hindu looks for is that of presence, the presence of God everywhere and in all things, and the presence of God in humankind. The Hindu believes that a person who is holy can transmit the effects of this experience to others. When two spiritual persons meet, the enrichment is mutual. The strongest effect of presence, of course, is found in experience in the ashram in direct relationship with the guru. Holiness of person provides a leaven. The guru, accepted by the Hindu as an incarnation of God, provides the guidance toward self-realization that cannot be achieved without spiritual help.

The Christian in dialogue with the Hindu must therefore be aware of the central significance of spiritual presence. Paulos Gregorios asks, "Are Asian Christians truly a manifest presence of God in Asian society?"[39] Are Christians truly *present* to Hindus in a Christlike sense? Among Hindus, the populace can recognize the presence of the authentic sannyasi, available to others as teacher and guide. Blessings pour forth from the sannyasi's presence. Yet his devotees must find their own spiritual paths through him.

Simplicity and serenity are learned in the presence of the holy person. These qualities are achieved through renunciation of material goods as a value. Detachment rather than comfort is sought. Rootedness in simple living exudes joy and happiness. Hospitality and openness are practiced without pretension. Powerlessness is a value that suggests a sense of timelessness. Quietness from rush and hurry, and the sacrifice of the desire for immediate solutions to problems, are characteristic of the sannyasi. A kind of blind faith that all will turn out well is due not so much to fatalism as to faith in the universe and the acceptance of suffering. The Indian *has* suffered much and *can* suffer much. A sense of the relativity of the world prevents the Hindu from giving tragic importance to most events. Westerners are impressed with the joy expressed by the Hindu even in abominable living conditions, and most especially with the simple and beautiful acceptance of his or her own death. Stillness and serenity among Hindus are due, often on a subconscious level, to the continual awareness of the divine. Two questions are often asked of the Christian by the simple and serene Hindu: Why does Christian prayer often suggest noise and activity? Why does the Christian priest so often appear as an organizer?

Simplicity and serenity are at the core of the nonviolence or ahimsa of the Hindu. Many values are associated with nonviolence: harmony and sharing, freedom from quarreling and narrow-mindedness, affirmation of the law of the spirit as opposed to the materialism that is violence to the spirit. Ahimsa demands that passion be overcome. It resists all violence, especially extreme violence like that of nuclear war. It regards both capitalism and communism as lacking the capacity to achieve the goals of nonviolence. In the words of Gandhi, persons are nonviolent only when they love those who hate them. And precisely here Christianity can go further in principle than Hinduism. Christianity offers the efficacy of suffering for others — even suffering unto death — as opposed to violence. Suffering unto death is a Christ principle. Nonviolence is not a "counsel of perfection" but a Christian principle of living. Gandhi caught the spirit of nonviolence, which is the spirit of Jesus. He went beyond the teaching of the Mahabharata, V, 1517, that "the sum of *duty* is to do nothing to others which if done to oneself would cause pain."[40] Yet Christians are accused of "violence of the spirit" in their assertion of the superiority of Christianity over all other religions. The Christian philosopher is asked to come out of an ivory tower and help to humanize the world as Christ did. In this context, the nonviolence of Gandhi has crucial religious significance.

Gandhi was opposed to the idea of some Hindus that service to others has the goal of earning happiness for the doer. His motive was more pure. In fact, he lived Christian nonviolence to the extent that he actually influenced Christian thought and practice. It cannot be denied that the history of the Christian West reveals the perpetration of war rather than passive resistance to violence. Gandhi gave the principle of nonviolence more strength, perhaps, than did any other individual in the modern world. In his negative attitude to the caste system, moreover, Gandhi sought both nonviolence here and now and a sadhanna for final human liberation. He taught that "nonviolence is a more active and real fight against wickedness than retaliation, the nature of which is to increase wickedness." Nonviolence is love, aimed at transforming the wicked by patient suffering. It requires discipline of body, mind, and life.

Gandhi's satyagraha is an extension of nonviolence. It requires three types of positive action: noncooperation, civil disobedience, and fasting. It is based on the principle that no one is beyond the reach of suffering love. There are, of course, those who believe that Gandhi's ahimsa is idealistic rather than realistic, that a breakthrough in human evolution would be necessary to make it practical. They propose that a compromise of Gandhi's principle is necessary to secure justice for the poor and the oppressed in India. At the least, they suggest, a revolution without bloodshed is required.[41]

The relationship of Gandhi's concept of nonviolence to Christian suffering is crucial to the interpenetration of Christianity and Hinduism in India. Gandhi openly professed the Sermon on the Mount, the center of Christ's teaching. Jesus, who lived the Beatitudes perfectly, suffered and died on the cross. Precisely here is a certain contrast between Christ and Krishna. The religious sanction given to suffering in the East by karma is different from the acceptance of suffering by the Redeemer who was never promised to the Hindu. In the past, Hindu rishis sought to establish noble causes by suffering, penance, and self-purification. But Christ died to win eternal salvation for all humanity and all creation. The suffering of Christ was totally for others.

The concept of a suffering God, the doctrine of the vicarious passion and death of Jesus, is somewhat of a stumbling block to the Hindu. Yet one finds in the Ramayana the story of the "blue-throated Siva" who took evil upon himself to save others. Hindu scholar V. A. Devasenapathi asks whether the Hindu who "overcomes all sense of I and mine" in suffering for others does not participate in the spiritual experience that finds its complete expression in the crucifixion of Christ.[42]

Surely there is blindness in the Christian who does not perceive the essential Christianity of this question! The fulfillment of the quest for salvation is Christ himself. Through his death and self-sacrifice, he established the new creation. He opposed injustice, paid the price with his death, and so humanized the world. His disciples in India are called to help their brothers and sisters by suffering with them. Who would deny a share of that call to Hindus who embrace the vocation of suffering for others?

The types of suffering that cry out to be alleviated in India are many: abject poverty; oppressive social and economic structures controlled by an elitist minority; neglect of the masses amid the material affluence of a minority. A radical change in Hindu thought on suffering is now coming about in India as the country slowly moves toward affirmation of human rights for all. The change is due to the influence of Gandhi and Hindus like him as well as to both Christian and communistic movements.

Christians at times feel a certain sense of failure in India when they consider that, after hundreds of years of missionary activity, comparatively few Indians are professed Christians. They feel that Christianity has scarcely touched the core of real life in India. They observe the achievement of the Hindu Vivekananda among his own people as he adapted the Christian teaching of love of one's fellowmen to Hinduism itself. But these Christians are also aware of the millions of Hindus who accept a suffering Christ and an "Our Father" who is accessible to his children. A Hindu professor could remark, for example, that "higher realities" are not very helpful in facing the reality of suffering all around us. "Krishna may be human in the mystic tradition, but Christ is nearer to the human sinner." Thus Hindus may miss what is close to them: the nearness of a personal God who loves them.[43]

Hindus are becoming dimly aware that Christianity in its purity is closely related to all who suffer — to beggars, the maimed, the sick. They are aware of the *problem* of suffering, just as they have always accepted the fact of suffering. Raimundo Panikkar goes so far as to say that a suffering God is an attraction to the Hindu. In the Hindu home, one may find the representation of Christ kneeling in Gethsemane. Pain and suffering, the Hindu sees, have entered into the heart of the Christian God who came to earth. The Christian has the courage to give suffering its place in the life of the God-Savior. God suffering, yet still God, is thus an attraction to the Hindu.[44]

To be sure, the problem of suffering and redemption is related to the problem of sin, and the Hindu concept of sin differs greatly from that of the Christian. For the Hindu, sin is scarcely a moral concept. Therefore, little urgency is brought to bear upon the problem of sin, and the need for a savior is not deeply felt. Unhappiness is not attributed to sin. The stars explain away certain types of problems, and on a deeper level, karma explains what happens to individuals. Interestingly enough, a Hindu professor of philosophy points out that it is bad psychology for the Christian to place emphasis on sin, especially when speaking to Indians who have been so long a subject nation! Christians should present the image of Christ, he declares, adding that Hindus themselves have three motives for doing good in rising order of significance: to seek a reward, to love God, and to suffer for others.[45] The last motive is one that is often denied to the Hindu except for the sannyasi.

Though sin is a cosmic concept for the Hindu, the Rigveda lists sinful acts to be avoided: falsehood, evil intentions, and cursing; theft, gambling, and debt; egoistic enjoyment, cruelty, and adultery. A contrast of these with the seven capital sins might be an interesting study! Gandhi was more aware of social sins than most Hindus are. He compared untouchability to the poison of arsenic. The Dharma Sutras speak of moral virtues of the individual, oddly enough in terms of freedom from evil: from anger, covetousness, hypocrisy, slander, and envy. Positive virtues stressed are: compassion, forbearance, purity, truth, liberality, peace, and subjugation of the passions. Social virtues center in dharma, or the duties and obligations of one's caste and state in life.

Hindus believe that their soul is delivered to union with the divine, normally after many reincarnations. In union with the Absolute they cast away their individuality. Hindus at their highest level of spiritual development accept the concept of grace, but karma is much more dominant in their everyday thought. When they speak of "redemption," they refer not chiefly to being freed from the consequences of individual sin, but from the limitations of the world, especially our limited knowledge.

Redemption also embodies the values of karma. Virtue is rewarded through karma, and forgiveness is presented as a virtue in the Gita. Divine forgiveness is experienced in reincarnation. Time is allowed for growth (a value the Hindu does not find in the Christian concept of only one life). Human beings are responsible for their actions, and virtue ultimately is rewarded.

In the long run, however, Hindu morality is always subordinate to cosmic concepts of the human being's relationship to the Absolute. Belief that the sinner is loved by God, that history is a real and purposive unity, and that divine grace is the source of unending hope are emphatically Christian.

5. KARMA AND PERSON

Karma is a concept basic to all approaches to Hinduism. It is defined by the Hindu philosopher as "the law of cause and effect." Karma is the acceptance of reality. Persons deserve their own reality because of their past life, either in a present or a former state. God is the source of this principle of justice that matches deserts with deeds. God is both the law-giver and the law. Individuals determine by their actions the nature of their destiny. Release from karma comes only when they have achieved self-realization or salvation: they are then no longer bound by time and space. A study of the responses to karma of Hindu villagers in India revealed the somewhat surprising belief that God cannot change karma. God forgives, but cannot take away due punishment. Many of these villagers believe, however, that humans can change their karma by worship in the temple.[46]

It is the conviction of many educated Hindus that the sense of karma can be related to the Christian sense of guilt. Karma can be creative or fatalistic, depending upon one's response to it. Individuals can move toward self-realization on their own initiative despite their karma. The positive aspects of karma are seen as acceptance and renunciation; the negative aspects, as apathy and fatalism.

Karma offers to Hindus a sense of duty to be accomplished. They are born into a caste and a community with obligations established in a social framework that calls them to be responsible human beings. Duty is based upon dharma, the doctrine of religion or of right order in the universe. The Hindu acceptance of karma renders them happy even in poverty and suffering. Because they believe they receive what they deserve, they are tolerant and forbearing of themselves and others. They are aware of the relativity of the world. Indeed they accept both their life and their death freely and even beautifully. They welcome death in anticipation of the karma they will experience in their next phase of existence. (In Freudian terms, these responses have been characterized as revealing that the Indian is narcissistic rather than punitive: they have a high libido and low aggressivity!)[47]

The renunciation that results from karma is also seen as a value by the Hindu. The Indian spirit of inner freedom is born of voluntary self-denial. Nonattachment is a corollary of renunciation. It encompasses both asceticism based on self-discipline and interior detachment. Even powerlessness is a value because humans have no reason to boast: all that they have comes from God. All is passing, and the sannyasi who renounces all is reverenced by all. The reason the Hindu respects the celibate sannyasi so profoundly is that the latter represents renunciation at the highest level of motivation. One of the reasons why Gandhi and thousands of other Indians accept the Sermon on the Mount so completely, moreover, is that it embodies renunciation so perfectly. Some Hindus respond totally to Christ's renunciation unto death. They comprehend that only Christ as incarnation of God can suffer unto death as he did. They understand the principle of total renunciation. They do not understand so well the Christian claim that Christ is the unique incarnation of God.

The more negative aspects of karma are apathy and a tendency toward fatalism. Gandhi spoke of the soul cowardice or "slave mentality" of the Indian. The proneness of the Hindu to flow with the tide rather than to act or to condemn is sometimes seen as passive submission in the face of wrong. The caste system separates person from person, and drives unselfish virtues into the family alone. Also, the notion that one cannot change one's karma often results in lack of initiative, falsely interpreted as the decision to live one's life on a higher spiritual and moral level. To be sure, some Indians view their country's historical retardation in action for self-improvement not as apathy but as an accident of history. But others — including

Vivekananda — view it as a fault in the Indian moral character. Of course, the so-called Hindu apathy reveals a paradox insofar as it results from an elemental faith in the universe! A primordial resignation in the face of suffering, starvation, and death can be an ambiguous virtue at best.

However, lack of involvement in life can result in a risk of heartlessness that is fatal. The problem of apathy can become colossal in nature and size to the point of fatal lack of concern for others. Subconsciously, some Hindus may feel no profound value in the principle of vicarious suffering taught by Christ. Karma may seem to contradict it. Fortunately, the interpretation of karma today does not result in withdrawal from life in India so much as it once did. Although Indian democracy is more political than social, the helplessness of the Indian in the colonial period no longer continues. Today Indians are less accepting of oppression than they ever were — even when they cannot actually conquer injustice. But the Hindu God who is both "the law-giver and the law" of karma is not the Christian God who loves and dies for all.

Christianity gave spiritual power to the concept of the free individual person, which underlies Greek and Roman history as an ideal. Practical service of others developed along with it until today concern for others is a worldwide ideal, whatever its achievement in everyday reality. Perhaps no religion has stressed the sacredness of human personality as Christianity has, for it has a complete foundation for human fellowship. Every human being is of value to Christ. All are part of his kingdom. Each person is a unique manifestation of God. The whole of creation converges on Christ. Therefore, Christianity teaches the relationship of the person to Christ and of person to person in knowledge and love. Everyone is therefore a relational reality, and the clear demand of Christ is for humanization. Thus the value of the person, the primacy of love in human relations, is a dominant and profound Christian teaching. The person is significant and lovable apart from all differences among human beings, because every human being is a part of the total Christ.

Hindus who may not believe in a personal God have difficulty in accepting the human being as a personal being in this Christian sense. They find it strange to support a concern for human freedom and dignity based on the concept that Jesus Christ initiated a new movement in the history of humankind. They do not understand the fellowship of Christians based on the relationship of persons. Leaders of the Hindu renascence of the nineteenth century, like Vivekananda, did understand. They found sources for concern for the person in their own scriptures and practiced service of their fellowmen without always recognizing the historical influence of Christ upon their actions.[48]

It is interesting that there is no word in the Indian languages that is the equivalent of the word "person." There is no precise equivalent of the Christian trinitarian mystery. The concept of the person as a reality of unique eternal value is strange to Hindus. They know of no communion of saints. The implications of "person" in dialogue between Hindu and Christian are therefore significant. And the implications of the Hindu belief in the identity of the atman within the human person and the Absolute are concomitantly significant. Similarly, both the equality of all persons before the Christian God and the inequalities of caste are significant. The duty of dharma and the love of Christ are not precisely the same. The Samaritan of the gospel is not the same as the Brahmin in his relationship to the untouchable. Reconciliation of all men and women in love is not a dominant teaching of Hinduism.

Moreover, there is little emphasis on the institution and more on the individual in Hindu spirituality. But "individual" is not to be confused with the Christian "person." Human dignity based on the human being as a child of God is a strong Christian concept. Equality of all is expressed in the Indian democratic Constitution but it does not exist in social practice. Fundamentally, human dignity for the Hindu is equivalent to the dignity of all creation. For the Christian, humanity is *unique* in dignity.[49] Because of this belief, disinterested love without thought of a return is the debt of each Christian to the other. Hinduism, at its highest level in the Gita, also teaches service without thought of reward, but not with precisely the same motive as Christianity.

Finally, Hinduism offers no universal morality based on the human being as person. Here is the root of social crisis in India. Morality is of caste, kinship, and position. The individual is valuable as a unit in the community. The social mentality of the Hindu is that of caste. On the other hand, Jesus preached universal morality based on the person, with the practice of love as the sole criterion.[50] The Christian contributes "person" to world spirituality as a basic factor in democratic culture as well as in worship.

The Christian and Hindu in dialogue, then, are called to relate the emphasis of each on various aspects of spirituality: mysticism with service; interiority with action: vertical spirituality with horizontal; experience in action with suffering; the significance of karma with that of the person. A pluralistic world today demands the interpenetration of all these values.

CHAPTER VII

Hope in the Spirit as Ground for Union of Christianity and Hinduism

IN the late 1980s one finds a seeming consensus in India among both Hindus and Christians that any profound understanding and interpenetration of these two great religious traditions will unveil a crucial spiritual offering of each to the other. As unfolded in the above chapters, Hinduism possesses a deep sense of interiority not only among its famous mystics but among its ordinary believers, many of whom are scarcely aware of their authentic inwardness. Western Christianity, on the other hand, is believed by many Christians as well as Hindus to have lost in great part its spirit of interiority. Hinduism can be a leaven, as we have seen, to raise Christianity to a deeper awareness of the sacred in everyday living. On the other hand, our consensus of Indian spiritual leaders reveals that the offering of authentic Christianity to India will be the prophetic dimension of equality, justice, and love as taught by Jesus Christ. We shall try to analyze why Hinduism is today more

156

ental Christian gift and explore tentatively rist offering in interpenetration with the Hinduism. Finally, we shall discuss the nderstanding of Hinduism and Christian- ether these be associated with the terms ation, indianization, or fecundation — he magnificent hope one feels all over stations of a new ecumenism, veiled in ywhere by the Holy Spirit.

an mystics are profoundly aware, as eliever is not, that the meeting of he core of the heart" through the pirit is one of the greatest hopes of rucial to both the identity crisis of present split between the inward ss of the contemporary Hindu. d Christian may produce, in the new child born in the love of the Trinity, but now still doubted in the mystery of the Absolute. Our consciousness of this mystery becomes daily more compelling:

> Far up the dim twilight fluttered
> Moth wings of vapor and flame.
> The lights danced over the mountain,
> Star after star they came.
> The lights grew thicker unheeded
> For silent and still were we.
> Our hearts were drunk with a beauty
> Our eyes could never see.[1]

1. SOME CLOSED ASPECTS OF HINDU SPIRITUALITY AND CULTURE

In previous chapters I have discussed both promising paths to the interpenetration of Christianity and Hinduism, and present obstacles to its consummation. I have emphasized the spiritual values of Hinduism and the obstructions to harmony raised by traditional Christianity. In this last chapter I should like to analyze a few of the obstacles that Hinduism sometimes places in the way of harmony, and to point out the values that Christianity, as represented by authentic followers of Jesus Christ, can offer in interpenetration with Hinduism. I shall discuss, first, certain closed aspects of Hindu spirituality and culture, and then turn to the prophetic dimensions of the teaching of Christ — equality, justice, love, and vicarious suffering. Finally, I shall touch briefly upon the evidences of mutual understanding of Christians and Hindus in India today, and the illuminating promise of what Raimundo Panikkar calls "spiritual fecundation" in his lifelong search for harmony among world traditions of East and West.

Christians in India are strongly aware of problematic aspects of Hindu culture, particularly as revealed in the age-old traditions of caste and family. They are also aware of the present split between these traditions and the actual life of many Indians in the everyday marketplace. They sense a certain contrast between these problematics and the prophetic and social dimensions of the faith of the true follower of Christ.

It is often stated that Hinduism *is* the social structure of India. Christianity, on the other hand, is a faith. Therefore, there is no need for opposition.[2] But such statements can be oversimplifications. It is true that India tolerates, with a certain degree of complacency, forms of social tyranny over its own people. Problems related to lower castes, harijans, illiterates, beggars, women, and tribals still exist, while vested interests and privileged classes are opposed to change. Many practices forbidden by law, particularly with regard to women's rights — bride price, for example — are still in existence. Orthodox Hindus are not always reconciled to the Christian concept of redressing these wrongs on the grounds of religious and moral principles.

Philosophically, many educated Hindus do not stress the need for change, because change for them is not real — it is, in a sense, mere illusion. And the villager imbibes this attitude from the philosopher. A basic philosophy that one *cannot* change certain things permeates the thinking of many Hindus. Therefore, to live without change often becomes an established way of life. Even the admirable levels of the Hindu full acceptance of life as it is often militate against changes that can lead to greater justice. Moreover, the basic teaching of the Rigveda that all paths lead to the same goal does not give strong force to movements for greater social improvement. Thus every type of change in India comes with slow development. In a country with a religious tradition of thousands of years, that which is old becomes conventional, and convention resists change. India remains wedded to ancient values and cultural customs. The Hindu sense of tradition and continuity can be at times almost idolatrous in its faithfulness to that which is old. Some Indians, who are Advaitans or Brahmins by birth, are opposed even to exploration of change. Such an attitude results in a lack of assimilation and adaptability that is reflected in the life of the lower castes. It also results in a type of caste pride that C. F. Andrews believed to be "as bad as racial pride elsewhere."[3] Sterner critics of Brahmins go so far as to say that "like the Pharisees, they are unwilling to change. The Pharisees never understood the Kingdom of God."[4]

Hindus of higher caste also desire to maintain the cultural status quo because they believe that, despite tension, it produces stability and happiness. The family is felt to be secure in a healthy state. The ideal life is believed to be reflected in the woman who follows her "lord" and sacrifices all for her family. The Ramayana and the Mahabharata still offer models for Hindu life today. Accompanying these sometimes unrealistic concepts is the provincial mentality that sometimes cares only for what happens in one's own caste, village, or family.

While almost 20 percent of the Indian people lead full and comfortable lives, the poor become poorer in a society crying out for cultural, social, political, and economic change. Ironically, the Hindu philosopher can sidestep the issue of lack of cultural and social development in India by calling it a "historical accident." Europe and Britain were adventurous; America had no civilization to resist change! As Leslie Newbigin points out, the Christian must agree with the Marxist against the Brahmin that "there is no understanding of the world apart from a changing world."[5] Christ cannot be identified with an unchanging society, but he can be identified with the unchanging universality and ultimacy of the religious experience of self-realization, of oneness of the human with the divine, which is central to the Hindu vision. Herein lies a seeming contradiction.

The Western Christian and the Indian Christian must examine carefully both the values and the blocks to be found in the Hindu structures of caste and family as they exist today. Otherwise mistakes and false judgments will be made in the Christian approach to the Hindu in dialogue.

It must be emphasized that "Hinduism *is* caste and caste is Hinduism." Caste is the social system. It is a logical necessity arising from the doctrine of karma, and karma is at the core of Hinduism.[6] Caste is thousands of years old. Untouchability, when it was first developed, meant segregation. Some persons were more civilized and powerful than others. Religion introduced an even stronger bar to separate the powerful from the powerless. Thus untouchability was sanctified. The average Hindu recognizes equality at the "soul level," but accepts variations and gradations among human beings at the "nature level." From the social point of view, the inequality of castes and classes that exists in Hinduism compares unfavorably with social equality as practiced among Christians today. The social consciousness of India today, as manifested in treatment of the poor and the oppressed, is sometimes inferior to that of fifty years ago.[7] To be sure, greed and the "need" to enter into competitive society influenced by Western capitalism are strong forces among wealthy Hindus who reject change. The caste system, with its justification in karma and dharma, suits well the interests of self-perpetuating ruling castes. Wealthy Hindus fear changes in lower caste communities. They express this fear as a danger to Hindu culture, and seldom confess it to be fear of conversion from caste exclusiveness and loss of their own financial supremacy. S. Suviseshamuthu compares this fear to the alarm of the Jewish populace who feared the demoniac healed by Christ. Humanly sinful, they dreaded the blessing to come.[8]

Caste distinctions have always remained dominant in the Hindu community. Liberalist movements have always produced countermovements of orthodoxy. The caste system, as expounded in the Dharmasastras, was "loaded" in favor of the higher castes, and especially Brahmins who were supposed to bear the heavy responsibility for social well-being. In the pessimistic words of a contemporary Indian, "casteism will never be wiped out." Moreover, hundreds of Brahmins still live with the Hindu temples as their only source of support, by good or by ill means.[9]

It is well, however, to point out in justice certain values of the caste system — values better perceived perhaps by the sociologist than by the prophet of a just society. It has been suggested that, because it may be impossible to suppress the caste system, a readaption of casteism may be more just in light of the Indian culture of thousands of years. In the pluralistic society of India, Hinduism as a way of life sometimes takes precedence over Hinduism as a religious doctrine. It is easy to oversimplify the evils of caste, particularly from the Western point of view. It has been demonstrated over and over again, for example, that intermarriages between members of different castes usually produce unhappy homes. The caste system is complex and ingrained. It is difficult for a non-Indian to understand the crucial differences in everyday living among diverse castes and subcastes. Perhaps injustices can be overcome without the complete destruction of casteism![10]

The fundamental attachment of Hindus to family life is closely related to the culture of the caste to which they belong. Family ties are strong. Joint families are common in the Indian villages where about 80 percent of the population lives, and where it would be unthinkable to marry outside one's caste. The individual is always a part of the family and the caste, bound by the codes of the group. Responsibility is shown for the young, concern for the old. Even irresponsible members of the caste are cared for. Yet, in such a social setting, the family system easily becomes the one goal to work for, and public service is neglected. National life can be left to look after itself!

While the concept of caste is being challenged in India today, many Indians feel that the establishment of caste is as strong as ever. It is ironic that some Indians object to race segregation in South Africa and at the same time hold to the sacredness of the caste tradition. Sixty-three percent of Indians live below the poverty level, receiving less than three rupees per day. Poverty, illiteracy, and unemployment afflict the majority of the population, while the minority, representing higher castes, live in comfort. Yet attempts to eradicate the caste system, from the time of the Buddha, have failed. Rabindranath Tagore was led to declare: "The regeneration of the Indian people, to my mind, directly and perhaps solely depends upon the removal of the condition of caste." Gross inequalities and cruel injustices under the caste system led Gandhi to denounce caste as vicious and to declare untouchability to be like "arsenic in pure milk." Other great Indians like Gokhale, Narayan, and Kripalani have joined vehemently in condemnation of the injustices of caste, and yet it remains strong not only among the wealthy but among other Indians as well.

2.   A TWO-TIER INDIAN SOCIETY

One of the results of the continuance of the age-old caste system of India side by side with technological and industrial developments influenced by the West is a type of two-tier society. The developing secular reality and the democratic constitution of the country are not integrated with the religious-cultural life of the people. The outside tier has accepted change, but the inside tier maintains the traditional structure of the caste system. Just as the stratification of Indian society is justified by the religious sanction of Hinduism, the theory that human nature is basically good and that evil is caused by ignorance or avidya negates any model of morality as related to caste. And so the "double" approach to life is maintained despite renewed attacks upon the legitimacy of the caste system throughout the twentieth century.[11]

This disturbance with regard to values leads some Hindus to two ways of living: a "Western" life in public and an "Eastern" life at home. A dichotomy exists between their prayer life and their social life. Worship is traditionally Hindu, for example, while dress is Western. Many wealthy Brahmins go to hotels to partake of food that violates their vegetarian standards. They visit temples or bathe in sacred rivers to be purified of their guilt. Some observers point out a dichotomy between the spiritual Hindu lifestyle of the "inside tier" and the growing corruption in the life of the marketplace.[12]

M. P. Pandit, internationally known director of Sri Aurobindo Ashram in Pondicherry, notes a breakdown in moral and ethical values in India today. He sees a " new society" in which Indians practice external forms of religion but do not have faith. Fear that something undesirable may happen if they fail to conform leads them to continue traditional Hindu practices. Pandit believes that Hindus today are too permissive, and that successive generations will have little faith.[13] He does not express, of course, the majority point of view.

3. CHRISTIAN PROPHETIC AND SOCIAL DIMENSIONS

If we turn now to the prophetic and social dimensions of Christianity in India today, we find a more open and understanding approach to Hindu culture and the caste system than has ever existed in the past.

In the teaching of Jesus Christ, God is the God of all equally. Human "rights" are a gift of God. All human works are of value. Witness to Christ involves action as well as speech. Values precede service, and the values of love and charity are qualitative. Hindu caste, on the other hand, is often based on a quantitative measure. The prophetic aspect of Christianity has undoubtedly influenced India through social involvement. Christians have demonstrated that religion is *not only* divine, and this idea has had tremendous consequences. It is not emphasized in the Gita. Whereas Hinduism stresses liberation from history, authentic Christianity stresses human liberation. Jesus, like the Buddha, had no social prejudices. Awareness of social need and commitment to it are Christian values that result in concern for the world in its temporal reality as opposed to underdevelopment.

The social dimension of religious life *within the community* of salvation is also Christian. Incarnational religion is by its very nature interhuman and committed to others, whether or not blood relations exist. The realization of God's plan for human beings in history is a part of salvation. Within Hindu philosophy, on the other hand, community is not necessary for salvation or self-realization. The individual can find personal salvation while India is bound in poverty, inequality, and religiosity. To be sure, Christian countries, like the Philippines and many South American countries today, and like European countries a century ago, have not always been conscious of the communal aspect of salvation. But true Christians cannot seek their own salvation alone. On the level of concept, Christian education in India has always stressed the communal and sharing aspects of salvation in Christ. Unfortunately, this teaching has been clouded, because often only the Indian elite could afford the best Christian education.

Vivekananda, in the nineteenth century, was one of the first Hindus to recognize the human problem in India, to realize that persons must serve God in their fellows, that human service is spiritual service. Christianity was his teacher. He was aware that Indians were arrested in their total development, that the *human* attitude was less privileged in India. "No religion on earth preaches human dignity more than Hinduism," said Vivekananda, "and no nation on earth treads upon the necks of human beings as India does."[14] He realized that, in order to raise the human level of Indian society, the traditions and institutions of Indian culture had to be challenged. And he did challenge them as he imbibed Christian attitudes. Yet some of the conditions he lamented still exist in India.

When one considers the socio-economic condition of India, one is tempted to say that both Hindus and Christians are "fiddling while Rome burns." The nature and causes of the present social fragmentation of India are definitely related to the economic system. We are reminded that Jesus was always concerned with concrete situations of the people. He sought for radical change in economic and political relationships when human need demanded it. He died on the cross because he dared to challenge the Pharisees, the powerful of his time. The same thrust is not so strong in the Hindu scriptures.[15] Nor do we find evidence there of the consciousness of social sin that is so deeply embedded within Christian tradition. The true Christian is concerned for all human beings on all levels — social, spiritual, economic, and political.

Today East and West are encountering each other as mysteries as well as economic and political anomalies. The interiority of the East and the social concern of the West are complementary, reciprocal, and convergent. The East sees Krishna as a "sacred mirror" of the preconscious depths of self. Christianity sees Christ as a mirror awakening humankind to the needs of brothers and sisters. Christianity demands the recognition of all human beings as persons. Christian presence in India has propagated the ideal of castelessness, accepted by many twentieth-century Indians as essential to the recognition of human personhood. Yet traditional Christianity (as opposed to ideal Christianity) has often been pointed out as a stumbling block to the achievement of the social goals of Christ. Samuel Rayan, for example, sees traditional Christianity as *the problem* that blocks human development in India.[16]

Christians are a block to human development in India when they fail as witnesses to Christian life, when they lack human qualities in everyday affairs. Asiatics tend to take the teachings of Christ literally. They look to Christians to live the message of Christ in their daily lives. They see Christianity as linked directly with Christ, not with the institutional church as such. Thus a Hindu remarked to the writer that he preferred a true sadhu, a true follower of Christ, to a hundred church officials. When Hindus are told that they do not always live what one reads in the Gita, they respond that Christians do not live what they read in the Bible! When Hindu converts do not observe their priest or minister practicing the values taught by Christ, they are likely to return to the Hindu sannyasi when they need the services of a religious guide. The greatest gift of Christians to the Hindu is to actually live their own faith.

When the famous scholar, S. Radakrishnan, declared that "Christians are ordinary people with extraordinary claims," he was getting to the heart of the matter: the true follower of Christ *is* extraordinary! In this sense, the Hindu has a right to insist that Christian witness be practiced in actuality, that social justice exist in the church, not in books. When social service becomes exploitation because leaders are friends of the exploiters, Christianity is misrepresented. The followers of Christ are not "the salt of the earth." The behavior of Christians can obstruct Christian goals. Sometimes, the more institutional the aspect of the church, the less it appears as true to Christ. Polarities can develop between institution and charism. At a meeting of bishops and theologians in Hyderabad in 1976, certain bishops who appeared as administrators felt that theologians who proposed prophetic aspects of ministry were destroying the church![17] The Hindu, on the other hand, expects the priesthood to be a vocation, not a profession. Witness to poverty is expected to be a value of the sadhu. The Asian turns a deaf ear to the preacher of the gospel who is an ally of an oppressive government.

According to Paulos Gregorios, the major accusation against Christians in India is that "faith in suffering as redemptive is an escape from responsibility to alleviate suffering." Gregorios declares that the New Testament is not merely a set of rules for Christians. "Christians have to act in history in terms of their understanding and in the context of their situation." The sign of the kingdom *today* is found wherever the oppressed are set free, the poor are made to rejoice, and injustice is vindicated.[18]

In India today, with its extreme poverty, its multireligious democracy, and its fast-changing society, the church is called to have a message for all suffering "nonpersons." Its goal cannot be the mere survival of itself as an institution. Jesus was revolutionary in upsetting the traditions of the "establishment" of his time. He spoke for the poor, the children, women, prostitutes, and persons of mixed blood. Thus he was a radical.[19] The church is called to encourage response to the needs of the poor. When money received from the West is used to strengthen existing institutions while the poor have no water and church leaders have running water in their rooms, the Hindu questions Christian witness. Christians are expected to fight the social sin that is an intrinsic evil in Indian social structures, particularly in villages where inhabitants are exploited by wealthy landowners. Needed reforms, such as the fight against corruption through economic pioneering, self-help, respect for law, community projects, and cooperatives are now being initiated by many Christian centers.

In India, politics means power. The poor are human beings when their votes are wanted at elections. But they are not persons when they are exploited by powerful landowners. Contact with the West has brought a democratic Constitution. But independence for the poor is slow in developing. The political ideology of the elite is partially a legacy of colonialism. Yet some emerging political and economic structures give hope. The church must strengthen and reinforce this hope. The future of India depends on the awakening of the masses of its people and the response to that awakening among present ruling classes.

4. CHRISTIAN EQUALITY

The teaching of Christ on the oppression of the poor and the suffering is unequivocal. To be true to Christ, the church must take a stand on social issues. It must adopt a strong base from which to teach as Christ taught and to witness to that teaching. That base must rest squarely on the fundamental message of Jesus Christ that is rooted in love for the Father manifested in equality, justice, and love for all persons. Hindus respond in sometimes diverse ways to the question of equality. Original castes were related to natural abilities, temperament, and function. Originally, there were no untouchables. Historically, conquered races became lower castes and untouchables. From the religious point of view, caste appeared only in a late hymn of the Rig Veda. As time progressed, Hindus rejected any challenge to the status quo of caste. Who one was had to do with caste background, and such identity established friends and enemies. With the onset of democracy, civic and political rights for all were guaranteed by the Indian Constitutions, but nevertheless caste and untouchability remained. Atrocities toward harijans continue to the present day, but untouchables are now awakening to and beginning to demand their rights. One of the reasons for this change is that educated Indian Christians are encouraging them to seek their rights. The coming struggle in India will be directed against wealthy landholding groups who refuse just wages to laborers.

Christian support of the oppressed in India must be based always on the actual teaching of Christ. Universal equality, the pursuit of liberation, and the development of all peoples demonstrate the equality of "all these little ones" of Christ. Authentic Christianity teaches the equal worth of all human beings and the glorification of God through love for one's neighbor. "Charity" cannot substitute for equality. It can be an easy way to maintain the status quo that cries out for structural change. "Charity" often denies equality. The educated segment of the Hindu population is sometimes the first to admit that the caste system produces inequality and injustice, while Christianity has never sanctioned social stratification.[20] For the true Christian, everything that a person has is a gift of God. No human being has a right to dominate others. A corollary of this principle is that all work has dignity because all human beings possess a dignity conferred not just by human right but by God. The establishment of equality among all Indians, when it is achieved, will be equivalent to the humanity taught by Jesus Christ, but expressed in Indian form.

To help to achieve this equality, the Indian Christian must be prepared to receive from the Hindu, not merely to give. The Christian must first affirm Hindus, then enter into interdependence with them. Without such a process, equality will not be achieved. The prophetic character of Christianity stands for fellowship, freedom, peace, and equality. It abhors racism, exploitation, imperialism, war, and *all* types of human inequality. It has a passion for social improvement. In India, it must give first priority to understanding of, affirmation of, and interdependence with the Hindu. The true Christian cannot be the great and triumphal savior.

The question of the Christian principle of equality has special reference to women. The Christian concept of human personality is *marked* in its teaching on the relationship between men and women. Authentic Christianity teaches reverence for the *person* of woman in a different manner than Hinduism. It is often said in India that Hindus "place woman on a pedestal and reverence her," but this concept is not to be confused with *personal* equality of man and woman. Christianity has done more to change the status of woman in India than any other force. Largely through the influence of Christian education, large numbers of Indian women have become teachers, nurses, and doctors. Christian influence has worked strongly against child marriage, and it has championed the rights of widows to remarry and daughters to share in the property of their families.

Even in many of the higher Hindu castes, the woman is almost completely subservient to her husband. She remains in the home, greeting visitors and then departing, while her husband and perhaps her mother-in-law entertain guests. The lot of rural women, on the other hand, is often a blot on Indian society. Born poor, they are often brought up in utter poverty, married by arrangement at the earliest opportunity to men as poor as themselves, condemned to work both in the home and for employers in the fields who can dismiss them if they seek a just wage or attempt to improve their status in life. These women often have unusual intelligence. They seek an opportunity to improve themselves, not "charity."[21]

It is well to remember that respect for the dignity of women as persons is not merely a cultural and historical development in either East or West. In the India of the Upanishads, women were apt spiritual pupils of the rishis. They were highly advanced in spiritual culture and considered worthy of profound religious instruction. The development of the caste system, however, changed the status of women in India. In the time of Christ in the Middle East, women were held in contempt. Ethical leaders of the day taught that "a man should not salute a woman in a public place, not even his own wife." It was held to be "better that the words of the law should be burnt than that they be delivered to women." In the daily service of the Hebrew synagogue men prayed, "Blessed art thou, O Lord, who hast not made me a woman." Women from their separate place responded: "Blessed art thou, O Lord, who hast fashioned me according to thy will."[22] Christ is the one who frees women in the West. The gospel accounts of the relationship of Jesus with women of all backgrounds is both radical and revolutionary. To be sure, the official church in the West has yet to "catch up" with Christ in the treatment of women. The established church still regards women as "second-class" members.

Catholic women religious in India, however, have had a monopoly in the education of Hindu women. Over a hundred sisterhoods, numbering forty thousand women, have been witnesses to the social and professional advancement of women as they have served in colleges and schools, hospitals, orphanages, maternity homes, hostels, leprosariums, and rescue homes. Their services are considered to be remarkable and unique by many Hindus who have adopted their respect for the personhood of woman while scarcely realizing their influence. The official church in India, like the church in the West, can contribute greatly to the equality of women and men in India if it will only develop its own position with regard to women religious and to all women.

First, the church must teach the spirituality of marriage in India. It has not done so in depth. As the basis of the Christian home, the spirituality of marriage is essential to the pastoral approach. Christians in India often continue practices of inequality of women with men that their families brought with them from the Hindu culture after their conversion to Christianity. The development of the spirituality of marriage among Christians will influence Hindu marriage customs just as Christian education in schools has done. Second, the church needs a theology of women, not just for India, but for the universal church. A clear understanding of the equality of men and women has never been developed within the total church.[23] The charisms of women should be recognized through liturgical rites to provide a new coherent ecclesiastical horizon for their activities within the church. Women can have a greater share in pastoral ministry (even while the church refuses to sanction the ordination of women to the priesthood). They can often replace priests in providing nonsacramental services.[24]

The entire question of equality of women can be referred to only briefly here. It has a special significance in india that it does not have in many Western counties because of the position of women in the East.

When we discuss the problem of equality of women and men within Hinduism, moreover, we have to be continually aware of the complexity of the question. Misunderstanding or misinterpretation of Hindu social and cultural history can lead easily to unjust condemnation of practices that have developed over centuries. Westerners are often unaware, for example, of fundamental differences between the social status of Hindu women and that of Muslim women in India, even though these women may live side by side within one town or city. The plurality of Indian society precludes facile generalizations with regard to women in society.

A warning is necessary, also, with regard to the whole question of human equality in East and West. In the above discussion, I have referred again and again to "authentic" Christianity and to the actual practice of Christianity, to the "theoretical" Hinduism of the Upanishads and the Rigveda and to the actual practice of Hinduism. These changes of plane, which one must deal with on the human level, must be kept in mental balance just as pluralities of society must be.

Historical and geographical planes also affect our judgments with regard to human equality. Christian Europe some centuries ago reflected no greater equality than the caste system of India today. In Latin America today, moreover, the majority of church leaders still support the privileged and wealthy classes. To state that the true follower of Christ can offer the Hindu a message of human equality is in no sense to state that Hinduism should be integrated into the Western fabric of life nor into the fabric of an "official" Christianity that is not always representative of the poor and loving Christ!

5. CHRISTIAN JUSTICE

When we consider the interpenetration of Hinduism and Christianity in India, justice must be closely interrelated with equality. As with all peoples, uniform and universal justice is not practiced among Hindus! Aside from the injustices of the caste system, in ordinary life the Hindu sometimes tends to believe that rules and regulations can always have an exception if one has enough influence with the authorities concerned. More to the point, the Hindu acceptance of equality at the soul level but not at the nature level sometimes militates against justice and strengthens the caste system. Educated Hindus recognize that they can learn much from Christians concerning social justice (while they insist that Christians must practice the justice they preach).

Hindus are aware that certain Indians tolerate with complacency social tyranny toward their own people; that many of the most brilliant of Indians turn their minds to pursuits that advance their personal fortunes at home and abroad, but neglect the pursuit of justice for their own people. The mammoth injustices of the aftermath of colonialism are often ignored: an elitist minority oppressing the masses, rural indebtedness, exploitation, deprivation of the essentials of life. One of the main reasons for a failure to respond to injustice has been the lack of a philosophy of social change and action.[25] Only at the turn of the present century was attention given by Hindus to social action. Gandhi, Vinoba Bhave, and Vivekananda, despite their influence, were even rejected by many of their Hindu compatriots because of their insistence on social justice.

On the other hand, we find a prominent, well-educated Hindu stating unequivocally that social action is always associated with the Catholic Church in India. Ka Naa Subramanyam points out that the *Mater et Magistra* of Pope John XXIII proposes a human approach to the socio-economic problems of the world as a whole on the basis of national and international social justice. This document touches on "every social problem that faces humankind today." Then Subramanyam adds that the social problems of India today are special concerns of *Mater et Magistra*. He declares that the church is not commissioned specifically to give the world a social system and create a paradise on earth, but he supports completely the words of John XXIII:

Though the Church's first care must be for souls, how can she sanctify them and share in the gifts of heaven if she does not concern herself too with the exigencies of man's daily life, with his livelihood and education, and his general temporal welfare and prosperity?

I shall refer briefly to the situation of injustice in India before outlining the teachings of Christ that Subramanyam believes to be the answer to all problems of social justice, always keeping in mind the words of a great Hindu leader that "Christianity is yet to be lived in India."[26] To be sure, the highest ideals of Hinduism also have still to be lived. The difference between the two, from this particular point of view, lies in the fact that the church for two thousand years has seldom failed to define the human values of Christ: its failures have been in their practice. Hinduism, on the other hand, had to initiate a renascence of human values in the nineteenth century in order to rediscover the values of justice and equality in the ancient Hindu Scriptures.

The political ideology accepted by the Indian elite today is partially a holdover from colonialism. Poverty and corruption have increased since the days of Nehru. Justice requires that the poverty-stricken, uneducated, and oppressed of India be given the means for self-help that their humanity demands. Case studies of injustice to the poor in Indian villages indicate that the only solution to their problems lies in a remodeling of their consciousness.[27] Paulo Freire's methods in Latin America may be helpful, but Indians must find their own way to equality and justice. The problem is especially acute in that practices of injustice in India tend to dissolve into the social structure of the caste system. There are those who insist that the only way to justice in India is to educate the wealthy to justice, for there has been only a 50 percent success in educating the poor to their rights![28] Perhaps only an approach as powerful and dramatic as Gandhi's will be successful. "If God were to appear in India," said Gandhi, "he would have to take the form of a loaf of bread!"

Christian justice in India is always complementary to Hindu interiority and sense of the sacred. If the two are divorced, the Hindu will not hear the voice of the Christian. The task of the

Christian in this exchange is to seek justice by taking seriously the temporal dimension of reality. Because they are human beings, and more so because they are followers of Christ, Christians have an obligation to be in the vanguard of the movement toward justice in India. Unless they share the common responsibility to treat their brothers and sisters justly, then they cannot help to make God present to others in a way that validates the divine existence. It is one thing to validate the existence of God for intellectuals, another thing to do so for the masses of poor of the world. The great leader of the Hindu renascence, Vivekananda, used to say, "Cure injustice and oppression first. Then talk about God." Vivekananda was often more Christian than Hindu!

Perhaps a more accurate way to express the relationship between the Hindu search for God and Christian justice is to say that human liberation is always linked to the divine plan. Christ and justice cannot be thought of as apart from each other. Most human beings find themselves to be (if they are honest) oppressor in one role and oppressed in another. If oppressed and oppressor can see themselves as "locked together in a single tragedy," and are prepared to respond to divine forgiveness and fellowship in Christ, there is no need to discuss whether justice precedes or follows the spiritual teaching of Christ: the two are one in both scripture and life.[29] Pope John XXIII stresses this new understanding of the Good News as the pursuit of the liberation of all peoples and of their development in his document *Peace on Earth*. The search for justice is a basic requirement for decent human existence without which growth to deeper values is impossible. This genuine Christian justice is not possessive: it is nonviolent.

Religious gestures of Christians are meaningless in India without active justice. "Charity" often offers a mere "band-aid" applied to suffering caused by basic violations of the dignity of persons. This type of "charity" is not enough. It does not touch causes. It is foreign to justice. The injustices of the caste system as well as the injustices of Western economic imperialism must be attacked at their roots. When ministers of the gospel ally themselves with oppressive governments or with landholders who rob the peasant, they do not ally themselves with Christ. We do not come to the fullness of the kingdom unless we join ourselves to the suffering, death, and resurrection of the corporate body of humanity, which is the body of Christ. The church is a barrier to Christ when it allies itself with those who keep the poor in subjection. In India there are 400 million uneducated people; less than 10 percent of the funds spent for education is spent for elementary teaching. True followers of Christ voice their disapproval of this type of injustice to the body of Christ. They respond to injustice not in theory but *in reality*. The humanity of Christ and their own humanity demand it.

The church is called upon today to promote a just world order. Indeed, it must offer revolutionary witness to justice. Evolutionary and counterrevolutionary concepts and actions are Christian. Christ opposed the society in which he lived because he refused to tolerate injustice to his brothers and sisters. The National Biblical, Catechetical, and Liturgical Centre in Bangalore published in 1978 a very heartening little book called *The Story of Thirty Years Struggle for Justice*. It is a consolidated account of seventy varied efforts over thirty years to end discrimination and injustice against Christians of scheduled caste origin. Here is justice in action! Christian ashrams in India are now being used to teach villagers their rights, to help them to organize in protest against unjust wages. Centers of Christian social action are training persons to be agents for change in the fight against poverty, ignorance, and unemployment.

Many Indian Christians are thus acting in history by adapting the teachings of Christ in scripture to the actual unjust situations in which they find themselves. They identify themselves with the victims of evil: they witness to the truth that where the oppressed are set free, the powerless are vindicated. They understand in the profoundest manner that Christ did what no other great religious leader ever did: he resisted domination and exploitation unto death on a cross. Until the end of the second century, Christianity was the religion of the poor. In India today, Christianity is still dominantly a religion of the poor. Millions of harijans have become Christians. But Hinduism is also a religion of the poor: only a comparatively small number of

Hindus are wealthy. Elimination of the caste system is one measure necessary to secure justice for the poor of India, whether Hindu or Christian. Marxism can never be the answer to the Indian problem of injustice. Both Christians and Hindus know this to be true. The answer to injustice is to humanize the world as Christ taught. This is why Christians must reject any assertion of superiority to Hinduism, which is violence of the spirit. The Indian appreciates the commitment of Christ to justice and love unto death.

Because poverty in India is a *total* cultural phenomenon, the demand upon Christians to transform society in freedom and justice is greater than in the West. Today the prophetic mission of the church in India is *not* fulfilled. The basic human rights of bread, equality, justice, and spiritual self-determination are not yet achieved. As M. M. Thomas has stated, "The Church should spiritually foster within its fellowship radical groups who consider their main social mission . . . in terms of cooperation with others in building the awareness of the people of their rights, in speaking truth to dehumanising power in the name of God's justice, and in defending human beings through involvement in conflict-situations."[30] Participant democracy must be achieved.

Paulos Gregorios, Orthodox metropolitan of Kerala, has expressed well the call for integration of all human activities with the quest for justice, freedom, and peace:

> If all human activities and abilities, including the development of science and technology, were subordinated to and integrated with the quest for justice, freedom, peace, and creative goodness, the human rule over the creation could mean a blessing for the whole universe.[31]

6. CHRISTIAN LOVE

For the Christian, equality and justice are meaningless unless they are grounded in the love of Christ. The scriptural command to "love your neighbor" is a love of mutuality. The loving devotion of bhakti found in the Bhagavad Gita differs from the love of Christ. The love of Krishna is more closely related to compassion than to mutuality. To be sure, the beautiful conversations between Krishna and Arjuna relate to the soul and God. But the love of all men and women for one another because all are a part of the living Christ is the new commandment of Jesus. This Christian gift creates a personal responsibility to all the world in love, a gift that is still partially nascent in Hinduism.

Jesus was unique in his perfect commitment to love for others unto death. He suffered, died, and rose again to redeem the human race, of which he was a member, from sin that was not his. By this ultimate sacrifice, he translated his love of the Father into practice, and established his church not as a "conqueror's bride" but as a "suffering servant." This type of love reaches deep into the heart where true conversion or metanoia takes place. It is the type of love that seeks to understand Hindus from *within*, to know how Hindus themselves penetrate the divine mysteries. The Christian love of agape can unite Hindu and Christian within "the cave of the heart" in the joy of Christ's resurrection.

In studying the bhakti approach to Krishna as Lord, A. J. Appasamy points out aspects of the Christian gift of love found in Hinduism.[32] Great Indians like Gandhi, in his *Songs from Prison*, have described the ideal of loving service to others:

> This and this alone
> Is true religion —
> To serve thy brethren:
> This is sin above all other sin,
> To harm thy brethren.[33]

On the whole, however, even the bhaktis have not always realized a love of God that requires unselfish service toward those who suffer. Authentic Christians can offer to the Hindu a message of love that is an antidote to the sometimes depressing effects of karma; a love that counteracts an impersonal conception of an Absolute Being who neither loves nor hates, neither acts nor is affected by the acts of others; a love that wipes out the fear of disaster inflicted by the gods; a love that compassionates all suffering creatures, whether or not they are faithful; and finally a love that goes to the uttermost depths to endure the

shame of the cross for all humans. The love of Christ unites with
the Hindu concept of a God who is Being-Awareness-Bliss
(Saccidananda). It points the way to bliss, and in doing so
transcends it. The love of Christ and the Father in the Spirit is
the active, never-ending giving of self in a love that lifts up all
men and women into union with the Trinity precisely because
they are the body of the living Christ.

The infinite love of Christ for all humans, not for a select few,
appeals to many Hindus. The tendency of the Hindu philosopher to see union with God as possible only for a select few who
have experienced years of self-discipline, meditation, and physical austerity is not appealing to the ordinary Hindu. The great
Hindu philosopher, T. M. P. Mahadevan, for example, told the
writer that only one person in a million reaches in the present
life the "final, plenary, complete, total experience of nonduality
which is reality."[34] Most men and women must go through an
innumerable series of rebirths. Authentic Christianity, on the
other hand, knows nothing of an esoteric circle of disciples,
even though some Christian theologians have taught that only a
minority of Christians are saved. Christ chose fishermen and
taught that every human being can realize the kingdom of God.
Christian love is qualitative, not quantitative. The widow's mite
is acceptable.

The Hindu responds positively to the unconditional love of
Christ for all humans expressed in St. John. Vivekananda spoke
harshly when he condemned the lack of selfless love among his
Hindu countrymen: "The blot on India's national flag is the
neglect of millions of people." And he added the words of
Christ, "If you cannot love man whom you see, how can you
love God whom you have not seen?"[35] Disinterested love without regard for reward or blessing in return is practiced by the
Hindu sannyasi who seeks the highest self-realization. The love
taught by Christ is none other than his own love for the Father,
a completely self-disregarding love that could express itself as
"Not my will but thine be done." This is the selfless love
appreciated by Hindus, whether they discover it in the Christian
or in the sannyasi.

It is well for Christians to be aware that Hindus do not always see them as a witness to Christ's selfless love. Gandhi told his Christian associates frankly that they should *live* the Sermon on the Mount. He himself was called a Christian by his Hindu associates because he *did* live the Sermon on the Mount. Gandhi looked for a poor church of Christ, not the triumphant church that he sometimes found in India. Christians in India should be encouraged, however, by the thought that millions of Hindus love and accept Christ without reservation. The challenge of these Hindus to the Christian is to live the love of Christ in actuality. Even those Hindus who reject the actual pursuit of equality, justice, and love for *all* humans as a non-Hindu concept expect Christians to pursue this goal that they themselves preach.

Unification, mutuality, and fellowship of Christian and Hindu can be found in loving understanding within the hearts of both. India does not yet understand the love of Father, Son, and Spirit in one self-giving. The love of bhakti was a later development of Hinduism in which Indians overcame in practice what they jettisoned in advaitic theory. Hindu swamis state freely that, although all great religions have profound values, *mutual love* is the great contribution of Christianity: the love of the Persons of the Trinity, and the love of men and women for one another. The ideal Christian is totally committed to love of others in community. Sharing with others is basic to the missionary idea itself that first brought committed Christians to India. The tradition of offering the mantra only to the qualified person is a practice contrary to the Christian mission of sharing with all others and helping all to seek salvation.[36] Sharing with all is also allied with healing all and forgiving all in Christian love. Forgiveness is not a common concept among Hindus, possibly because sin does not have the implications it has among Christians: it is viewed only as a deterrent to self-realization or salvation.

Among Hindus, the chief orientation of love and sharing lies within a narrow circle: I, my family, my caste. Although Hindu family relationships are admirable, the goals of the spiritual lives of individual family members are often based on philosophical rationalizations of spiritual experience rather than on openness to love for all. Thus the values of horizontal spirituality are sometimes lost in the personal search for self-realization. The worst effects of a completely vertical approach to God are evident when love and service of those outside the family or caste are seen as actual impediments to God-realization.

Paradoxically, however, Hindus are greatly impressed when they observe Christians devoting themselves to the service of others in love. These Christians reveal to Hindus the essence of Christian love; they demonstrate that the church does not exist for itself. They reveal that Christians can be sadhus and sannyasis, a fact that is extremely important in establishing a spiritual bridge between Christian and Hindu. Selfless love of Christians also impresses Indians with a positive outlook toward the world. It helps to turn them away from the Hindu idea that the greatest spiritual goal is release from the world. The good Christian reveals a joy in action and involvement in the world of men and women for the love of Christ. This mission of the Christian is not just a generalized concept of love; it is care for individuals in particular situations. Christ always served others in particular ways. He was the concrete manifestation of the love of the Trinity through both knowledge and action. Western Christianity often takes for granted the love of the Father, if not the love of Christ. It is well to remember that no religion of India except Christianity emphasizes the concept of God as Father, men and women as brothers and sisters, and a community of all human beings as a sacred value.

Paulos Gregorios writes that if the new creation in Christ is to break forth in India not beyond history but within history, Asian Christians must be a manifest presence of Christ in Indian society. They must embrace their vocation to suffer in behalf of their fellow men and women. Then, echoing St. Paul, Gregorios asks:

> If God be for us, who can be against us? Can colonialism, imperialism, neo-colonialism, racism, economic injustice, trans-national corporations, the military-industrial complex — can any of these enemies withstand the power of God? If they are evil, they will be destroyed; and we must join the fight against them. It is the love of Christ that is the ground of our hope.[37]

If Indian Christians are willing to follow Christ in his suffering, death, and resurrection, the millions of Hindus who already accept Christ but not the church will join with these Christians in understanding and love to bring forth the mystery that is waiting to be born in the East. And Christians will be able to speak in understandable language to the millions of Hindus to whom Christ is the "unknown God" of cosmic revelation.

7. CHRIST IN THE SPIRIT AS GROUND OF HINDU-CHRISTIAN UNION

If the everlasting Christ who existed from the beginning in loving union with the Father through the Spirit is the meeting point of Hindu and Christian; if this same Christ was incarnated as Jesus and suffered, died, and rose again for the redemption of all men and women; if this same Christ is alive today in the body of humankind and in the whole universe — then the Christian church is called to unite the body of Christ with the truth of the Spirit revealed to Hindus by God over thousands of years. Indian Christians are aware of this calling. They are searching in the Spirit to unite themselves with their Hindu brothers and sisters in love through an exchange of the spiritual gifts each has received from God. They trust in the Spirit that this union will produce a new manifestation of the still unknown mystery of the eternal Christ. They await with hope this new creation.[38]

Various approaches have been devised in the search for loving union between Hindu and Christian on spiritual, liturgical, and theological levels. Terms used are merely terms: they cannot define mystery. Yet each term is pregnant with meaning. Many Indian Christians speak of inculturation, indigenization, and indianization in their efforts to foster understanding of the Christian faith in India. Each of these words has positive and negative aspects. "Indianization" is considered by some Christians to be an artificial term. Christ comes to India directly from the Father, not from any other culture. Therefore it is meaningless to "indianize" a Western Christianity. "Inculturation" and "indigenization" are more acceptable words, for they suggest the growth of Christianity *within* India itself, not a faith or belief imposed from outside the culture. Yet these terms still imply a hint of transformation rather than confirmation of a faith rooted in India from the beginning through cosmic revelation. Other Indians, less sanguine in their approach, insist that Christianity itself must be "christianized." If Christianity is truly, always, and everywhere the universal manifestation of the incarnate Christ, then there will be no need to adopt linking or connecting terms of an artful or contrived nature.

Raimundo Panikkar has offered a creative and unique suggestion in the word "fecundation" that negates the violence of spirit that implies superiority. Christians do not come to Hindus to convert them; they do not come with a superior gift from West to East. Rather, they meet the Hindu in the love of Christ, ready to share and to receive. They offer the truth of Christ, and they receive the truth that God has given to the Hindu over centuries of profound spirituality. Christians thus live in actuality the mutuality of Christian love. They await in faith the birth of the new child of Christian and Hindu, the new creation in Christ.

It will be helpful to look briefly at the types of spiritual exchange between Christian and Hindu suggested above. D. S. Amalorpavadass, in his essay *Gospel and Culture*,[39] defines inculturation or indigenization as "the integration of the church in a socio-cultural-religious milieu, the incarnation of the church in a place, time, and people." This inculturation is an incarnational procedure, implemented in all areas: local community, lifestyle, art, architecture, theology, spirituality, and the triple ministry of word, liturgy, and service. It is centered in an ecclesial pluralism based on social, cultural, religious, and theological pluralism leading eventually to pastoral pluralism. It realizes the universality of the church through particularities and localization. It is a providential occasion for real renewal because religious colonialism is finished! Inculturation of this type would have to be developed over a transitional period, indefinite in length. It would always assume that the message of Christ arises within Indian culture itself. The mystery of Christ would be experienced as emerging through the total richness of the Indian heritage. Indigenization would thus progress slowly by trial and adaptation, always accepting of the values of the Hindu culture just as the early Christians accepted the values of Greco-Roman culture.

Special problems arise because Indian Christians are said to be alienated today from their own culture. Indigenization will take them back to what they rejected when they were converted from Hinduism! Ninety percent of them came originally from outcast communities with a desire to improve their social status as concomitant with their following of Christ. Hinduism has absorbed Indian culture, moreover, to such an extent that no strict line can be drawn between the two. In accepting Indian culture, will Christianity absorb Hinduism too? This is the question asked by Indian Christians. The 10 percent of Indian Christians whose roots are in the Sanskrit culture will be more able, in the process of inculturation, to accept what can be reaffirmed in their Hindu roots. As for the majority of Christians, on the other hand, it has been pointed out that they may actually rejoice in returning to the religious festivals, dances, songs, and parables in which they once participated. The St. Thomas Christians of Kerala are an excellent example of a Christian community that was never separated from its cultural roots. They represent, moreover, the strongest Christian community in India.

Indigenization in the liturgy is basic to Christian inculturation based on true renewal.[40] It is interconnected with indigenization in spirituality and theology. When the Indian Christian community can express itself in genuine Indian forms of worship, it will be able to integrate that expression with its quest for God and with the evolution of a genuine Indian Christian theology. Liturgy is "a sum total of the efficacious signs of salvation among men and women and of worship of God through Christ." The reformed liturgy of the Catholic Church reveals simplicity, brevity, variety, intelligibility, and spontaneity. At the level of the universal church, these qualities are blessed and meaningful. But at the level of the local church, the signs used in the liturgy are meaningful only when they are a genuine expression of the community's faith and worship, fellowship and service. They must be drawn from the cultural and religious heritage of the people. Because of the great regional diversity of India, pluriformity in the liturgy is demanded. Beneath a plurality of liturgical forms, a basic unity of worship will prevail. Bede Griffiths reminds us that we must trust in liturgical reforms.[41] Inculturation in worship is taking place continually in India in small basic communities and in ashrams. The experiments of these worshiping communities are illuminating the Christian liturgy in India. Cardinal Joseph Parecattil points out that "to become increasingly aware of God's presence in us and to realize in an ever more vivid manner the value of renunciation in the Indian context and according to indigenous standards are the touchstones of the genuine Indian Christian."[42] Precisely here we find the link between liturgy and spirituality in Indian inculturation of Christianity.

In the process of inculturation, Christians should never forget that they are still strangers in India. Therefore indigenization must progress slowly, perhaps with a step backward for each step forward. On the whole, Indian Christians are still embedded in Western religious customs, and some Indian Christians complain that too many *Westerners* in India are involved in efforts toward indigenization.[43] The assimilative process must be taken seriously. It is a two-way traffic between Christianity and Hindu culture, not a fascinating novelty offering grounds for Western experimentation! It requires a knowledge of the Eastern Christian tradition (and even Oriental biblical studies) as well as of Hindu culture. Moreover, no Christian in India is a *pure* Christian and no Hindu is a *pure* Hindu. There is no "pure" religion in India. As often expressed above, millions of Hindus accept Christ and the gospel, but not the church. Indigenization must take place in the spirit of Christ. It must be honest and it must be Indian: foreign elements should not intrude. The Asiatic mentality is different from the Western. Westerners must live *within* the Indian culture for many years before they can understand *interiorly* that pure rationality cannot reach the Indian spirit in a profound way. Witness is essential. The spirituality of the Indian responds by a kind of "osmosis" to the spirituality of holy persons. Indigenization therefore rests to a great extent on communion between Christian and Hindu "within the cave of the heart." It is difficult to set boundaries and limitations in the process of inculturation, but all superficialities should be eliminated. Christians must be aware of ambiguities. Inculturation cannot be commanded. In a country in which the Christian church has been called "an island in a sea of Hinduism," inculturation of Christianity will be ultimately a spontaneous outcome of the spiritual lifestyle of Indian Christians living within their own culture.

Because adaptation of methods of Indian prayer, worship, and spirituality have been discussed in previous chapters, I shall allude here only to the relationship of these Indian approaches to Christianity in the context of our present discussion of inculturation. Indian resistance to inculturation of Christianity sometimes arises because Indians fear destruction of their own culture. Though they love the traditional music, dance, and drama of Hinduism, they are sometimes fearful when Indian traditions are used to proclaim the Christian gospel, because they know instinctively that Hindu tradition and Indian culture are so closely related as to be inseparable. If Christianity were "naturalized" in India, they would lose their fear of a faith that they know to be universal.

Thus inculturation without fear of controversy must be a basic goal of the Christian. Art, music, poetry, and architecture can speak to the spirit of the Hindu as logical argument never can. Just as Hinduism is a way of life, a new Christianity can also become an Indian way of life if the Hindu mind and heart are understood. Interreligious prayer and dialogue are fruitful only when neither Christian nor Hindu has the slightest desire to prove the other wrong. Robert De Nobili discovered through experience long ago that stories and parables revealed Christ to the Brahmins he associated with as theology taught in the native Tamil language and based on the Vedas never could. Yoga and Hindu methods of meditation are warmly accepted by Indian Christians because they feel them to be their own ancient heritage. They are at home with these Hindu practices. Hindu prayers, symbols, and images lead Indians to spiritual freedom and openness. They do not feel free kneeling in straight pews, singing Anglo-Saxon hymns!

Western nuns in India tell humorous stories of the mistakes

they make before they understand the true meaning of inculturation. A group of religious sisters in the village of Anand in
Gujarat, for example, presented a play in which they dressed
the children of Indian land laborers in "angel" costumes as they
would have done in a public school in London.[44] Western
customs used in Indian religious worship have often been no
more than caricatures. Magnificent adaptations of Hindu customs for Christian feast day celebrations, however, are now
being developed in India. For example, the Hindu festival of
lights can be adapted to a Christmas-Epiphany paraliturgical
celebration in a truly Indian context that appeals to all Indians,
whatever their faith.[45] Also, indigenous symbols and ceremonies, now sometimes used in the Indian Christian funeral rite,
by their very nature draw both Christians and Hindus to the
liturgical service for the departed.[46] Numerous examples of this
type may be cited.

Such interrelationships render Hindus and Christians more
at home with each other in everyday life simply because they
find communion in ceremonies and symbols they both understand and love. When Christians and Hindus meditate together
on the Bhagavad Gita in silence, both can become open to profound mystery. God can come down to embrace humankind.
Christians then seek more deeply for the everlasting Christ
who is nearer to them than they are to themselves. The real
Christ is more universal than the Christian ordinarily conceives
him to be. The real Christ is everywhere. He is in the Gita and in
the Upanishads.[47]

Krishna is the Hindu concretization of Bhagavan, God coming down. Krishna is a mythological figure. He is not Christ. But
a meditative acquaintance with the Krishna of the Gita can lead
a Christian to growth in communion with the reality of the
living, transhistorical Christ. Hindus are often more aware of
this mystery of inward spiritual sharing than many Christians
are. Perhaps this is why millions of Hindus unhesitantly accept
Christ as their own chosen God. Nor do they confuse Krishna
with Christ. In fact, their understanding of Christian faith is
often amazing. The writer once asked a Hindu rickshaw driver
who had a tiny image of Mary pinned to his car whether Mary

was to him a goddess like the Hindu Kali. "No," he responded immediately. "Mary is the mother of Christ. She answers our prayers." His response was as accurate and precise as that of the educated Hindu engineer who told the writer that he worships an image of Jesus Christ daily in his home.

Theology is normally a development that follows liturgy and spiritual development in time. It analyzes the origins and teachings of a more or less organized religious community. It studies the relationship of God to the world within that community. Indian Christian theology is in an ongoing stage of development in an increasingly complex, pluralistic, independent India. Here we can only allude briefly to its growth, particularly within the present century. An Indian Christian theology promises today to be a profound contribution not only to India but to the universal church.

Before the twentieth century, the strongest impetus for the creation of an Indian Christian theology came from Hindus.[48] Throughout history Hinduism has been strongly assimilative. Among Hindu names associated with the study of Christianity, outstanding are: Ram Mohan Roy, Keshub Chandra Sen, M. C. Parekh, Shanker Nath, Mahatma Gandhi, Sarvepalli Radhakrishnan, and Ramakrishna Paramahamsa. It is pointed out by theologian Klaus Klostermaier that many attempts by the above Hindus to present Christ to their countrymen in terms understandable to them were rejected as "hinduization of Christianity" by "pagans." Thus the "official church" lost genuine opportunities for development of an Indian Christian theology (whatever the unorthodox approaches of these writers) and for articulation of India's "groaning of the Spirit." Today the message of Christ probably is propagated in India by more Hindus than by Christians!

A significant beginning of Indian Christian theology was not initiated until the turn of the present century. An Indian convert, Brahmabhandab Upadhyaya, contributed to the development of a Christian theology on the conceptual basis of the Hindu Sankara's Advaitic Vedanta philosophy. Other twentieth-century Christian theologians were P. Johanns, J. Fallon, and G. Antoine, all associated with the so-called Calcutta School. More contemporary are J. Neuner, R. De Smet, G. Gispert-Sauch, H. O. Mascarenhas, J. A. Cuttat, J. B. Chettimattam, M. M. Thomas, and Paul Devanandan. Many of these writers adopted the basic approach of utilizing the Vedanta in its various branches in attempts to integrate elements of Indian tradition with Western Christian backgrounds. Klostermaier suggests that A. J. Appasamy, late bishop of the Church of South India, is outstanding with regard to the volume of writings and breadth of treatment of Indian Christian theology as a whole. His best known work is *The Gospel and India's Heritage.*

However, four writers may be pointed out who have published in the second half of the century and who have had a strong influence on Indian Christian theology today. Jules Monchanin (Swami Parama Arubi Anandam), Henri Le Saux (Swami Abhishiktananda), and Dom Bede Griffiths have all reemphasized the necessity of sannyasa as aboriginal Christian experience in India. Raimundo Panikkar, son of a Hindu father from Kerala and a Catholic mother from Spain, has achieved perhaps the most profound and creative accomplishment to date in the field of Indian Christian theology.

Panikkar's contribution to Indian theology is so comprehensive that it may only be hinted at in these pages. *The Unknown Christ of Hinduism* (published in 1964, with a new revised edition in 1981) is the basis of his theology developed over a period of twenty-five years.[49] In it he describes the Hindu-Christian encounter on both ontological and existential levels, revealing a living presence of Christ in Hinduism; the complementary question of the doctrinal relationship between Christianity and Hinduism; and the concrete manifestation of the presence of "Christian" truth within Hinduism. Panikkar concludes with a statement of the possibility of unveiling "Christian" truths within Hinduism so that the unveiled truth may be ready to receive the revealed fullness of Christ. In numerous works that have followed *The Unknown Christ*, Panikkar developed a "christology for the future," or rather a Christophany, which he calls *The Supername*. At the same time, he is preparing a similar work from an Indian perspective, which he calls *Rāmamandala*. His ultimate goal is the mutual understanding and fecundation of diverse world traditions. *The Trinity and the Religious Experience of Man* (1973) explores further the basic ideas of *The Unknown Christ* with particular reference to the margas, or paths to God, of the great world religions.

I have stressed the contribution of Panikkar to Indian Christian theology because I believe that our present study of Christianity and Hinduism leads directly to his theory of "mutual fecundation" of the Hindu and Christian traditions. The terms "inculturation" and "indigenization," on the other hand, do not imply the same mutual sharing in love resulting in new birth.

In *The Trinity and the Experience of Man*,[50] Panikkar clarifies the theological approach to the concept of mutual fecundation through the Trinity. He points out that what we ordinarily call "Christianity" is only one form of living and realizing the Christian faith. The distinction between essence and form is crucial today. We have no right to identify a particular sociological form of living our religion with the Christian faith. The vital process of growth constitutes the very kairos or destiny of the modern world. The deepening and universalization of Christianity is necessary today to prepare the way for the mutual fecundation not only of Christianity and Hinduism, but of all major Eastern and Western religions. This union can take place only in the Trinity, through which the living, moving breath of Father, Son, and Spirit maintains the life of the universe through every moment of every day and beyond time.

In previous chapters I have explored the challenge to the Christian church offered by millions of Indians who accept Christ, but not the church. I have followed Christ in the land of the Hindu, and Christ in the kingdom beyond the official church. The values of dialogue, reciprocity, complementarity, and ecumenism in the search for harmony between Eastern and Western spirituality; the need for understanding amid the tensions created by pluralism as opposed to narrow approaches to dogma, by decentralization of church government as opposed to centralization, by freedom and responsibility as related to authority and law within the church — all these have received my concern. I have discussed the need for growth toward understanding among religions rather than false syncretism of beliefs.

With faith in this principle, I have explored the sense of the sacred and of interiority, the centrality of cosmic revelation and of nondualism, and the profound significance of symbols among Hindus. Concomitantly, I have suggested the need for Hindus to explore the values of rationality and of the seriousness of history to Western Christians. Because Eastern religions can accept with complacency contrarieties that often appear to be contradictions to the Western Christian, I have studied combinations of values that ordinarily bring forth differing responses from East and West: mysticism and service, interiority and action, vertical and horizontal spiritualities, experience and suffering, karma and person. I have analyzed some ambiguities and closed aspects of Hindu culture, and I have attempted to relate them positively to Christian social and prophetic dimensions — to equality, justice, and love.

And so I arrive at a firm hope in the love of Christ in the Spirit as a ground of Hindu-Christian communion. I have faith that this union will one day emerge in the mystery of an Indian faith that will unveil the glory of the Christ who always discloses himself to those who seek him with their whole hearts. Christ belongs to all men and women. All belong to him. But Hindu and Christian must suffer, die, and rise again in the glory of the God whom both adore. After that, the self-revelation that God has made to the East since ancient days will at last unite Banaras to Bethlehem, Krishna to Christ.

Notes

Chapter I

1. Quoted in Clifford Manshardt, *The Mahatma and the Missionary*, Henry Regnery, 1969, p. 69.
2. Louis Fischer, ed., *The Essential Gandhi*, Vintage Books, New York, 1962.
3. Quoted in Eddy Asirvatham, *Christianity in the Indian Crucible*, YMCA Publishing House, Calcutta, 1957, Foreward.
4. Bede Griffiths, Shantivanam Ashram, Tiruchirappalli, Tamil Nadu, India. Interviews, March 29–30, 1980.
5. Raimundo Panikkar, Varanasi, Uttar Pradesh, India. Interviews, March 5–6, 1980; Santa Barbara, California, June 1982.
6. See Raimundo Panikkar, "Confrontation between Hinduism and Christianity," *New Blackfriars*, 50 (January 1969), 197.
7. V. A. Devasenapathi, "Hinduism and Other Religions," in *Hinduism*, Punjabi University, Patiala, India, 1969, p. 106.
8. Raimundo Panikkar, "Contemporary Hindu Spirituality," *Philosophy Today*, 3 (1959), 112–27.
9. Quoted in A. J. Appasamy, *The Gospel and India's Heritage*, Macmillan, London, 1942, p. 23.
10. Sarvepalli Radhakrishnan, *Eastern Religions and Western Thought*, Oxford University Press, New York, 1959.

Chapter II

1. Klaus Klostermaier, *Hindu and Christian in Vrindaban*, SCM, 1969, p. 112.
2. Claude D'Souza, S. J., Loyola College, Madras, India. Interview, January 11, 1980.
3. Ka Naa Subramanyam, *The Catholic Community in India*, Macmillan, Calcutta, 1970, p. 35.
4. Bede Griffiths, *Christian Ashram: Essays Towards a Hindu-Christian Dialogue*. Quoted in V. A. Devasenapathi, *Hinduism*, Punjabi University, Patiala, India, 1969, p. 111.

5. George Gispert-Sauch, S. J., Vidya Jyoti Institute, Delhi, India. Interview, September 16, 1980.
6. Francis Acharya, *Kurisumala, A Symposium on Ashram Life*, Kurisumala Ashram and Asian Trading Corporation, Bangalore, India.
7. D. S. Amalorpavadoss, National Biblical, Catechetical, and Liturgical Centre, Bangalore, India. Interview, April 17, 1980.
8. T. M. P. Mahadevan, Madras, India. Interview, January 28, 1980.
9. Tirumandiram, 2104. Quoted in V. A. Devasanapathi, "Hinduism and Other Religions," *Hinduism*, p. 112.
10. Raimundo Panikkar, *The Trinity and the Religious Experience of Man*, Darton, Longman, and Todd, London, 1973, p. 5.
11. M. P. Pandit, Sri Aurobindo Ashram, Pondicherry, India. Interview, October 22, 1980.
12. D. S. Amalorpavadoss, *Gospel and Culture*, Bangalore, India, p. 14.
13. *The Unknown Christ of Hinduism*, Second Edition, Orbis Books, Maryknoll, N.Y., 1981, p. 93.
14. Raimundo Panikkar, Varanasi, Uttar Pradesh, India. Interview, March 5, 1980.
15. Swami Tapasyananda, Sri Ramakrishna Math, Madras, India. Interview, August 7, 1980.
16. Sharda Rao, "Who is Inside and Who is Outside?" *National Christian Council Review*, March 1980, p. 125.
17. Ishwar Prasad, Christnagar, Varanasi, Uttar Pradesh, India. Interview, March 7, 1980.
18. Joseph Neuner, De Nobili College, Pune, India. Correspondence, September 3, 1980.
19. Raimundo Panikkar, "Confrontation between Hinduism and Christianity," *New Blackfriars*, 50 (January 1969), 197–204.

Chapter III

1. Ignatius Hirudayam, Aikya Alayam Ashram, Madras, India. Interview, January 15, 1980.
2. Sundar Clarke, Bishop, Church of South India, Madras, India. Interview, October 21, 1980. George Soares, S. J., De Nobili College, Pune, India. Interview, June 24, 1980.
3. Christopher Durai Singh, United Theological College, Bangalore. Interview, April 28, 1980.
4. Theological Consultation, Asian Christian Peace Conference, Colombo, Sri Lanka, October 23–27, 1980.
5. Interview, Madras, India, August 7, 1980.
6. New American Library, New York, 1963.
7. See, for example, Raimundo Panikkar, *The Trinity and the Religious*

Experience of Man, Orbis Books, Maryknoll, N.Y., 1975; Bede Griffiths, *Vedanta and Christian Faith*, Dawn Horse Press, Los Angeles, 1973.
8. *Declaration on the Relation of the Church to Non-Christian Religions*, 3.
9. Margaret Chatterjee, Professor of Philosophy, University of Delhi. Interview, September 18, 1980.
10. Stephen Fuchs, Institute of Indian Culture, Andheri, Bombay. Interview, July 15, 1980.
11. Bede Griffiths, Shantivanam Ashram, Tiruchirappalli, Tamil Nadu, India. Interview, March 30, 1980. Also, correspondence, May 29, 1982.
12. Albert Nambiaparambil, Varanasi, Uttar Pradesh. Interview, March 7, 1980.
13. Herbert Jai Singh, United Theological College, Bangalore. Interview, April 19, 1980.
14. Christian Literature Society, Madras, 1970, p. 196.
15. Raimundo Panikkar, "Confrontation between Hinduism and Christianity," *New Blackfriars*, 50 (1969), 197–204.
16. Abhishiktananda, *Hindu-Christian Meeting Point*, ISPCK, Delhi, 1969, pp. 94–111.
17. A. J. Appasamy, ed., *Temple Bells*, Calcutta, n.d.
18. Samuel Rayan, Vidya Jyoti Institute, Delhi. Interview, September 22, 1980. P. K. Sundaram, Institute for Advanced Philosophy, University of Madras. Interview, February 4, 1980.
19. A. S. Appasamy, *Fifty Years' Pilgrimage of a Convert*, Christian Literature Society, Bangalore, 1940, pp. 95–102.
20. Bede Griffiths, *Return to the Centre*, Fount Paperbacks, William Collins and Son, London, 1978, pp. 99–101.
21. Paul Puthanangady, Kristu Jyoti College, Bangalore. Interview, April 30, 1980.
22. Orbis Books, Maryknoll, N.Y., 1973.

Chapter IV

1. T. M. P. Mahedevan, "Hindu Metaphysics" in *Hinduism*, K. R. Sundararajan, ed., Punjabi University, Patiala, India, 1969, pp. 18–40.
2. Raimundo Panikkar, Varanasi. Interview, March 6, 1980.
3. Margaret Chatterjee, University of Delhi. Interview, September 18, 1980.
4. J. Moffitt, "God as Mother," *Cross Currents*, 28 (1978), 129–33.
5. Swami Bramchari Paramatha Chaitanya, Madras. Interview, November 25, 1980.
6. See Raimundo Panikkar, *The Trinity and the Religious Experience of*

Man, Christian Literature Society, Madras, 1970.

7. Raimundo Panikkar, Varanasi. Interview, March 6, 1980. Christian Troll, De Nobili College, Pune. Interview, June 29, 1980.
8. Bede Griffiths, Shantivanam Ashram, Tiruchirappalli, Tamil Nadu, India. Interview, March 30, 1980.
9. A. J. Appasamy, *The Gospel and India's Heritage*, pp. 188–90.
10. Sebastian Painadath, Jyothis Centre for Dialogue, Cochin, Kerala. Interview, November 10, 1980.
11. Swami Ranganathananda, president, Ramakrishna Math, Hyderabad, "Vivekananda and Human Development in India," lecture, Triplicane Cultural Academy, Madras, February 4, 1980.
12. Interview, February 19, 1980.
13. Bede Briffiths, interview, March 29, 1980.
14. Samuel Rayan, Vidya Jyoti Institute, Delhi. Interview, September 14, 1980.
15. See Mar Joseph Powathil, "Some Pastoral Problems and Inter-Church Relationship in India," *Christian Orient*, 3 (1982), 6–7.
16. Vincent Miranda, Dhyana Ashram, Mandavali, Madras. Interview, October 14, 1980.
17. A. J. Appasamy, *Sundar Singh*, pp. 146–92.
18. Matthew Lederle, Snehasadhan, Pune. Interview, June 30, 1980.
19. Claude D'Souza, president, All India Catholic University Federation, Loyola College, Madras. Interview, January 10, 1980.
20. P. K. Sundaram, interview, February 4, 1980.
21. M. P. Pandit, Sri Aurobindo Ashram, Pondicherry, India. Interview, October 22, 1980.
22. Quoted in Arthur Jones, "West's Church Must Go East," *National Catholic Reporter*.
23. J. B. Pratt, quoted in Eddy Asirvatham, *Christianity in the Indian Crucible*, p. 146.
24. S. Venkatachalam, Bharatiya Vidya Bhavan, Madras. Interview, January 31, 1980.
25. T. K. John, Vidya Jyoti Institute, New Delhi. Interview, Madras, September 10, 1980.
26. D. S. Amalorpavadass, National Biblical Catechetical, and Liturgical Conference, Bangalore. Interview, May 1, 1980.
27. Sundar Clarke, Church of South India, Madras. Correspondence, October 7, 1980.
28. Theodore Bowling, De Nobili College, Pune. Interview, July 2, 1980.
29. Subhash Anand, interview, June 24, 1980.
30. Xavier Irudayaraj, St. Paul's Seminary, Tiruchirappalli, Tamil Nadu. Interview, March 29, 1980.
31. D. S. Amalorpavadass, *Gospel and Culture*, pp. 39–40.

32. S. S. Raghavachar, "Hindu Mysticism," in *Hinduism*, pp. 76–81.
33. Quoted by Swami Ranganathananda, Ramakrishna Math, Hyderabad. Lecture, February 4, 1980.
34. D. S. Amalorpavadass, interview, May 1, 1980.
35. Sebastian Kappan, Centre for Social Reconstruction, Madras. Interview, November 26, 1980.
36. Xavier Koodapuzha, interview, November 4, 1980.
37. J. A. Cuttat, quoted in "The Incarnate Word, Exemplar of Religious Encounter," Joseph Mattam, *Land of the Trinity*, Theological Publications in India, 1975, p. 185.
38. Joseph Vadakkan, Trichur, Kerala, N.C. News Service, February 9, 1979.
39. Sebastian Kappan, interview, November 26, 1980.
40. D. S. Amalorpavadass, *Gospel and Culture*, pp. 51–53.
41. M. M. Thomas, *The Acknowledged Christ of the Indian Renaissance*, Christian Literature Society, Madras, 1970, pp. 141–42.
42. See, for example, Francis Acharya, ed., *Kurisumala, A Symposium on Ashram Life*.
43. T. M. P. Mahadevan, "Metaphysics," in *Hinduism*, pp. 19–31.
44. R. C. Zaehner, quoted in "Christ, the Fulfillment of the Religious Quest," Joseph Mattam, *Land of the Trinity*, Theological Publications in India, 1975, p. 112.
45. Adolf Esteller, St. Xavier College, Bombay. Interview, July 12, 1980.
46. Raimundo Panikkar, *The Trinity and the Religious Experience of Man*, Orbis Books, Maryknoll, N.Y., 1973, pp. 2–5.
47. Raimundo Panikkar, "Confrontation between Hinduism and Christianity," *Blackfriars*, 50 (January, 1969), 197–204.
48. D. S. Amalorpavadass, *Gospel and Culture*, pp. 37–38.
49. Walter M. Abbott, ed., *The Documents of Vatican II*, Guild Press, New York, 1966, pp. 612–13.
50. Aelred Pereira, Jesuit Provincial House, Andheri, Bombay. Interview, July 15, 1980.
51. Raimundo Panikkar, *The Trinity and the Religious Experience of Man*, Preface, pp. xiv–xvi.

Chapter V

1. Joseph Mattam, "Christ, the Fulfillment of the Religious Quest," in *Land of the Trinity*, Theological Publications in India, 1975, p. 115.
2. Francis Vineeth, Dharmaram College, Bangalore. Interview, June 2, 1980.
3. Michael Amaladoss, "Towards an Indian Christian Spirituality," in

Indian Spirituality in Action, Asian Trading Corporation, Bombay, 1973, p. 115.

4. D. S. Amalorpavadass, *Praying Seminar,* National Biblical, Catechetical, and Liturgical Centre, Bangalore, n.d., pp. 42–44.

5. A. J. Appasamy, *The Gospel and India's Heritage,* Macmillan, London, 1942, pp. 31–35.

6. Eddy Asirvatham, *Christianity in the Indian Crucible,* pp. 127–30.

7. Raimundo Panikkar, "Confrontation between Hinduism and Christianity," *New Blackfriars,* 50 (January 1969), 197–204.

8. Raimundo Panikkar, "Contemporary Hindu Spirituality," pp. 112–27.

9. Sister Zita Martens, St. Joseph's School, Bombay. Interview, July 16, 1980.

10. David E. Stewart, Assembly of God Church, Madras. Interview, August 27, 1980.

11. T. M. P. Mahadevan, "Hindu Metaphysics," in K. R. Sundararajan, ed., *Hinduism,* Punjabi University, Patiala, 1969, pp. 22–26.

12. M. M. Thomas, *The Acknowledged Christ of the Indian Renaissance,* p. 168.

13. V. A. Devasenapathi, Centre for Advanced Study of Philosophy, University of Madras. Interview, January 25, 1980.

14. Xavier Koodapuzha, St. Thomas Apostolic Seminary, Kottayam, Kerala. Interview, November 4, 1980.

15. M. M. Thomas, *Towards a Theology of Contemporary Ecumenism,* Christian Literature Society, Madras, 1978, pp. 94–96.

16. Raimundo Panikkar, *The Unknown Christ of Hinduism,* rev. ed., Orbis Books, Maryknoll, N.Y., 1981.

17. Bede Griffiths, *Return to the Centre,* pp. 99–101.

18. G. Gispert-Sauch, Vidya Jyoti Institute, New Delhi. Interview, September 16, 1980.

19. Bede Griffiths, *Return to the Centre,* pp. 86–87.

20. Carlos Valles, St. Xavier College, Ahmedabad, Gujarat. Correspondence, August 10, 1980.

21. Bede Griffiths, *Return to the Centre,* pp. 145–46.

22. Joseph Mattam, "The Incarnate Word, Exemplar of Religious Encounter," in *Land of the Trinity,* pp. 103–4.

23. M. M. Thomas, *The Acknowledged Christ of the Indian Renaissance,* pp. 187–92.

24. See *The Trinity and the Religious Experience of Man,* Orbis Books, Maryknoll, N.Y., 1973; *The Unknown Christ of Hinduism,* rev. ed., Orbis Books, 1981.

25. For the above quotations, see Introduction to *The Unknown Christ of Hinduism.*

26. St. Irenaeus, *Against Heresies.*

27. K. P. Chellappan, University of Madras Post-Graduate Centre,

Tiruchirappalli, Tamil Nadu. Interview, March 28, 1980.

28. Swami Ranganathananda, president, Ramakrishna Math, Hyderabad. Lecture, February 4, 1980.
29. Swami Tapasyananda, president, Sri Ramakrishna Math, Madras. Interview, August 7, 1980.
30. M. M. Thomas, *The Acknowledged Christ of the Indian Renaissance*, p. 125.
31. Abhishiktananda, *Hindu-Christian Meeting Point*, rev. ed., ISPCK, 1976, pp. 90–91.
32. Joseph Neuner, De Nobili College, Pune. Correspondence, September 8, 1980.
33. Albert Nambiaparambil, secretary, Dialogue Commission, Catholic Bishops Conference of India, Cochin, Kerala. Interview, March 7, 1980.
34. A. J. Appasamy, *The Gospel and India's Heritage*, p. 262.
35. Raimundo Panikkar, "Confrontation between Hinduism and Christianity," pp. 197–204.
36. Bede Griffiths, Shantivanam Ashram, Tamil Nadu. Correspondence with V. A. Devasanapathi, July 23, 1980.
37. See K. M. Munshi, *Hinduism, A Way of Life*.
38. Gaspar Koelman, interview, June 27, 1980.
39. Swami Tapasyananda, interview, August 7, 1980.
40. Francis Acharya, Kurisumala Ashram, Kerala. Interview, November 5, 1980.
41. Quoted in Vandana, "Indian Theologizing and the Role of Experience," *Jeevadhara*, vol. 53, p. 244.
42. T. M. P. Mahadevan, "Hindu Metaphysics," p. 29.
43. Swami Ranganathananda, Ramakrishna Math, Hyderabad. Lecture, February 4, 1980.
44. *The Complete Works of Swami Vivekananda*, 5th ed., Almora, 1931, vol. 4, pp. 51f.
45. M. Amaladoss, "Towards an Indian Christian Spirituality," p. 117.
46. M. P. Pandit, interview, October 22, 1980.
47. Raimundo Panikkar, "Confrontation between Hinduism and Christianity," pp. 197–204.
48. A. J. Appasamy, *Tamil Christian Poet*, Lutterworth Press, London, 1966, p. 69.
49. Sister Munira Khan, Bandra, Bombay. Interview, July 18, 1980.
50. R. D. Immanuel, *Influence of Hinduism on Indian Christians*, Jabalpur, India, 1950.
51. George Proksch, Gyan Ashram, Andheri, Bombay. Interview, July 15, 1980.
52. Adolph Esteller, interview, July 12, 1980.
53. Matthew Lederle, "Interpreting Christ through Indian Art," in *Indian Spirituality in Action*, pp. 130–39.

Chapter VI

1. T. M. P. Mahadevan, "Metaphysics," in *Hinduism*, K. R. Sundararajan, ed., Punjabi University, Patiala, 1969, p. 20.
2. Bede Griffiths, "Mystical Theology in the Indian Tradition," *Jeevadhara*, 53 (1979), pp. 262–71.
3. Quoted in A. J. Appasamy, *The Gospel and India's Heritage*, Macmillan, London, 1942, p. 143.
4. A. J. Appasamy, *Fifty Years Pilgrimage of a Convert*, Christian Literature Society, Bangalore, 1940, pp. 94–95, 110.
5. Marcus Braybrooke, *The Undiscovered Christ*, Christian Literature Society, Madras, 1973, pp. 45–46. See also Bede Griffiths, *Christ in India*, p. 91.
6. Abhishiktananda, *Towards the Renewal of the Indian Church*, K. C. M. Press, Cochin, 1970, pp. 1–14.
7. Samuel Rayan, Vidya Jyoti Institute, Delhi. Interview, September 22, 1980.
8. Joseph Mattam, *Land of the Trinity*, pp. 159–62.
9. See Raimundo Panikkar, *The Unknown Christ of Hinduism*, Darton, Longman, and Todd, London, 1964, pp. 6–34; also, "Christianity and World Religions," in *Christianity*, Punjabi University, Patiala, 1969.
10. See Raimundo Panikkar, *The Trinity and the Religious Experience of Man*, Orbis Books, Maryknoll, N.Y., 1973, pp. 41–69.
11. V. A. Devasenapathi, University of Madras. Interview, January 25, 1980.
12. Vandana, "Panditji Dada Saheb," in *Indian Spirituality in Action*, Asian Trading Corporation, Bombay, 1973, p. 178.
13. S. Radhakrishnan, *Eastern Religions and Western Thought*, New York, 1959, p. 57.
14. Interview, February 19, 1980.
15. Quoted in A. J. Appasamy, ed., *Temple Bells*, Calcutta, n.d.
16. Xavier Irudayaraj, St. Paul's Seminary, Tiruchirappalli. Interview, March 29, 1980.
17. Alfred De Souza, Indian Social Institute, New Delhi. Interview, September 17, 1980.
18. Fidelis D'Lima, St. Sebastian Friary, Madras. Interview, May 15, 1980.
19. A. J. Appasamy, *Sundar Singh*, Christian Literature Society, Madras, 1958, 1966, 1970, pp. 185–239.
20. Bede Griffiths, *Return to the Centre*, Collins, 1978, pp. 99–110.
21. M. M. Thomas, *The Acknowledged Christ of the Indian Renaissance*, pp. 140–41.
22. Interview, Madras, September 10, 1980.

23. Joseph Neuner, Pontifical Athenaeum, Pune. Correspondence, September 3, 1980.
24. G. Gispert-Sauch, Vidya Jyoti Institute, Delhi. Interview, September 23, 1980.
25. "Prayer in Asian Traditions," FABC Paper no. 11, Hong Kong, 1978.
26. National Biblical, Catechetical, and Liturgical Centre, Bangalore, n.d.
27. ISPCK, Delhi, 1967, 1969, 1972, 1975.
28. *Prayer with the Harp of the Spirit*, Kurisumala Ashram, Kerala, 1980.
29. Ishwar Prasad, Christnagar, Varanasi. Interview, March 7, 1980. Ishwar Prasad now lives as a hermit; Krist Panthi has developed on different lines.
30. T. K. John, interview, September 10, 1980.
31. K. R. Sundararajan, "Hindu Ethics," in *Hinduism*, Punjabi University, Patiala, 1969, p. 55.
32. Bede Griffiths, *Vedanta and Christian Faith*, Dawn Horse Press, Los Angeles, 1973, p. 54.
33. George Soares, De Nobili College, Pune. Interview, June 24, 1980.
34. S. Suviseshamuthu, Christian Arts and Communication Service, Madras. Interview, August 20, 1980.
35. For the above ideas, see M. M. Thomas, *Towards a Theology of Contemporary Ecumenism*, pp. 35–36, 44–45, 98, 112–15, 133, 194.
36. D. S. Amalorpavadass, *Praying Seminar*, pp. 21–22.
37. *Sundar Singh*, 1958, 1966, 1970.
38. Sister Vinaya, Rajkot, Gujarat. Interview, February 9, 1980.
39. Paulos Mar Gregorios, "Bible Study Outlines," in *Jesus Christ in Asian Suffering and Hope*, pp. 95–99.
40. A. J. Appasamy, *The Gospel and India's Heritage*, pp. 168–70.
41. Samuel Rayan, interview, September 25, 1980.
42. "Hinduism and Other Religions," in *Hinduism*, pp. 123–25.
43. K. P. Chellappan, University of Madras, Tiruchirappalli, Tamil Nadu. Interview, March 28, 1980.
44. Raimundo Panikkar, "Confrontation between Hinduism and Christianity," *New Blackfriars*, 50 (1969), 197–204.
45. V. A. Devasenapathi, University of Madras. Interview, January 25, 1980.
46. Abraham Ayrookuzhiel, "An Enquiry into the Idea of God and Pattern of Worship in a South Indian Village," reprint, pp. 16–18.
47. Philip Spratt, *Hindu Culture*, quoted by George Soares, interview, June 24, 1980.
48. Swami Ranganathananda, "Vivekananda and Human Development in India," February 4, 1980.
49. Aelred Pereira, interview, July 15, 1980.
50. Sebastian Kappen, interview, November 26, 1980.

Chapter VII

1. George Russell (AE), "The Unknown God."
2. Matthew Lederle, Snehasadhan Ashram, Pune. Interview, June 30, 1980.
3. *Representative Writings*, Marjorie Sykes, ed., National Book Trust, New Delhi, 1973, p. 11.
4. Vincent Miranda, Dhyana Ashram, Madras. Interview, October 14, 1980.
5. Leslie Newbigin, *Behold I Make All Things New*, Christian Literature Society, Madras, 1968.
6. M. M. Thomas, *The Acknowledged Christ of the Hindu Renaissance*, Christian Literature Society, Madras, 1970, pp. 291–305.
7. M. P. Pandit, Sri Aurobindo Ashram, Pondicherry. Interview, October 28, 1980.
8. S. Suviseshamuthu, interview, August 20, 1980.
9. Vincent Miranda, interview, October 14, 1980.
10. Hilary Rodriguez, pastor, St. Andrew Church, Bombay. Interview, July 11, 1980.
11. George Soares, De Nobili College, Pune. Interview, June 24, 1980.
12. Bishop Christopher Robinson, Anglican Church of North India, Delhi. Interview, September 19, 1980.
13. M. P. Pandit, interview, October 21, 1980.
14. Quoted by Swami Ranganathananda, president, Ramakrishna Math, Hyderabad. Lecture, Triplicane Cultural Academy, Madras, February 4, 1980.
15. Samuel Rayan, Vidya Jyoti Institute, Delhi. Interview, September 25, 1980.
16. Interview, September 25, 1980.
17. Joseph Pathrapankal, Dharmaram College, Bangalore. Interview, April 30, 1980.
18. Paulos Gregorios, "Suffering and Hope in the Light of the Cross and Resurrection," in *Jesus Christ in Asian Suffering and Hope*, pp. 50–57.
19. D. S. Amalorpavadass, National Biblical, Catechetical, and Liturgical Center, Bangalore. Interview, May 1, 1980.
20. P. K. Sundaram, Institute for Advanced Philosophy, University of Madras. Interview, February 12, 1980.
21. T. Pamasini Asuri, "Rural Women in India," pp. 25–30.
22. See William Temple, *Readings in St. John's Gospel*, p. 59, and B. F. Wescott, *The Gospel According to St. John*, Baker Book House, Grand Rapids, Michigan, 1980, p. 74.
23. George Soares, interview, June 24, 1980.
24. Study Committee on Ministries (CBCI), *The Renewal of Ministry in*

the Church, National Biblical, Liturgical and Catechetical Centre, Bangalore, 1976.

25. Ka Naa Subramanyam, *The Catholic Community in India*, pp. 106–7.
26. M. P. Pandit, interview, October 21, 1980.
27. Gladys D'Souza, "Poverty and Oppression at Erranyapallya," in *Jesus Christ in Asian Suffering and Hope*, pp. 16–24.
28. Vincent Miranda, interview, October 14, 1980.
29. See Charles West, *The Power to Be Human*, Macmillan, New York, quoted in M. M. Thomas, *Towards a Theology of Contemporary Ecumenism*, Christian Literature Society, Madras, 1978, pp. 262–63.
30. M. M. Thomas, *Revolution in India and Christian Humanism*, Forum for Christian Concern for People's Struggle, New Delhi, 1978, pp. 13–14.
31. Quoted by Philipos Thomas in review of Paulos Gregorios's "The Human Presence: An Orthodox View of Nature," in *Indian Journal of Theology*, 39 (1980), 108–10.
32. A. J. Appasamy, *The Gospel and India's Heritage*, pp. 64–70.
33. Gandhi wrote these lines in Yervada Jail, Pune, in 1930.
34. T. M. P. Mahadevan, Madras. Interview, January 28, 1980.
35. Quoted by Swami Ranganathananda, "Vivekananda and Human Development in India." Lecture, Triplicane Cultural Academy, Madras, February 4, 1980.
36. Swami Tapasyananda, interview, August 7, 1980.
37. Paulos Mar Gregorios, "Bible Study Outlines," in *Jesus Christ in Asian Suffering and Hope*, p. 94.
38. Raimundo Panikkar, Varanasi, interview, March 6, 1980.
39. National Biblical, Catechetical, and Liturgical Conference, Bangalore, 1978, pp. 19–20, 25, 32–50, 55.
40. See D. S. Amalorpavadass, *Towards Indigenization in the Liturgy*, National Biblical, Liturgical, and Catechetical Centre, Bangalore, 1973.
41. Bede Griffiths, Shantivanam Ashram, Tiruchirappalli. Interview, March 30, 1980.
42. Joseph Cardinal Parecattil, Preface to *Indian Spirituality in Action*, Asian Trading Corporation, Bombay, 1973.
43. Joseph Maciel, pastor, St. Peter church, Bombay. Interview, July 9, 1980.
44. Sister Munira Khan, St. Joseph Convent, Bandra, Bombay. Interview, July 18, 1980.
45. Jude S. Pereira, *The Festival of Lights in India and the Christian Epiphany Celebration of the Liturgical Year*, Pontifical Athenaeum of St. Anselm, Rome, 1955.
46. Theodore Pereira, *Towards an Indian Christian Funeral Rite*, Asian Trading Corporation, Bangalore, 1980.
47. Sebastian Painadath, interview, November 10, 1980.

48. For an excellent brief review of this subject, see Klaus Klostermaier, "Indian Christian Theology," *Clergy Review* 54 (1969), 175–98.
49. See *The Unknown Christ of Hinduism*, Darton, Longman, and Todd, London, and Orbis Books, Maryknoll, N.Y., rev. ed., 1981.
50. *The Trinity and the Religious Experience of Man*, Orbis Books, Maryknoll, N.Y., 1973.

Selected Bibliography

BOOKS

Abhishiktananda, Swami (Henri Le Saux). *The Further Shore*. Delhi: I.S.P.C.K., 1975.

——. *Guru and Disciple*. London: S.P.C.K., 1974.

——. *Hindu-Christian Meeting Point*. Delhi: I.S.P.C.K., 1976.

——. *Prayer*. Delhi: I.S.P.C.K., 1975.

——. *Saccidananda: A Christian Approach to Advaitic Experience*. Delhi: I.S.P.C.K., 1974.

——. *Towards the Renewal of the Indian Church*. Ernakulam, Cochin: K.C.M. Press, 1970.

Acharya, Francis. *Prayer, With the Harp of the Spirit*, vol. 1. Kerala: Kurisumala Ashram, Vagamon, 1980.

Ahmad-Shah, A. *Theology, Christian and Hindu*, Lucknow, 1966.

All India Seminar: Church in India Today. New Delhi: C.B.C.I. Center, 1969.

Amalorpavadass, D. S., ed. *Ecumenism in Perspective*. Bangalore: N.B.C.L.C., 1976.

——. *Gospel and Culture: Evangelization and Inculturation*. Bangalore: N.B.C.L.C., 1978.

——, ed. *Ministries in the Church in India: Research Seminar and Pastoral Consultation*. New Delhi: Ashok Place, 1976.

——, ed. *Praying Seminar*. Bangalore: NBCLC, n.d.

——, ed. *Research Seminar on Non-Biblical Scriptures*. Bangalore: N.B.C.L.C., 1974.

——. *Theology of Evangelization in the Indian Context*. Bangalore: N.B.C.L.C., 1973.

——. *Towards Indigenisation in the Liturgy*. Bangalore: N.B.C.L.C., 1973.

Andrews, C. F. *Representative Writings*. Marjorie Sykes, ed. New Delhi: National Book Trust, 1973.

Appasamy, A. J. *The Gospel and India's Heritage*. London: Macmillan, 1942.

203

————. *My Theological Quest.* Bangalore, 1965.
————. *Sundar Singh.* Madras: Christian Literature Society, 1958, 1966, 1970.
————. *Tamil Christian Poet. Life and Writings of H. A. Krishna Pillai.* London: Lutterworth Press, 1966.
————, ed. *Temple Bells.* Delhi: YMCA Press, n.d.
Appasamy, A. S. *Fifty Years' Pilgrimage of a Convert.* Bangalore: Christian Literature Society, 1940.
Appasamy, Paul. *Legal Aspects of Social Reform.* Madras: Christian Literature Society, 1929.
Asirvatham, Eddy. *Christianity in the Indian Crucible.* Calcutta: YMCA Publishing House, 1957.
Baago, Kaj. *Pioneers of Indigenous Christianity.* Bangalore: Christian Institute for the Study of Religion and Society, 1969.
Baird, Robert D., and Bloom, Alfred. *Indian and Far Eastern Religious Traditions.* New York: Harper and Row, 1972.
Behari, Bankey. *Sufis, Mystics, and Yogis of India.* Bombay: Bharatiya Vidya Bhavan, 1962.
Bhave, Vinoba. *Talks on the Gita.* London: Allen and Unwin, 1960.
Braybrooke, Marcus. *The Undiscovered Christ. Recent Developments in the Christian Approach to India.* Madras: Christian Literature Society, 1973.
Brown, Judith M. *Men and Gods in a Changing World. Some Themes in the Religious Experience of Twentieth Century Hindus and Christians.* London: Student Christian Movement Press, 1980.
Chenchiah, P. *Rethinking Christianity in India.* Madras, 1959.
Chethimattam, John B. *Consciousness and Reality: An Indian Approach to Metaphysics.* Bangalore, 1967.
Chinmayananda, Swami. *Kindle Life.* Madras: Chinmaya Publications Trust, 1977.
Chinmulgund, P. J., and Mirashi, V. V., eds. *Review of Indological Research in the Last Seventy-Five Years.* Pune, 1967.
Colaco, J. M., ed. *Jesus Christ in Asian Suffering and Hope.* Madras: Christian Literature Society, 1977.
Cronin, Vincent. *A Pearl to India: Life of Robert de Nobili.* New York: Dutton, 1959.
Dechanet, J. M. *Christian Yoga.* Bombay: St. Paul Publications, 1960.
de Mello, Anthony. *Sadhana, A Way to God.* Gujarat Sahitya Prakash Anand, India, 1978.
De Smet, Richard, and Neuner, Joseph, eds. *Religious Hinduism.* Allahabad, India, 1966.
Dasgupta, Surendranath. *A History of Indian Philosophy.* London, 1963.

Dhavamony, Mariasusai, ed. *Evangelization, Dialogue and Development: Selected Papers of International Theological Conference, Nagpur, India, 1971.* Rome: Gregorian University Press, 1972.

————. *Love of God According to Saiva Siddhanta: A Study in the Mysticism and Theology of Saivism.* London: Oxford University Press, 1971.

Eliade, Mircea. *Yoga: Immortality and Freedom.* London: Kegan Paul, 1958.

Farqhuar, J. N. *Modern Religious Movements in India.* New York: Garland Publications (reprint), 1980.

Fernandes, Walter, ed. *People's Participation in Development.* New Delhi: Indian Social Institute, 1980.

Gandhi, Mahatma. *The Essential Gandhi.* Louis Fischer, ed. New York: Vintage Books, 1962.

————. *My Autobiography, or the Story of My Experiments with Truth.* Ahmedabad: Navjivan Press, 1948.

Geffré, Claude, and Dhavamony, Mariasusai. *Buddhism and Christianity.* Concilium: Religion in the Seventies Series. New York: Seabury Press, 1979.

Graham, Aelred. *Contemplative Christianity.* New York: Seabury Press, 1975.

————. *Zen Catholicism.* New York: Harcourt Brace Co., 1963.

Griffiths, Bede. *Christ in India: Essays Toward a Hindu-Christian Dialogue.* New York: Scribners, 1966.

————. *The Golden String.* New York: Kenedy, 1954.

————. *The Marriage of East and West.* Springfield, Illinois: Templegate, 1982.

————. *Return to the Centre.* Collins, Fount Paperbacks, 1978.

————. *Vedanta and Christian Faith.* Los Angeles: Dawn Horse Press, 1973.

Hoefer, Herbert E., ed. *Debate on Mission.* Madras: Gurukul Lutheran Theological College and Research Institute, 1979.

Hooker, Roger. *Outside the Camp.* Madras: Christian Literature Society, 1972.

————. *Voices of Varanasi.* London: Church Missionary Society, 1979.

Hughes, Catharine R., ed. *The Smokeless Fire.* New York: Seabury Press, 1974.

Indian Spirituality in Action. Bombay: Asian Trading Corporation, 1973.

Irudayaraj, Xavier, and Sundaram, L., eds. *Inter-Faith Dialogue in Tiruchirappalli.* Madras: SIGA, 1978.

Johanns, P. "To Christ Through the Vedanta," *Light of the East Series,* 4, 7, 9, 19. Ranchi, 1942–44.

Kappen, Sebastian. *Jesus and Freedom*. Maryknoll, N.Y.: Orbis Books, 1977.

Keshub, Chandra Sen. *Lectures in India*. Calcutta, 1901.

Klostermaier, Klaus K. *In the Paradise of Krishna*. Philadelphia, 1971.

————. *Kristavidya*, Indian Christian Thought Series, no. 8. Bangalore: C.I.S.R.S., 1967.

————. *Salvation, Liberation, Self-Realization*. Madras: University of Madras Press, 1974.

Mahadevan, T. M. P. "The Christian Image in India," in *Debate on Mission*, Herbert E. Hoefer, ed. Madras, 1979.

————. "Hindu Metaphysics," in *Hinduism*, K. R. Sundararajan et al., eds. Patiala: Punjabi University, 1969, pp. 18–40.

————. *Invitation to Indian Philosophy*. Livingston, N.J.: Arnold Heinemann, Oriental Books, 1978.

————. "Social, Ethical, and Spiritual Values in Indian Philosophy," in *The Indian Mind: Essentials of Indian Philosophy and Culture*, Charles A. Moore, ed. East-West Center Press, University of Hawaii, 1967, pp. 152–73.

————. "Vedantic Meditation and Its Relation to Action," in *Contemplation and Action in World Religions*. Seattle and London: University of Washington Press, pp. 72–85.

Maharshi, Bhagavan Sri Ramana. *Who Am I?* T. M. P. Mahadevan, trans. South India: Tiruvannamalai, 1976.

Mattam, Joseph. *Land of the Trinity*. Bangalore: Theological Publications in India, 1975.

May, Peter. *Banaras and Bethlehem*. Madras: Christian Literature Society, 1959.

Mazoomdar, F. C. *The Life and Teachings of Keshub Chandra Sen*. Calcutta, 1931.

Merton, Thomas. *The Asian Journal of Thomas Merton*. New York: New Directions, 1968.

————. *Zen and the Birds of Paradise*. New York: New Directions, 1968.

Moffitt, John. *Journey to Gorakhpur: Reflections on Hindu Spirituality*. London: Sheldon Press, 1973.

Muller, Max. *The Upanishadas*. New York: Ramakrishna Press, 1962.

Neuner, Joseph, ed. *Christian Revelation and World Religions*. London, 1967.

————. "The Transcultural Church," in *The Word in the Third World*, James P. Cotter, ed. Washington, D.C., 1968, pp. 134–58.

Neuner, Joseph; Anand, Subhash; Hoefer, Herbert. *Mission in India*. Pune: Ishvani Kendra Series, no. 7, 1979.

Newbigin, Leslie. *Behold, I Make All Things New*. Madras: Christian Literature Society, 1968.

Nikhilananda, Swami. *Hinduism*. New York: Ramakrishna-Vivekananda Centre, 1958.

Osborne, Arthur, ed. *The Collected Works of Ramana Maharishi*. Tiruvannamalai, 1968.

Otto, Rudolf. *Indian Religion of Grace and Christianity*. New York, 1960.

Panikkar, Raimundo. "Action and Contemplation as Categories of Religious Understanding," in *Contemplation and Action in World Religions*, Y. Ibish and I. Masculescu, eds. Seattle: University of Washington Press, 1978, pp. 85–104.

————. "Christianity and the World Religions," in *Christianity*. Patiala: Punjabi University, 1969, pp. 78–127.

————. "The European University Tradition and the Renascent World Cultures," in *A Challenge to the European University*. World Council of Churches, Geneva, 1967, pp. 72–87.

————. *The Intra-Religious Dialogue*. New York: Paulist Press, 1978.

————. *Myth, Faith, and Hermeneutics*. New York: Paulist Press, 1979.

————. "Time and Sacrifice: The Sacrifice of Time and the Ritual of Modernity," in *The Study of Time, III*, J. T. Fraser, ed. New York: Springer, 1978, pp. 683–727.

————. *The Trinity and the Religious Experience of Man*. Madras: Christian Literature Society, 1970. Maryknoll, N.Y.: Orbis Books, 1973, 1975.

————. *The Unknown Christ of Hinduism*. New and revised edition. Maryknoll, N.Y.: Orbis Books, 1980.

Parekh, M. C. *A Hindu's Portrait of Jesus Christ*. Rajkoth, 1953.

Pereira, Jude S. *The Festival of Lights in India and Its Suitability in Expressing the Content-Message of the Christian Epiphany Celebrations of the Liturgical Year*. Rome: Pontifical Athenaeum of St. Anselm, 1955.

Pereira, Theodore. *Towards an Indian Christian Funeral Rite*. Bangalore: Asian Trading Corporation, 1980.

Prabhavananda, Swami. *The Sermon on the Mount according to Vedanta*. Madras: Sri Ramakrishna Math, 1964.

Radhakrishnan, Sarvapalli. *Eastern Religions and Western Thought*. London: Oxford University Press, 1955.

————. *The Principal Upanishads*. London: Allen and Unwin, 1953.

Rajagopalachari, C., ed. *Mahabharata*. Bombay: Bharatiya Vidya Bhavan, 1958.

————. *Ramayana*. Bombay: Bharatiya Vidya Bhavan, 1958.

Ramakrishna. *The Gospel of Sri Ramakrishna*. Swami Nikhilananda, trans. New York: Ramakrishna-Vivekananda Centre, 1951.

Rao, Mark Sunder. *Ananyatva*. Indian Christian Thought Series, no. 2. Bangalore: C.I.S.R.S., 1964.

Renou, Louis, ed. *Hinduism*. New York: Braziller, 1961.

Roy, Ram Mohan. *The Precepts of Jesus: Guide to Peace and Happiness*. See Klaus Klostermaier, "Indian Christian Theology," *Clergy Review*, 54 (1969), 175–98.

Sen, K. M. *Hinduism*. London: Penguin Books, 1961.

Soares Prabhu, George. "Jesus Christ Amid the Religions and Ideologies of India Today," in *Ecumenism in India: Essays in Honor of M. A. Thomas*, Mathai Zachariah, ed. Delhi: I.S.P.C.K., 1980.

Staffner, Hans. *The Open Door, A Christian Approach to World Religions*. Bangalore: Asian Trading Corporation, 1978.

Subramanyam, Ka Naa. *The Catholic Community in India*. Madras: Macmillan, 1970.

Sundararajan, K. R., et al., eds. *Hinduism*. Patiala: Punjabi University, 1969.

Tagore, R. *Gitanjali*. London: Macmillan, 1967.

Thomas, M. M. *The Acknowledged Christ of the Indian Renaissance*. Madras: Christian Literature Society, 1970.

———. *Revolution in India and Christian Humanism*. Forum for Christian Concern for People's Struggle. New Delhi, 1978.

———. *Salvation and Humanisation*. Madras: Christian Literature Society, 1971.

———. *Towards a Theology of Contemporary Ecumenism*. Madras: Christian Literature Society, 1978.

Urampachal, Thomas Paul. *Organized Religion According to S. Radhakrishnan*. Rome: Gregorian University, 1972.

Vithayathil, Varkey J. *The Origin and Progress of the Syro-Malabar Hierarchy*. Kottayam, Kerala: Oriental Institute of Religious Studies, 1980.

Vivekananda, Swami. "Christ the Messenger," in *Selections from Swami Vivekananda*. Calcutta, 1963, pp. 316–33.

Whaling, Frank. *An Approach to Dialogue: Hinduism-Christianity*. Lucknow, 1966.

Zaehner, R. C. *Christianity and Other Religions*. New York: Hawthorn Books, 1964.

———. *Hindu and Muslim Mysticism*. University of London: Athlone Press, 1960.

———. *Hinduism*. London: Oxford University Press, 1966.

PERIODICALS

Abhisiktananda, Swami (Le Saux, Henri). "An Approach to Hindu Spirituality," *Clergy Review*, 54 (1969), 163–74.
Anand, Subhash. "Evangelical Poverty and Our Mission in India Today," *Vidyajyoti*, November 1976, 461–65.
————. "A Prolegomenon to Theologizing in India Today," *Vidyajyoti*, February 1979, 50–58.
————. "Some Missiological Implications of the Concept of Incarnation," *Vidyajyoti*, January 1978, 35–41.
————. "The Universal Call to Contemplation," *Vidyajyoti*, October, 1977, 414–18.
Arapura, J. G. "The Use of Indian Philosophical Traditions in Christian Thought," *The Indian Journal of Theology*, 29 (1980), 67–73.
Arulsamy, Saverimuthi. "Diksa in Saiva Siddhanta," Reprint, Bangalore.
————. "Theology in Indian Languages," Reprint, Bangalore.
Ashe, G. "Christian Approach to Vedanta," *Month*, 2 (1949), 234–47.
Ayrookuzhiel, Abraham. "An Enquiry into the Idea of God and Pattern of Worship in a South Indian Village," Christian Institute for Study of Religion and Society, reprint, Bangalore.
————. "The Living Hindu Popular Religious Consciousness and Some Reflections on It in the Context of Hindu-Religious Dialogue," *Religion and Society*, 26 (1979), 5–25.
Bulcke, C. "Catholic Approach to Hinduism," *Clergy Monthly Supplement*, 6 (1963), 279–82.
Christian Orient. Journal of Eastern Churches for Creative Theological Thinking. vols. 1–3, 1980–82. Liturgy, Ecclesiology, Spirituality, Ecumenism. Kottayam, Kerala, St. Thomas Apostolic Seminary.
Bhajanananda, Swami. "Hindu Upasana vis-à-vis Christian Meditation," *Dharma*, 2 (1977), 217–30.
Chethimattam, John B. "Four Patterns of Theological Experience," *Jeevadhara*, 9 (1979), 277–88.
Colaco, P. S. "Sri Aurobindo, A Philosopher of Reconciliation," *Modern Schoolman*, 28 (1951), 291–99.
Cousins, E. "The Trinity and World Religions," *Journal of Ecumenical Studies*, 7 (1970), 476–98.
De Smet, Richard V. "The Indian Ascertainment of the Godhead," *Indica*, January 16, 1979.
————. "Pathways for Evangelization in India," *Lumen Vitae*, 29 (1974), 403–17.

————. "Recent Developments in the Christian Approach to the Hindu," *Lumen*, 29 (1974), 515.

————. "Some Governing Principles of Indian Philosophy," *The Philosophical Quarterly*, Amalner, India, January 1963, 249–58.

de Sousa, P. "Blessed Trinity in Hinduism and Christianity," *Worldmission*, 24 (1973), 50–52.

Dhavamony, Mariasusai. "Christian Experience and Hindu Spirituality," *Gregorianum*, 48 (1967), 776–91.

Dooley, P. "A Hindu Concept of Salvation," *American Benedictine Review*, 18 (1967), 504–16.

E.D.M. "Ramakrishna Movement," *Month*, 185 (1948), 351–54.

Gathier, Emile. "Hinduism and Christian Thought," *Cross Currents*, 3 (1953), 142–48.

Grant, S. "Hindu Religious Experience," *Way*, January 1978.

Griffiths, Bede. "Dialogue with Hinduism," *New Blackfriars*, 46 (1965), 404–10.

————. "Mystical Theology in the Indian Tradition," *Jeevadhara*, 9 (1979), 262–77.

————. "Hindus Welcome Dialogue Proposal." *Tablet*, 217 (1963), 1276.

Kappen, Sebastian. *Socialist Perspectives*. Centre for Social Reconstruction, Madras. "Towards a Strategy of Socialist Reconstruction," December 1978; "Marxism in the Indian Context," February 1979; "Socialism Through Community Action," 1980.

Klostermaier, Klaus K. "Hindu-Christian Dialogue," *Journal of Ecumenical Studies*, 5 (1968), 21–44.

————. "A Hindu-Christian Dialogue on Truth," *Journal of Ecumenical Studies*, 12 (1975), 157–71.

————. "Indian Christian Theology," *Clergy Review*, 54 (1969), 175–98.

————. "A Sketch of a Hindu-Christian Theology of Love," *Journal of Ecumenical Studies*, 9 (1972), 750–76.

————. "The Structure of an Indian Christian Theology," *Clergy Review*, 54 (1969), 188–98.

Mercier, J. "Presenting Christianity," Address at Interreligious Convention, Ramakrishna Mission, Bombay, 1963, *Clergy Monthly Supplement*, 7 (1964), 150–53.

Moffitt, John. "The Bhagavad Gita as a Way-Shower to the Transcendental," *Theological Studies*, 38 (1977), 316–31.

————. "A Christian Approach to Hindu Beliefs," *Theological Studies*, 27 (1966), 58–78.

————. "Christianity Confronts Hinduism," *Theological Studies*, 30 (1969), 207–24.

——. "God as Mother in Hinduism and Christianity," *Cross Currents*, 28 (1978), 129–33.

——. "Incarnation and Avatara: An Imaginary Conversation," *Journal of Ecumenical Studies*, 14 (1977), 260.

Neuner, Joseph. "Towards an Indian Theology," *Clergy Monthly Supplement*, 6 (1963), 313–25.

Panikkar, Raimundo. "Advaita and Bhakti, Love and Identity in a Hindu-Christian Dialogue," *Journal of Ecumenical Studies*, 7 (1970), 299–309.

——. "The Bostonian Verities: A Comment on the Boston Affirmations," *Andover Newton Quarterly*, 18 (1978), 145–53.

——. "Confrontation between Hinduism and Christianity," *New Blackfriars*, 50 (1969), 197–204.

——. "The Contribution of Christian Monasticism in Asia to the Universal Church." *Cistercian Studies*, Vanves, France, 1975, pp. 73–84.

——. *Cross Currents: Panikkar in Santa Barbara*, 29, 1979. Articles by Panikkar: "The Myth of Pluralism: The Tower of Babel — A Meditation on Non-Violence," 197–230; "Some Words Instead of a Response," 193–96; "Response to Harold Coward," 190–92.

——. "Have 'Religions' the Monoply on Religion?," *Journal of Ecumenical Studies*, 3 (1974), 515–17.

——. "Hinduism and Christianity," *Cross Currents*, 13 (1963), 87–101.

——. "Hinduism and Christianity," *Jubilee*, January 1966, pp. 29–33.

——. "Indology as a Cross-Cultural Catalyst," *Numen*, 18 (1971), 173–79.

——. "Man as a Ritual Being," *Chicago Studies*, 16 (1977), 7–10.

——. "The New Innocence," *Cross Currents*, 27 (1977), 7–28.

——. "Non-Dualistic Relation between Religion and Politics," *Religion and Society*, 25 (1978), 53–63.

——. "Philosophy and Revolution: The Text, the Context, and the Texture," *Philosophy East and West*, 3 (1973), 315–22.

——. "The Rhetoric of Intrareligious Dialogue," *Jeevadhara*, 8 (1978), 367–80.

——. "Rtatattva: A Preface to Hindu-Christian Theology," *Jeevadhara*, 49 (1979), 6–63.

——. "The Silence of the Word: Non-Dualistic Polarities," *Cross Currents*, 24 (1974), 164–71.

——. "The Theandric Vision," *Monastic Studies*, 8 (1972), 67–74.

——. "Toward a Typology of Time and Temporality in Ancient Indian Tradition," *Journal of Ecumenical Studies*, 24 (1974), 161–64.

————. "The Vitality and Role of Indian Philosophy Today," *Indian Philosophical Quarterly*, 5 (1978), 673–92.

Parel, A. J. "Religious Syncretism in India," *Thought*, 32 (1957), 261–79.

Pathrapanikal, Joseph. "Christianity as a 'Way' according to the Acts of the Apostles," Bangalore: Dharmaram College, reprint.

Rao, Sharda. "Who Is Inside and Who Is Outside?," *National Christian Council Review*, March 1980.

Rayan, Samuel. *Anawim*. Centre for Social Reconstruction, Madras. "Caesar and God," no. 23; "Jesus and Imperialism," no. 26.

Soares, George M. *Anawim*. Centre for Social Reconstruction, Madras. "The Miracles of Jesus: Subversion of a Power Structure?," no. 14.

Vellanickal, Mathew. "Individual Churches: the Biblical Perspective," *Jeevadhara*, reprint.

————. "New Ministries for the Church in India," Pan-Asian Colloquium on New Ministries for the Church in Asia, Hong Kong, *Indian Theological Studies*, February-March 1977.

Vikrant, Swami. "Mysticism — Christian and Hindu," *Jeevadhara*, September-October 1979.

Zachariah, Mathew. "Christian Education and Cultural Transformation in India," *Journal of Christian Education Papers*, 49 (1974), 1–18.

Zaehner, R. C. "Can Mysticism Be Christian?," *New Blackfriars*, 46 (1964), 21–31.

————. "Christianity and the World Religions," *Blackfriars*, 41 (1960), 256–71.

DOCUMENTS, LECTURES, LETTERS, MANUSCRIPTS

Ananthaswami. "Jnana Marga and Pure Advaita," Lecture, Birth Centenary of Bhagavan Sri Ramana Maharshi, Asthika Samajam Venus Colony, Madras, October 4, 1980.

Ayrookuzhiel, Abraham. "Religion, Spirituality, and Aspirations of the People," C.I.R.S. Biennial Council, Bangalore.

————. "A Study of the Religion of the Hindu People of Chirakkal, Kerala," Empirical Survey of the Religion of the People of Chirakkal, Bangalore, March 1977.

Arrupe, Pedro. *On Inculturation*. Letter to Jesuits from the Superior General of the Society of Jesus, May 14, 1978.

Sri Aurobindo Society. *Auroville*, 1980.

Chethimattam, J. "Morality Beside and Beyond Religion: An Indian

Approach to Morality," in *American Catholic Philosophical Association Proceedings*, vol. 51, 1977.

"Conclusions of the Asian Colloquium on Ministries in the Church (Hong Kong)," Manila, Philippines, 1977.

De Smet, Richard V. "The Indian Understanding of Man," Presidential Address, Indian Philosophical Congress, University of Pune, November 5–8, 1970.

———. "Origin: Creation and Emanation," International Society for Metaphysics," Jerusalem, August 18–22, 1977.

Ecumenical Dialogue of Third World Theologians. Theological Conferences I, Dar es Salaam, Tanzania, 1976; II, Accra, Ghana, 1977; III, Colombo, Sri Lanka, 1979.

Federation of Asian Bishops' Conferences: Evangelization in Modern Day Asia, Taipei, 1974; Ministries, Heralding a New Era, Hong Kong, 1977; Assembly on Prayer in Asia, Calcutta, 1978.

Fernandez, Walter. "The Indian Catholic Community," *Pro Munda Vita Dossier*, January 1980.

Founders of Philosophy. Publications Division, Ministry of Information, Government of India, 1975.

Gispert-Sauch, G. "Ananda, Hedone, and the Holy Spirit," Theological Conclusion to an Indological Research on the Vedic Concept of *Ananda*. Vidyajyoti Institute, Delhi, 1977.

Griffiths, Bede. Unpublished correspondence with D. V. A. Devasanapathi.

Hirudayam, Ignatius. "Prayer in Asian Traditions," F.A.B.C. Paper no. 11, 1978.

Indian Culture and the Fullness of Christ. Study-Week Papers, Madras Cultural Academy, 1957.

King, Ursula. "Indian Spirituality, Western Materialism: An Image and Its Function in the Reinterpretation of Modern Hinduism," International Congress of the History of Religions, Lancaster, England, August 1975.

Nambiaparambil, Albert. "The Ground of Transvaluation — A Reflection on Dialogue Experience — A Philosophical Interpretation," lecture, Mexico, 1979.

Ranganathananda, Swami. "Swami Vivekananda and Human Development in India," lecture, Triplicane Cultural Academy, Madras, February 4, 1980.

Study Committee on Ministries, C.B.C.I. "The Renewal of Ministry in the Church," NBCLC, Bangalore, 1976.

Soares, George Prabhu. "Towards an Indian Interpretation of the

Bible," paper presented at Biblehashyam Symposium, Kottayam, Kerala, December 27–31, 1979.

Story of Thirty Years Struggle for Justice, National Convention of Christian Leaders on Plight of Christians of Scheduled Caste Origin, NBCLC, Bangalore, 1978.

Index

215